FICTIONS OF FORM IN AMERICAN POETRY

FICTIONS OF FORM
IN AMERICAN POETRY

Stephen Cushman

PRINCETON UNIVERSITY PRESS

PRINCETON, NEW JERSEY

PUBLISHED BY PRINCETON UNIVERSITY PRESS, 41 WILLIAM STREET,
PRINCETON, NEW JERSEY 08540
IN THE UNITED KINGDOM: PRINCETON UNIVERSITY PRESS, CHICHESTER, WEST SUSSEX

LIBRARY OF CONGRESS CATALOGING-IN-PUBLICATION DATA

CUSHMAN, STEPHEN, 1956–

FICTIONS OF FORM IN AMERICAN POETRY / STEPHEN CUSHMAN.

P.   CM.

INCLUDES BIBLIOGRAPHICAL REFERENCES AND INDEX.

ISBN 0-691-06963-8

1. AMERICAN POETRY—HISTORY AND CRITICISM—THEORY, ETC.

2. LITERARY FORM.   I. TITLE.

PS303.C87   1993   811'.009—DC20   92-39503

THIS BOOK HAS BEEN COMPOSED IN ADOBE SABON

PRINCETON UNIVERSITY PRESS BOOKS ARE PRINTED
ON ACID-FREE PAPER, AND MEET THE GUIDELINES FOR
PERMANENCE AND DURABILITY OF THE COMMITTEE ON
PRODUCTION GUIDELINES FOR BOOK LONGEVITY
OF THE COUNCIL ON LIBRARY RESOURCES

PRINTED IN THE UNITED STATES OF AMERICA

3   5   7   9   10   8   6   4   2

For my two triads

ANNE, BIGELOW, CHARLOTTE

and

SANDRA, SAMUEL, SIMON

To be in any form, what is that?
   —*Whitman*

CONTENTS

ACKNOWLEDGMENTS

MANY PEOPLE shaped this book. For their thorough readings of various chapters, I am grateful to Sidney Burris, J. C. Levenson, David Levin, Austin Quigley, and David Wyatt; for his devoted attention to the entire manuscript, I am especially grateful to Jahan Ramazani. The American Council of Learned Societies and the National Endowment for the Humanities provided fellowship support, as did the University of Virginia during two summers. For other kinds of support and encouragement, I owe much to John Hollander, Raymond Nelson, and Patricia Meyer Spacks. At Princeton University Press, Robert Brown has been especially helpful. Always generous with their time, Ruth Estep, Sheri Morris, Rosemary Sheuchenko, Joy Shifflette, and Barbara Smith generated copy after copy of the manuscript at successive stages. I appreciate the skill and diligence of Dan Philippon, who checked the manuscript, Becky Standard, who copyedited it, and Audrey Kinsella, who prepared the index.

A portion of chapter 6 appeared in *American Literature* (December 1987), and I thank the editors of that journal for their careful work. I acknowledge with pleasure the New York University Press editions of Whitman's poetry and prose, which I used and from which I quote.

Excerpts from the poetry of Emily Dickinson are reprinted by permission of the publishers and the Trustees of Amherst College from *The Poems of Emily Dickinson*, Thomas H. Johnson, ed., Cambridge, Mass.: The Belknap Press of Harvard University Press, Copyright © 1951, 1955, 1979, 1983 by the President and Fellows of Harvard College. Excerpts from *The Complete Poems of Emily Dickinson* edited by Thomas H. Johnson. Copyright 1929, 1935 by Martha Dickinson Bianchi; Copyright © renewed 1957, 1963 by Mary L. Hampson. By permission of Little, Brown and Company. Excerpts from *Emily Dickinson Face to Face* by Martha Dickinson Bianchi. Copyright 1932 by Martha Dickinson Bianchi. Copyright © renewed 1960 by Alfred Leete Hampson. Reprinted by permission of Houghton Mifflin Co. All rights reserved. Excerpts from the letters of Emily Dickinson reprinted by permission of the publishers from *The Letters of Emily Dickinson*, edited by Thomas H. Johnson, Cambridge, Mass.: The Belknap Press of Harvard University Press, Copyright © 1958, 1986 by the President and Fellows of Harvard College.

Grateful acknowledgment is given to New Directions Publishing Corporation for permission to quote from the following copyrighted works of Ezra Pound. *ABC of Reading* (All rights reserved). *The Cantos*

(Copyright © 1934, 1937, 1940, 1948, 1956, 1959, 1962, 1963, 1966, and 1968 by Ezra Pound). *Collected Early Poems* (Copyright © 1976 by the Trustees of the Ezra Pound Literary Property Trust). *Pound/Ford* (Copyright © 1971, 1972, 1973, 1982 by the Trustees of the Ezra Pound Literary Property Trust). *Guide to Kulchur* (Copyright © 1970 by Ezra Pound). *Literary Essays* (Copyright 1918, 1920, 1935 by Ezra Pound). *Personae* (Copyright 1926 by Ezra Pound). *The Rome Broadcasts: "Ezra Pound Speaking"* (Copyright © 1978 by the Trustees of the Ezra Pound Literary Property Trust). *Selected Letters 1907–1941* (Copyright 1950 by Ezra Pound). *Selected Prose 1909–1965* (Copyright © 1960, 1962 by Ezra Pound, Copyright © 1973 by the Estate of Ezra Pound).

Grateful acknowledgment is also given to New Directions Publishing Corporation for permission to quote from the following copyrighted works of William Carlos Williams. *Collected Poems: Volume I, 1909–1939*. Copyright 1938 by New Directions Publishing Corporation. Copyright © 1982, 1986 by William Eric and Paul H. Williams. *Interviews with William Carlos Williams: "Speaking Straight Ahead."* Copyright © 1936, 1939, 1957, 1976 by the Estate of William Carlos Williams. Reprinted by permission of New Directions Publishing Corporation. *Paterson.* Copyright © 1946, 1948, 1949, 1951, 1958 by William Carlos Williams. *Selected Essays.* Copyright 1954 by William Carlos Williams.

Excerpts from *The Collected Poems 1927–1979* by Elizabeth Bishop, Copyright © 1979, 1983 by Alice Helen Methfessel, are reprinted by permission of Farrar, Straus & Giroux, Inc. Excerpts from *The Collected Prose* by Elizabeth Bishop, Copyright © 1984 by Alice Methfessel, are reprinted by permission of Farrar, Straus & Giroux, Inc.

For excerpts from the poetry of A. R. Ammons, acknowledgment is made to W. W. Norton & Company, Inc. for permission to quote from the following sources: *Collected Poems, 1951–1972* (Norton, 1972); *Lake Effect Country* (Norton, 1983); *Ommateum* (Dorrance, 1955); *The Snow Poems* (Norton, 1977); *Sphere: The Form of a Motion* (Norton, 1974); *Sumerian Vistas* (Norton, 1987); *Tape for the Turn of the Year* (Cornell, 1965; Norton, 1972).

Excerpts from "Summer Place" by A. R. Ammons are reprinted by permission from the *Hudson Review* 30, no. 2 (Summer 1977). Copyright © 1977 by the Hudson Review, Inc.

For permission to reproduce the watercolor by A. R. Ammons, I am grateful to the artist.

Finally, I turn to my family, particularly the two members of it who cannot yet read but who, over the years in which the pieces of this book appeared and grew, appeared and grew steadily with them.

FICTIONS OF FORM IN AMERICAN POETRY

ONE

FICTIONS OF FORM IN AMERICAN POETRY

SURVEYING the "Literary Characteristics of Democratic Times," Tocqueville claims that "the inhabitants of the United States have, then, at present, properly speaking, no literature."[1] In his reflections, published in the second part of *Democracy in America* (1840), he continues his inventory of the new nation's scant literary holdings, ignoring, among others, Irving, Cooper, and Bryant, whose reputations were well established by the time of his arrival in May 1831, and declaring unequivocally, "The only authors whom I acknowledge as American are the journalists" (2:56). But Tocqueville also prophesies that this situation will change, that America will generate a literature with a character "peculiarly its own," adding that it is not "impossible to trace this character beforehand." Among his many shrewd and useful insights appears this description of the style and form of American literature to come:

> Taken as a whole, literature in democratic ages can never present, as it does in the periods of aristocracy, an aspect of order, regularity, science, and art; its form, on the contrary, will ordinarily be slighted, sometimes despised. Style will frequently be fantastic, incorrect, overburdened, and loose, almost always vehement and bold. Authors will aim at rapidity of execution more than at perfection of detail. Small productions will be more common than bulky books; there will be more wit than erudition, more imagination than profundity; and literary performances will bear marks of an untutored and rude vigor of thought, frequently of great variety and singular fecundity. The object of authors will be to astonish rather than to please, and to stir the passions more than to charm the taste. (2:59)

Although at least one of Tocqueville's foretellings is mistaken, since Melville's *Moby-Dick* and Pound's *Cantos* suggest that American fiction and poetry value large productions and "bulky books" as much as, if not more than, small ones, Tocqueville prophesies here with uncanny accuracy. As one thinks over the history of American poetry since this passage was written and considers the examples of Whitman's 1855 *Leaves of Grass*, Dickinson's poems, Moore's poems, Eliot's *Waste Land*, Cummings's poems, Pound's *Cantos*, Crane's *The Bridge*, Williams's *Paterson*, Roethke's *The Lost Son*, Olson's *Maximus Poems*, Ginsberg's *Howl*, Lowell's *Life Studies*, Tolson's *Harlem Gallery*, Berryman's *Dream Songs*, and Ammons's *Sphere*, the chain of adjectives "fantastic, incorrect, overburdened, and loose, almost always ve-hement and bold" repeats itself like an unavoidable refrain. Even Frost, Stevens, and Bishop, whose work may not seem immediately implicated by this refrain, must be included among poets who seek "to astonish rather than to please, and to stir the passions more than to charm the taste."

Two of Tocqueville's assertions, one explicit and one implicit, bear particular importance for this study. The explicit assertion about liter-ature in democratic ages is that "its form, on the contrary, will ordi-narily be slighted, sometimes despised." In context, this statement means that in their efforts to astonish and to stir the passions, American writers will not bother themselves with formal strictures observed in "periods of aristocracy" that value "an aspect of order, regularity, sci-ence, and art" or the confining rigors of traditional craft and technique. Although this statement is truer of some poets in the list above than of others, Tocqueville's formulation that American writers will slight and even despise form is problematic. Certainly, American poets, the object of this discussion, have shown a collective tendency to slight, and in extreme cases despise, inherited poetic forms, but the gist of Tocque-ville's statement is that, therefore, American poets slight or undervalue the formal aspects of their art in general, and this is not true. If any-thing, American poets overvalue the formal aspects of their art, invest-ing those aspects with tremendous significance. This overvaluation, which persists throughout the period between Tocqueville's *Democracy in America* and the present, generating so many vehement and bold poems, as well as vehement and bold explanations of those poems, is one of my main concerns.

A second main concern involves the implicit assertion of Tocque-ville's description, the assertion that a necessary link exists between slighted form or fantastic style and democracy in America, or, more ac-curately, the idea of democracy in America. In Tocqueville's thinking, the slighting or despising of traditional literary form stands as a synec-doche for the promotion of rapid execution over perfection and wit over erudition, as well as for "an untutored and rude vigor of thought" that frequently demonstrates its "great variety and singular fecundity." In turn, these literary characteristics stand as synecdoches for the general characteristics—social, economic, political, psychological—of demo-cratic times. Tocqueville's implicit linking of literary form to democracy anticipates Whitman's by at least fifteen years, but by the time Whitman announces in his 1855 preface that "the United States themselves are essentially the greatest poem," the merging of literary form with na-tional myth has become explicit.[2]

Here arise two further considerations for a study of American poetry from Emerson and Whitman to the present. The first involves the generic nature of verse itself, not just American verse of the nineteenth and twentieth centuries. In the idiom of modern linguistics, Antony Easthope formulates this generic definition: "So, in several ways, one of which is entirely specific to it, poetry contains repetitions in the signifier which thus work to foreground the signifier. This feature can stand as a definition of poetry."[3] Although I would argue that this is a definition of verse, not of poetry, which necessarily involves not just form but also figure or trope, it is useful nonetheless. The features of poetic form—the nature of lineation, the presence or absence of meter and rhyme, the cooperations of sound and sense, syntactic and rhetorical patterns, fixed forms—can never be subordinated to some more significant aspect of the poem because there is no more significant aspect of the poem as a piece of verse. Verse distinguishes itself by exhibiting its schematic repetitions.

The second consideration has to do specifically with American poetry of the nineteenth and twentieth centuries. Since American poets tend to overvalue the formal aspects of their art, it follows that they also tend to overestimate the synecdochic relationship between those formal aspects and various ideas of America. It is one thing to trace in the style of a writer an implied set of notions of, and attitudes toward, America, but it is quite another to evaluate critically the polemical statements of Whitman, Pound, Williams, or Ginsberg, statements that use notions of America as explicit justifications for various aesthetic ideologies. For example, when Roethke, equally adept at metrical and nonmetrical forms, explains in his essay "Some Remarks on Rhythm" (1960) that "there are areas of experience in modern life that simply cannot be rendered by either the formal lyric or straight prose," he implies a procedure for reading.[4] Instead of proceeding from the technical aspects of style to an implied notion of American experience, the reader encounters first a notion of that experience from which, Roethke argues, a certain appropriate style, with certain formal aspects, ought to follow.

Such an argument is a fiction, or rather a series of fictions: a fiction about modern life (parts of it are inaccessible to certain literary forms), a fiction about literary forms (certain forms can do things other forms cannot), and a fiction about the relationship between them (the poet ought to find the right form for modern life). To call these assumptions "fictions" is not to judge their truth value, not to call them wrong or false.[5] Instead, it is to suggest that American poetry defines and distinguishes itself not only by the unique ways in which it foregrounds signifiers but also by the unique ways in which it promotes the significance of its own formation. Statements such as Roethke's operate alongside a poem, establishing a figurative discourse that relates to the poem as a patient's associations in therapy about a dream relate to the dream itself: although not strictly part of the original, they often develop or extend the original, appearing to analyze or explain but instead compounding precisely that which needs to be analyzed or explained.

The fictions of form in American poetry arise, then, from both the heightened significance American poets attach to form as it organizes a given poem or poems and the figurative significance they attach to form as it relates to the world outside the poem, the world or worlds they think of as America. In their discussion of contemporary American poetic schools and techniques, Harold Bloom and David Bromwich treat these fictions harshly: "Am[erican] poetry since the end of World War II is an epitome of this reverse Emersonianism: no other poets in Western history have so self-deceivingly organized themselves along the supposed lines of formal divisions." Not at all shy about judging the truth value of "the supposed lines of formal divisions," which have been so important to American poets not just since World War II but since Emerson, Bloom and Bromwich recall Tocqueville in a significant way. Quoting Emerson's injunction "Ask the fact for the form" ("Poetry and Imagination") to claim that recent American poets have reversed it "to beg the form for the fact," they conclude with the question "For what, finally, can poetic form mean to an Am[erican]?"[6]

Posed as a rhetorical question, this query corners the reader, demanding an answer such as "nothing" or "not much." These are certainly the answers Tocqueville would expect, having described American writers who will slight or despise the obstacles form places between them and the bold expression of their rude, untutored vigor. But whereas Tocqueville describes, wrongly as it turns out, the secondary importance he believes Americans will attach to form, Bloom and Bromwich prescribe that Americans ought not to attach to it the primary importance that many do. According to them, the American poet overvalues form as a defense against the recognition of this essential truth: "Every Am[erican] poet who aspires to strength knows that he starts in the eveningland, realizes he is a latecomer, fears to be only a secondary man." The implication, then, is that only a secondary poet considers form primary. Support for this belief could come from Emerson's statement that "it is not metres, but a metre-making argument that makes a poem," a statement that many have read as a justification for organicism, but one that could also mean that poetic form of any kind should not matter compared with "a thought so passionate and alive."[7]

This is an attractive position. It rests on a long tradition of distinguishing between mere versifiers and true poets, a tradition including

Emerson's statement in "The Poet" (1844) that "we do not speak now of men of poetical talents, or of industry and skill in metre, but of the true poet" (W 3:8–9). In the specific context of Emerson's thought, or a Bloomian account of Emerson's thought, this position gathers the added power of Romantic rhetoric, which pits the loftiness of individual sublimity against the smallness of social conventions, including the literary conventions of poetic form. The culmination of this thinking comes in the magisterial dismissal, "neither closed nor open forms could be anything but an evasion."[8] But this formulation is inadequate for at least two reasons. First, although it strives to correct the overvaluation of poetic form, it does so by undervaluing poetic form. This is true of many discussions of poetry and individual poems, discussions that mistakenly assume that what a poem "says" can be extracted from its formal husk. Bloom's own work, so often admirable and incisive, is especially guilty, as his tracking of figurative patterns leads from the prose of Emerson or Freud to the verse of Whitman or Stevens as though these were interchangeable kinds of discourse.

Second, if it is true that neither closed nor open forms could be anything but an evasion, then of all people Bloom, the master classifier of evasions, should realize how significant poetic forms are. He should realize that the more American poets concentrate on form, in both theory and practice, the more meaning accrues to whatever it is they are evading by means of form. For him the explanation is simple: formal preoccupations mask anxiousness about poetic strength and originality. No doubt, to a large extent this is true. But any poet emerging now in any country necessarily emerges in Bloom's belated eveningland; and yet, according to Bloom and Bromwich, no other poets in Western history have been so preoccupied with formal issues. If this last statement is true, then there must be some connection between the Americanness of these poets and their preoccupations.

One last interesting aspect of the discussion by Bloom and Bromwich is that it marks an end point of the literary historical narrative that begins with Tocqueville. Between the 1830s, when the latter predicts American writers will be indifferent to form, and the 1970s, when the former find American poets organizing themselves along the lines of formal divisions, at least one aspect of American poetry changes dramatically. Especially remarkable is the language various commentators have used to describe the engines and motives behind this change. In it the idioms of psychopathology abound. Predictably, Bloom and Bromwich speak of "a welter of wholly shared anxieties that unite the feuding camps."[9] But they are not alone in adopting this tone. In *The Continuity of American Poetry* (1961), Roy Harvey Pearce describes the history of American poetry as the history of "the American poet's compulsion (or obligation) again and again to justify his existence as poet." As a result of this compulsiveness, he concludes, "American poetry is characteristically tendentious, over-committed, programmatic, self-conscious, often—even in its moments of grandeur—provincial and jejune."[10] In *Lucifer in Harness* (1973), Edwin Fussell sketches "a literary situation dominated by deprivation and therefore by excessive national self-consciousness and resentment, manageable only by desperate remedies born of frustration and tension."[11] Discussing experimentalism in American poetry, John Hollander notes that "an obsession with form has been widespread in American poetry" and argues that "the *sine qua non* of originality has led to an almost obsessive concern, in American poetry in particular, with metrical format."[12] Finally, Daniel Hoffman details in rather grisly terms "the fratricidal intensity" that characterizes quarrels among various American poetic schools and groups.[13]

Anxiety, compulsion, self-consciousness, desperation, frustration, tension, obsession, fratricidal intensity: these terms probe the dark side of the American will toward poetic independence, a will that Emerson's address "The American Scholar" (1837) first voices so aggressively in public: "Our day of dependence, our long apprenticeship to the learning of other lands, draws to a close" (W 1:81). The synchronization of Emerson's exhortations and Tocqueville's unflattering survey is no coincidence. Although the history of American poetry includes the earlier accomplishments of, among others, Bradstreet, Taylor, Freneau, Wheatley, Bryant, and Poe, each of whom manifests a certain self-consciousness about the role of a poet in the New World, American poetic self-consciousness becomes acute with Emerson's reaction to the same void Tocqueville observes. This acuteness not only makes the language of psychopathology appropriate to the critical discussions mentioned above; it also saturates the reexamination of poetic form that Emerson initiates.

In his remarks about the fratricidal intensity of contemporary disagreements, Hoffman goes on to comment that such intensity "reflects a peculiarly American situation."[14] This statement belongs to the large body of commentary by writers who attempt to define the Americanness of American poetry. For example, having acknowledged only journalists as American authors, Tocqueville classifies other writers as "aliens" who "amuse the mind, but . . . do not act upon the manners of the people" (2:56). Also written from a foreigner's perspective, Auden's essay "American Poetry" (1955) calls the diversity of such poets as Longfellow and Whitman "an American phenomenon" and proceeds with a statement that anticipates Pearce's quoted above: "To some degree every American poet feels that the whole responsibility for contemporary poetry has fallen upon his shoulders, that he is a literary aristocracy of one." But it is in a longer passage that Auden approaches American fictions of poetic form:

> Just as in their political thinking Americans are apt to identify the un-democratic with monarchy, so, in their aesthetics, they are apt to identify the falsely conventional with rhyme and meter. The prose of Emerson and Thoreau is superior to their verse, because verse in its formal nature protests against protesting; it demands that to some degree we accept things as they are, not for any rational or moral reason, but simply because they happen to be that way; it implies an element of frivolity in the creation.[15]

Like Tocqueville, Auden recognizes the analogy between American political thinking and aesthetics, but he differs by criticizing implicitly the reductive, humorless aspect of the analogy, especially its failure to recognize and enjoy a frivolity that is the opposite of acute self-consciousness, anxiety, compulsion, obsessiveness, and the rest.

For another English poet, Robert Graves, the essence of the American poet is restlessness: "Whitman did much the same [as Blake], though for different reasons: he epitomizes the restless American habit, first noted in the eighteenth century, of moving adventurously west across the trackless prairie, scratch-farming as one goes, instead of clinging to some pleasant Pennsylvanian farm, improving crops and stock by careful husbandry, and building a homestead for one's children and grandchildren." Significantly, Graves's playful extended metaphor comes in the midst of a polemical paragraph on the "heresy of free verse." He, too, recognizes the knotting of psychological, sociological, and formal threads in American poetry. Not surprisingly, Graves's polemic ends in an affirmation of an American poet who managed to confine his restlessness to the limits of traditional prosody: "Robert Frost's poems, which combine traditional metres with intensely personal rhythms, show the advantage of staying put and patiently working at the problem."[16]

But the most serious, extended attempts to define the Americanness of American poetry have come, naturally enough, from Americans.[17] For Pearce, the "'Americanness' of American poetry is, quite simply, its compulsive 'modernism'—or, with some poets in the twentieth century, its compulsive 'traditionalism,' which is, ironically enough, a form of 'modernism.'" Hyatt Waggoner explains that "focusing on Emerson seemed to me originally, and still seems, to throw more light on the question of what's *American* about American poetry than any other approach could have."[18] For Fussell, Americanness lies in an ambivalence toward Great Britain that manifests itself in the radical tradition of poetic technique. Albert Gelpi suggests that American poets are "challenged by their culture and so driven more deeply than others into the erotic and instinctual resources of the individual psyche."[19] For Hoffman, the peculiarly American situation of contemporary poetry necessarily involves the fierce competition to be number one: "A nation of over two hundred million requires, as in politics, boxing, rock music, and all else, that a poet be king of the cats, or be ignored." Finally, for Bloom the "American poetic soul emerges as the Coleridgean moon of imagination . . . but with the destructive American Emersonian difference, an antithetical flight or repression away from art and nature alike, towards the solipsistic grandeur that is a new Gnosis."[20]

The critical urge to isolate the essential Americanness of American poetry surely reveals some of the same nervous self-consciousness that characterizes the poetry itself. But this does not mean that such an urge is necessarily unproductive or wrongheaded, as long as it acknowledges that an essential Americanness may be a mirage. Instead, it means that American poetry has succeeded in making fictions about itself that persuade its readers that its uniqueness transcends merely geographical boundaries. For many readers, such as Fussell, that uniqueness depends primarily on developments in poetic form: "Therefore we can say that the soul of American poetry dwells in its rhythm, and that we can approach that soul, however imperfectly, through metrical analysis." For other readers, such as Bloom and Bromwich, "the issue of form is as always bogus."[21] In the present study, I want to avoid both these positions, one of which succumbs too uncritically to the fictions American poetry generates about itself and the other of which dismisses those fictions too glibly. Alternatively, I suggest that the uniqueness of American poetry lies not so much in its forms as in its formalism and in the various attitudes that formalism reveals.

2

"Formalism" has gathered many different meanings and associations, both positive and negative, from the history of twentieth-century literary criticism. In much recent Anglo-American criticism of twentieth-century poetry, "formalist," or its more recent derivative, "New Formalist," describes poets who prefer traditional prosodic forms, poets such as Robinson, Frost, Ransom, Crane, Tate, Wilbur, Nemerov, Hecht, and Hollander.[22] Used in this way, the term denotes the opposite of "antiformalist" or "informalist" poets, such as Pound, Williams, Olson, Ginsberg, Ammons, and Charles Wright, who discard traditional forms in favor of freer ones. Between these poles, Stevens, Moore, Eliot, Cummings, Hughes, Roethke, Bishop, Hayden, Berryman, Lowell, Brooks, Dickey, Ashbery, Merwin, James Wright, Kinnell, Rich, and

Plath arrange themselves in various ways, depending on what poem or part of a career is under consideration. In this context, the connotations of "formalist" depend, of course, on whether or not one sides with either the cooked or the raw, as Lowell dubbed the two poles.

But "formalism" can be used in a way that denies this polarity and more fully illuminates one aspect of American poetry. As Denis Donoghue has remarked about Williams, for example, "Nor is 'informal art' adequate to Williams, who was just as formal as Stevens but practised a different sense of formality."[23] Likewise, James Breslin argues that Williams's "approach is formalist in the sense that he brackets content in order to focus on 'the elementary construction of the modern poem.'"[24] Used this way, "formalism" implies a profound engagement with various aspects of poetic form, regardless of whether they are traditional or avant-garde. Also, it suggests a degree of seriousness, even solemnity, that is antithetical to the frivolity Auden associates with conventional prosody.

The example of Williams is a good one, and I have considered it at greater length elsewhere.[25] Although he went out of his way to disparage and revile the use of conventional prosody by American poets, he never lapsed into the casual offhandedness about poetic form that the terms "antiformalist" or "informalist" would suggest. Instead, he devoted much of his attention and energy to promoting with an intense earnestness his own formal experiments, an earnestness that bordered on preoccupation and obsession. In this way, Williams's formalism may have been extreme, but if so, it was simply a more obvious example of a tendency shared by many American poets named above.

Stevens presents another interesting case. Although his greatest poems tend to fall into approximations of blank verse, it is often a loose blank verse at best. He is not nearly as devoted to traditional fixed forms as Yeats or Auden, and so is not as much a formalist, in the first sense, as they are. But he does share with Williams a tendency toward the second kind of formalism, as this passage from "Two or Three Ideas" (1951) reveals:

> If one keeps in mind the fact that most poets who have something to say are content with what they say and that most poets who have little or nothing to say are concerned primarily with the way in which they say it, the importance of this discussion becomes clear. I do not mean to imply that the poets who have something to say are the poets that matter; for obviously if it is true that the style of a poem and the poem itself are one, it follows that, in considering style and its own creations, that is to say, the relation between style and the unfamiliar, it may be, or become, that the poets who have little or nothing to say are, or will be, the poets that matter.[26]

In the same year he published "Two or Three Ideas," Stevens read "The Relations between Poetry and Painting," later included in *The Necessary Angel* (1951), in New York at the Museum of Modern Art. Citing passages from this latter essay and from a 1946 letter to José Rodriguez Feo, Marjorie Perloff demonstrates that Stevens, at least on some occasions, prefers to identify himself with poets who have something to say, not with poets, such as Pound or Williams, who are more interested in the way they say things.[27]

Nevertheless, the broader kind of formalism stamps the above passage from "Two or Three Ideas" in two unmistakable ways. First, it assumes "that the style of a poem and the poem itself are one." Although here "style" reaches beyond prosody to include other elements of voice, such as trope, diction, and rhetoric, Stevens believes that the poem necessarily foregrounds its signifiers in ways that deny their transparency. Style is not merely the secondary ornamentation of poetic statement; it is the primary reality of the poem.

Second, Stevens distinguishes between poets with something to say, who are content to say it, and poets with nothing to say, who are concerned primarily with the way they say it. In this somewhat facetious formulation, the second kind of poets are formalists who bracket content to concentrate on the construction of the poem. Of course, Stevens dissembles when he identifies them as having nothing to say, since what they have to say is that the construction of a poem represents the encounter between the imagination and reality. Furthermore, in the long final sentence of his paragraph, with its hedgings and qualifications ("it may be, or become, that the poets who have little or nothing to say are, or will be, the poets that matter"), Stevens confronts the consequences of his own unraveling argument, as the statement that the poem and its style are one necessarily means that the way of saying something matters as much as what is said. No good poets could be content only with what they say.

The reception of American poetry bears Stevens out. The canonical poets have not been content with simply saying what they have to say; they have also been deeply concerned with the way they say it. They are not only, or even primarily, poets of statement but also of style and form. The best examples here are Eliot and Pound, poets whose statements have alienated many readers, but whose experiments with style and form have secured them places in the American poetic canon. Conversely, Emerson and Thoreau come to mind as poets who valued, at least in their own verse, statement over stylistic and formal innovation and so, in the canon of American literature, are more important for their prose than their verse.

If the major American poetry from Emerson and Whitman to the present is broadly formalist on at least one level, whether or not it always adheres to traditional prosody, then the next question is what kind of critical approach best illuminates the nature and significance of that formalism. Unfortunately, the waxings and wanings of various theoretical approaches over the last twenty years have kindled some of the same hostility among critics that characterizes competition among poets. Mutual antagonism brings loss to all, for no one gains when a new insight begets new blindness or, more dangerous for readers of poetry, deafness. If some approaches appear to need reminding that the writing and reading of poetry bind themselves to more general human activities, other approaches appear to need reminding that certain events take place in poems that do not take place in all kinds of human utterance and inscription.[28]

Least useful are those approaches that insist on binary pairings of opposites, such as formalist and antiformalist, cooked and raw, or closed and projective. Certainly, these binary descriptions identify differences, but the differences they identify are superficial and not the differences that make a difference. All too often the binary approach leads to platitudes about poets who use traditional forms to insulate themselves from historical experience and those who use experimental forms to plunge themselves into the midst of historical experience.

Instead, a more appropriate response to the formalism of American poetry would reflect what Breslin calls "an historically informed formalist criticism."[29] Just as the term "formalist" can be misunderstood in its application to specific poems and poets, so can it in its application to criticism. In his essay "Beyond Formalism" (1966), Geoffrey Hartman tries to correct some misunderstandings, arguing against F. W. Bateson's definition of *formalism* as "a tendency to isolate the aesthetic fact from its human content" by defining it instead "simply as a method . . . of revealing the human content of art by a study of its formal properties":

> This definition does not say that form and content are separable; nor does it infer that the human and the formal could not be caught and exposited as one thing by a great interpreter. It does suggest that the literary scholar establishes a priority which has procedural significance and which engages him mediately and dialectically with the formal properties of the work of art. I do not know whether the mind can ever free itself genuinely of these procedural restraints—whether it can get beyond formalism without going through the study of forms.[30]

Although Hartman argues here about the nature of formalist criticism, much of what he says also has important implications for a discussion of formalist poetry.

Bateson's charge against formalist criticism, that it isolates the aesthetic fact from its human content, sounds remarkably like the usual charge against so-called formalist poetry, poetry that uses traditional forms. Lowell, for example, worries about poets of his generation who "have gotten terribly proficient" at using fixed forms, but whose "writing seems divorced from culture somehow." Claiming that these poems in fixed forms "can't handle much experience," he concludes by urging that "there must be some breakthrough back into life."[31] For both Bateson the critic and Lowell the poet, formalism implies a set of habits and assumptions that deny the humanity of art. Hartman's redefinition of formalism as a method of revealing humanity by studying form answers not only the critic but also the poet: the characteristic formalism of American poetry reveals human content, and often national attitudes, through its attention to its own formal properties.

But to some even a redefined and enlightened formalism remains unacceptable, as it appears to turn form into fetish. Hartman quotes this criticism from Trotsky's *Literature and Revolution* (1925): "'Having counted the adjectives,' says Trotsky of the formalist, 'and weighed the lines, and measured the rhythms, a Formalist either stops silent with the expression of a man who does not know what to do with himself, or throws out an unexpected generalization which contains five per cent Formalism and ninety-five per cent of the most uncritical intuition.'" Trotsky levels his charges against the formalist critic, but Victor Erlich summarizes the analogous case against the formalist writer: "Ever since 1930 'formalism' has been in Soviet parlance a term of censure, connoting undue preoccupation with 'mere' form, bourgeois 'escapism' and like offenses."[32]

In the context of Marxist debate, Terry Eagleton has summarized and challenged the traditional Marxist opposition to formalism, an opposition "attacking that inbred attention to sheerly technical properties which robs literature of historical significance and reduces it to an aesthetic game." Extending Georg Lukács's statement in *The Evolution of Modern Drama* (1909) that "the truly social element in literature is the form," Eagleton argues against a reductive version of antiformalism: "It is against this danger that Lukács's comment is meant to warn: the true bearers of ideology in art are the very forms, rather than abstractable content, of the work itself. We find the impress of history in the literary work precisely *as literary*, not as some superior form of social documentation."[33] One might argue, reasonably enough, that these assertions hold for epic narratives, realistic novels, or modern plays, but not for lyric poems that not only foreground their own patterning but also, in many of the cases this book will examine, insist on commenting, explicitly or obliquely, on that patterning. Such poems, the argument might continue, have succumbed to a formal narcissism beyond the reach of the historical world.

But John Hollander has demonstrated richly and repeatedly that when poems talk to, and about, themselves, they do so "not to evade discourse about the rest of the world, then, but to enable it." Specifically, Hollander concerns himself with what he calls the fictional "ulteriority" of poems that comment on themselves, as their self-descriptions turn to allegories about what lies beyond them. What I am interested in here is a broader kind of ulteriority, one that includes the allegories generated by self-descriptive poems, as well as the various links and analogies between poets' notions of poetic form and their notions of America and Americanness. If Hollander is correct in arguing that "poetry gets to be the poetry of life by successfully becoming first the poetry of poetry," as the example of Stevens suggests that he surely is, then it follows that in certain ways the poems with the most profound connections to America are often those that appear at first to have the least to say about it.[34]

3

The American preoccupation with form, and the inevitable slippages in the meaning of the word "form," began with Puritanism and religious dissent, as the objects, rituals, and language of the Anglican Church became the focus of criticism, but with Emerson the examinations of religious and literary forms converge most obviously. F. O. Matthiessen describes this convergence as a "breakdown of the distinctions between poetry and belief."[35] At this point, I want to sample the various connotations of Emerson's notions of form and to reassess the nature and significance of his supposed antinomianism.

Not only do the connotations of "form" vary from context to context in Emerson's writing, but they also vary from stage to stage in his career. In a journal entry for May 26, 1837, he muses on his own individuality: "As a plant in the earth so I grow in God. I am only a form of him."[36] The phrase "only a form" suggests a lesser material version of a spiritual ideal and anticipates a statement in "The Poet" (1844) that typically blurs the boundaries between art and religion: "It is a proof of the shallowness of the doctrine of beauty as it lies in the minds of our amateurs, that men seem to have lost the perception of the instant dependence of form upon soul" (W 3:3). The model behind such statements is Platonic, and it casts form in a secondary, derivative role.

But from these relatively neutral uses of "form," it is a short step to more pejorative connotations. In "The American Scholar" (1837), as one result of the fabled breaking up of the One Man into many men, "the priest becomes a form" (W 1:84). Likewise, a sentence in "The Divinity School Address" (1838) anticipates the criticisms of formalism discussed above: "Whenever the pulpit is usurped by a formalist, then is the worshipper defrauded and disconsolate" (W 1:137). In the same address, he warns of the Lord's Supper that if "no heart warm this rite, the hollow, dry, creaking formality is too plain" (W 1:140). Finally, the address culminates in a stirring passage that, once again, speaks of religion in terms that include art: "The question returns, What shall we do? I confess, all attempts to project and establish a Cultus with new rites and forms, seem to me vain. . . . Rather let the breath of new life be breathed by you through the forms already existing. For if once you are alive, you shall find they shall become plastic and new. The remedy to their deformity is first, soul, and second, soul, and evermore, soul. A whole popedom of forms one pulsation of virtue can uplift and vivify" (W 1:149–50). The injunction to "let the breath of new life be breathed by you through the forms already existing" is especially interesting, since it signals a reluctance to abandon altogether the old forms, no matter how hollow, dry, and creaking.

This passage mixes the conservative with the radical into Emerson's unique blend, but the result of such mixing is not always so reassuring. Sometimes it contains an ambivalence that, later in the history of American poetry, germinates into less manageable feelings, such as anxiousness and obsession. In "Experience" (1844), for example, he makes this formulation: "Human life is made up of the two elements, power and form, and the proportion must be invariably kept if we would have it sweet and sound" (W 3:65). In the later essay "Fate" (1860), these two elements will be called freedom and fate or limitation, and it is not at all clear that the proportion between them can be "invariably kept," despite Emerson's cherished fiction of compensation, or that the keeping of proportion can guarantee the sweetness and soundness of human life. Instead, Emerson describes humanity as "a stupendous antagonism, a dragging together of the poles of the Universe," reasoning that "if Fate follows and limits Power, Power attends and antagonizes Fate" (W 6:22).

First comes the conception of form as passively dependent on soul, then a belief that soul can reclaim existing forms that have forgotten their dependence on it, and finally an image of power, or soul, as the constant attendant and antagonist of fate, or form. This succession dramatizes the rebellion of Emerson's notion of form against the original hierarchical scheme that placed it safely in a subordinate position. In Emerson's late mythology, his ambivalence toward form is figured as the clashing of two equal opponents. But although that ambivalence roots itself in Emerson's personal history and private concerns, it also corresponds to an aspect of national character that Matthiessen traces to a statement by Tocqueville: "'Democratic nations naturally stand more in need of forms than other nations, and they naturally respect them less.'"[37] Emerson's mythologized ambivalence is simply a more vivid version of a general condition. What has been dismissed as secondary refuses to accept its subordinate position.

Furthermore, Emerson's ambivalence toward form—whether poetic form, ecclesiastical form, existential form (fate or limitation), or material form (the opposite of soul or the ideal)—makes what many have judged to be his antinomianism more complex.[38] But in the midst of general agreement, a dissenting voice is that of Sacvan Bercovitch: "Perhaps the most misleading commonplace of recent criticism is that our major literature through Emerson is Antinomian."[39] A statement from "Self-Reliance" (1841) supports the position that Emerson may not be quite as much against the law (*anti* + *nomos*) as some seem to think: "The populace think that your rejection of popular standards is a rejection of all standard, and mere antinomianism; and the bold sensualist will use the name of philosophy to gild his crimes. But the law of consciousness abides. . . . If any one imagines that this law is lax, let him keep its commandment one day" (W 2:74). These are not the sentiments of one who believes that faith alone is necessary for salvation or that the moral law does not pertain to him. They reveal instead a serious commitment to that law, a law originating outside the self in a transcendent source on which the self depends. Emerson does not refuse to be bound by moral law, but instead binds himself even more tightly to a more inclusive, more exacting version of that law.

In this way, his attitude toward moral law is like his attitude toward form. Here and there he may reject specific examples of law or form—although the passage from "The Divinity School Address" shows that he can be reluctant to do even that—but he does so only to substitute his own gigantic law or form, the one he calls fate. As a result, he becomes the prototype of many a later American poet whose apparent rejection of one law doubles as a serious commitment to an even more demanding one, as one kind of formalism yields to another.[40] At the same time, he also enacts on an individual level the American rejection of an unsatisfactory law (the word "Laws" returns like a refrain throughout the Declaration of Independence) and the subsequent development of an exaggerated litigiousness.

But Bercovitch also has something slightly different in mind: "If Emerson differs from the chauvinist by his Romantic self-reliance, he differs equally from the Romantic Antinomian by his reliance on a national mission."[41] This is indeed an important difference, as it links Emerson's reevaluation of anterior laws and forms to his sense of America, what it is and what it should be. In making this link, Bercovitch points to what I have been calling the fiction of form, an imaginative creation that imbues aesthetic ideology with a sense of national significance. Now, not all American poets after Emerson are "intensely nationalistic," as Fussell points out; in fact, some are "scarcely national."[42] Whitman, Williams, Pound, and Crane, for example, make their sense of national mission much clearer than do Dickinson, Frost, Stevens, and Moore. But this does not mean that the formalism of the latter operates in an ideological vacuum. It simply means that their fictions may be more subtle and elusive.

For example, when Stevens concedes that the poets who matter most may turn out to be those with nothing to say, he subverts, willingly or unwillingly, poets who would say something, presumably about themselves, their experiences, their beliefs and opinions, all of which point toward what it means to be an actual citizen of an actual society, toward what Stevens would consider aspects of reality rather than the imagination. These are precisely the aspects Stevens commits himself to avoiding, as he makes plain in "The Noble Rider and the Sound of Words" (1942):

> Reality then became violent and so remains. This much ought to be said to make it a little clearer that in speaking of the pressure of reality, I am thinking of life in a state of violence, not physically violent, as yet, for us in America, but physically violent for millions of our friends and for still more millions of our enemies and spiritually violent, it may be said, for everyone alive.
>
> A possible poet must be a poet capable of resisting or evading the pressure of the reality of this last degree, with the knowledge that the degree of today may become a deadlier degree tomorrow.

Somewhat later Stevens then repeats this conclusion even more explicitly: "The truth is that the social obligation so closely urged is a phase of the pressure of reality which a poet (in the absence of dramatic poets) is bound to resist or evade today."[43] Stevens's insistence than a poet must evade reality, especially the aspects of reality operating in wartime America, opens him to the charge that his preoccupation with the imagination, or with the style of the poems it generates, typifies bourgeois escapism. But a more sympathetic reader might explain Stevens's evasion another way, arguing that, far from operating in a vacuum, his formalism springs directly from his vision of "the nature and fate of actual

society" in America. In so doing, it gathers as much national significance as the more positive missions of Emerson or Whitman.

Emerson's figurative image of this mission comes in "The Poet": "Yet
America is a poem in our eyes; its ample geography dazzles the imagination, and it will not wait long for metres" (W 3:38). Like Whitman's
echoing statement that the United States "themselves are essentially the
greatest poem," Emerson's image assumes that the nature and fate of
actual society are compatible with the poetic imagination and, beyond
it, with poetic form. Furthermore, the triangulation of America, imagination, and form does not derive from glib optimism. Emerson's catalogue mixes the celebratory tone Whitman later amplifies with sobering
fact: "Our log-rolling, our stumps and their politics, our fisheries, our
Negroes and Indians, our boats and our repudiations, the wrath of
rogues and the pusillanimity of honest men, the northern trade, the
southern planting, the western clearing, Oregon and Texas, are yet un-
sung" (W 3:37–38). Behind what sounds like the rhetoric of boosterism,
Emerson refers directly to examples of "life in a state of violence" when
he mentions "our Negroes and our Indians," a phrase that suggests that
"Negroes" and "Indians" are objects of American experience rather
than subjects who experience America. In 1831, for example, Nat
Turner led a slave rebellion in Virginia that killed fifty-seven whites and
led to suppression in which at least one hundred blacks were killed. In
1832 the Black Hawk War pushed Sauk and Fox Indians west across
the Mississippi, and between 1836 and 1842 the United States waged an
unpopular war against the Seminoles in Florida.

For Emerson what must be sung about America necessarily includes
these and other consequences of "the wrath of rogues and the pusillanimity of honest men." Likewise, Whitman's imagination does not
evade the pressure of violent reality, as in the passages from "Song of
Myself" (1855) about the wreck of the *San Francisco*, the hounded
slave, the mashed firemen, the old artillerist, or the massacre of Captain
Fannin's soldiers by the Mexicans after his surrender at Goliad, March
1836:

> None obeyed the command to kneel,
> Some made a mad and helpless rush . . . . some stood stark and straight,
> A few fell at once, shot in the temple or heart . . . . the living and dead
>   lay together,
> The maimed and mangled dug in the dirt . . . . the new-comers saw
>   them there;
> Some half-killed attempted to crawl away,
> These were dispatched with bayonets or battered with the blunts
>   of muskets;

A youth not seventeen years old seized his assassin till two more came
    to release him,
The three were all torn, and covered with the boy's blood.

At eleven o'clock began the burning of the bodies;
And that is the tale of the murder of the four hundred and twelve
    young men,
And that was a jetblack sunrise.[44]

Although one hundred years and several wars later the scale of violence
here might seem small to Stevens, he cannot be thinking of too many
more graphic instances of the pressure of reality.

Perhaps Stevens would applaud this passage as an example of the poetry of statement that focuses on what it has to say rather than on the
way it says it; or perhaps he would reject the passage as an example of
war poetry that fails to resist adequately the pressures of factual reality,
as his own war poems appear to do. In an undated prose statement, he
admits that the "poetry of war and the poetry of a work of the imagination are two different things." In the poetry of war the consciousness of
fact usurps the imagination and its poetry that "constantly illustrates
the fundamental and endless struggle with fact." Stevens might argue
that in yielding to the pressure of reality, Whitman's imagination has
been displaced by the consciousness of fact, or at least "fact as we want
it to be" or "fact as everyone is at least satisfied to have it be."[45]

But such an argument would misread Whitman. Among the achievements in the "tale of a jetblack sunrise" are those that are wholly imaginative and stylistic. By manipulating syntax, for example, Whitman
manufactures the illusion of a factual consciousness presenting a journalistic account. As James Perrin Warren has demonstrated, Whitman's
verse generates many of its characteristic effects by manipulating the frequency of finite verb elements.[46] In the passage above, the frequency of
finite verb elements reaches a level that is uncharacteristically high for
Whitman, as each line contains at least one complete sentence or independent clause. Syntax grounds the passage firmly in the temporal realm
of events and action, while alliteration, among other devices, foregrounds its signifiers and distinguishes it from journalistic reportage.

The point is that the poetry of reality and the poetry of imagination,
as of statement and of style, are not mutually exclusive as far as Emerson and Whitman are concerned. At the moment in literary history Matthiessen calls the American Renaissance, history and formalism cooper-
ate. Their fiction is that history is the source of form, that what America
is and does cannot help but find its way into meters and "the free
growth of metrical laws" (*CRE* 714) that Whitman praises in his preface. Conversely, those freely growing metrical laws reflect back an

image of historical America. But for Stevens America is not a poem in our eyes, as it subjects the imagination to the withering pressures of factual reality. His fiction is that history and the imagination are not generally compatible, so that it is the job of the poet not to sing but to struggle against the real America.

4

Ever since Pearce's study, the question of continuity has been prominent: Is the history of American poetry properly a narrative of forces, principles, and impulses that have operated uninterruptedly from the beginning? In his discussion of mythic and Adamic impulses, Pearce answers yes. Likewise, Waggoner's emphasis on Emerson and Emersonianism is a narrative of essential unity. For Fussell the history of American poetry is dialectical, "the history of recurrent explosions . . . alternating with longer periods of conciliation and consolidation."[47] He locates the two major explosions in 1855 and 1912, but to these dates 1956 surely must be added, as it saw the publication of Ginsberg's *Howl*. Although Fussell's narrative includes interruptions and disjunctions, a larger continuous narrative subsumes them.

But since Emerson and Whitman, different versions of the relationship between formalism and America have emerged. In organizing my discussion, I have chosen to be selective, rather than comprehensive, looking in depth at four poets who are not usually associated with one another. In making this choice, I have sacrificed the encyclopedic approach of Pearce, Waggoner, Bernard Duffey, or David Perkins in *History of Modern Poetry*.[48] I have also foregone the taxonomic approach of Mutlu Konuk Blasing in *American Poetry*, who sorts representative poets into four categories headed by Poe, Emerson, Whitman, and Dickinson in an attempt "to view the field of American poetry cleared of the centering figure of Emerson."[49] I admire and have benefited from these studies, but in the limited space of this book I have opted to begin with a brief discussion of Whitman, who will serve here as both foreground and a point of comparison throughout, and then to consider at greater length four poets who represent difficult, complicated instances of both formalism and Americanness. If my grouping appears unorthodox, the heterodoxy is necessary, for it enables me to challenge some of the critical truths propounded by the studies I have named.

The first poet is Dickinson. In the century after her, the demands of poets' public personae have produced much that is of mixed value for their readers. The lecture, the reading, the essay, the radio broadcast, and the interview all contribute to a vast body of material that begins where the poem ends. Sometimes illuminating, sometimes obscuring, this material often encroaches on the poem itself by calling attention too aggressively to some of its parts and distracting from others. Even more private media, such as the journal, the notebook, and the letter, take on a particular kind of significance in the hands of poets who know that they are recognized as poets, that their biographies will be written, their letters collected, their notebooks and journals purchased by libraries and edited by scholars. Inevitably, a discussion of what poetic form means to poets will draw heavily on this material, since often its function is to explain, even to defend, the poem to its readers. Explanations and defenses become especially important when they edge away from hard analysis, exposition, and denotation toward metaphor, ellipsis, and connotation because, after all, the latter constitute the element in which poets best reveal meaning. The fictions of form often reside in the gaps between poet and poem or poem and reader, gaps between intention and realization.

But in Dickinson's case too much is missing. The public persona, the consciousness of an audience, the need to explain and defend, the sense of a larger national mission such as Emerson's or Whitman's—none of these provoked her into commenting on her unique brand of formalism. One can only wonder what would have happened had she felt it necessary to justify her meters, rhymes, and dashes as Williams felt he had to justify his variable foot. Instead, her readers have only letters, a few prose fragments, memoirs by her brother's lover's daughter, a scholar's reconstruction of her "years and hours," necessarily incomplete biographical studies, and the 1,775 poems. Even Hopkins, in many ways her likeness in anonymity and isolation, left so much more.

Beyond Dickinson lie the modernists and a multitude of polemical essays and manifestoes. With the emergence of so much poetic self-evaluation, a peculiar situation arises. One of Eliot's biographers, Peter Ackroyd, describes it, commenting on the appearance of the first book-length study of Eliot, George Williamson's *The Talent of T. S. Eliot* (1929): "A process was beginning here which is unique in twentieth-century poetry: of a poet setting the context and the principles for the description and critical evaluation of his own work."[50] Whitman's strategy of writing reviews of his own work, reviews that were then published anonymously or under someone else's name, no doubt anticipates this twentieth-century process, but certainly Ackroyd is correct in believing that with the moderns the process becomes overt.

Because Dickinson established almost no context and no principles for the description and critical evaluation of her work, description and evaluation, in at least one way, are greatly simplified: her own account of her intentions does not interfere. But with the moderns, the fictions of form double and blur. One must reckon not only with an insistent, intimidating formalism in the poems, but also with insistent, intimidating explanations by the poets. That these two kinds of fiction rarely resolve themselves into one is inevitable. Williams presents one obvious example of this blurring, but chapter 4 approaches modernist formalism by taking up the example of Pound. Since Pound generated so much written material in addition to verse, this chapter, more than the rest, examines letters, essays, and related media, such as radio broadcasts, in arguing, among other points, the inadequacy of associating Pound solely with the experimental or avant-garde pole of any binary opposition. Not only is he deeply involved with traditional prosody, but his own brand of formalism suggests an ulterior fiction that is both pragmatic and conservative. Furthermore, in Pound's case the ideological aspects of Americanism are especially complex.

Beyond modernism lies the terrain that reaches to the present. Chapter 5 considers Bishop. Like Roethke, Berryman, and Lowell, Bishop does not align herself exclusively with particular formal camps. In her work, as in theirs, the supposed polarities of closed and open forms are not stable. Although all these poets demonstrate their facility with traditional metrical forms, none maintains Frost's strict loyalty to them. The example of Williams was as important to Roethke as those of Yeats and Eliot and to Lowell as those of Eliot and Tate. Even Bishop, so often associated with the influences of Moore and Stevens, appreciated Williams deeply.

Like Dickinson, Bishop did not go out of her way to mythologize her own formalism, and like Stevens she sometimes seems to work at evading the pressures of reality, both historical and personal. But if the explicit self-descriptions of Pound and other modernists appear to have yielded to silence in the instance of Bishop, it is only because those descriptions have been modified and disguised. As for a sense of nationality implicit in her formalism, Bishop provides an intriguing case, especially since her ties with Canada complicate her Americanness. As Pound bridled at Whitman and his vision of historical America, so Bishop reacts against Pound and his. In this way, the ideological dimension of her formalism is similar to that of Dickinson, whose response to another outspoken male precursor, Emerson, resulted in a camouflaged national identity.

Chapter 6 enters the realm of the contemporary with the example of Ammons, whose work in several ways represents an inevitable culmination of American formalism. Unlike many of his contemporaries, Ammons has not published work in both closed and open forms. Whereas Ashbery, Kinnell, Merwin, James Wright, Rich, and Plath all in some way repeat Lowell's shift from strictly traditional prosody to looser structures, Ammons has devoted his powers exclusively to free verse. Even Ginsberg, whose conversion to free verse anticipated Lowell's, worked seriously with traditional forms for several years.

Furthermore, unlike many other poets of his generation Ammons has published only a few pages of critical prose. But since his earliest published efforts in 1951 he has meditated persistently on form within the poems themselves. In scrutinizing his own techniques and structures, Ammons has examined repeatedly their figurative, fictional powers. His formalism exceeds the basic preoccupation with form and style that is the lowest common denominator of American poetry and makes itself an explicit subject of his poems. Like Pound, Ammons has much to say about poetic form, but like Bishop he reacts against the modernist manifesto by inventing his own version of the *ars poetica*. Meanwhile, in Ammons's many evocations of America and Whitman, especially in *Sphere: The Form of a Motion* (1974), it would appear that the synecdochic relationship between form and nationality recognized by Tocqueville still operates, but it would also appear that the national mission of Emerson and Whitman has necessarily altered. Crane's *The Bridge* (1930) shows the ambiguous consequences for a modernist of trying to recover that mission in its original form; yet even in his extreme formalism, which acknowledges the instability of structures within the poem and without, Ammons retains a sense of national mission.

The foursome of Dickinson, Pound, Bishop, and Ammons includes several possible pairings. Dickinson and Ammons identify themselves with home, whereas Pound and Bishop opted for expatriation. Pound and Bishop write in both metrical and nonmetrical verse, whereas Dickinson and Ammons do not. Dickinson and Bishop are women whose formalism avoids public debate, whereas Pound and Ammons are men whose formalism engages in it, specifically with respect to Whitman. Bishop and Ammons represent the emergence of the professional poet in America, with various awards, grants, and university teaching positions to their names, whereas, for many reasons, Dickinson and Pound do not. But if these pairings demonstrate convenient symmetries and similarities, they do not unify the four, and this lack of unity is precisely the point. If there exists an occasional likeness between or among these poets, there remain deep, persistent differences. If the progression from Dickinson to Pound to Bishop to Ammons exhibits continuity, it is the continuity of continuous change, as Whitman's original pairing of America and formal innovation undergoes reexamination and rearrangement.

TWO

WALT WHITMAN'S SIX CHILDREN

THREE FAMOUS descriptions of his own formal practices illustrate Whitman's preference for what he calls "indirection" or "suggestiveness." Two appear in the 1855 preface to *Leaves of Grass*, which associates nationality with the notion of form in its opening paragraph: "[America] is not so impatient as has been supposed that the slough still sticks to opinions and manners and literature while the life which served its requirements has passed into the new life of the new forms" (*CRE* 709). In the first description, Whitman likens his own formal schemes to various flowers and fruits: "The rhyme and uniformity of perfect poems show the free growth of metrical laws and bud from them as unerringly and loosely as lilacs or roses on a bush, and take shapes as compact as the shapes of chestnuts and oranges and melons and pears, and shed the perfume impalpable to form" (*CRE* 714). Although for many readers this sentence constitutes a *locus classicus* of American organic theory, it raises a disturbing question: Why is it that a poet who continually renounces stylistic ornamentation, along with "the smooth walks, trimm'd hedges, poseys and nightingales of the English poets" (*Democratic Vistas* [1871]; *PW* 2:416–17), should link his verse to the carefully cultivated (the chestnut excepted), and even (in the case of lilacs and roses) ornamental, products of gardens, groves, and orchards?

Whitman's relationship to the ornamentation of "stock 'poetical' touches" (*Specimen Days and Collect* [1882]; *PW* 1:22) is complicated, and I shall return later to some of the questions it poses. As for the second self-descriptive passage of the 1855 preface, he chooses a domestic image: "He [the greatest poet] swears to his art, I will not be meddlesome, I will not have in my writing any elegance or effect or originality to hang in the way between me and the rest like curtains" (*CRE* 717). The simile "like curtains," enlarged in the next sentence to "the richest curtains," carries a particular resonance for a poet who values the opera and theater, in which curtains, at least on the proscenium stages of nineteenth-century New York, define the boundaries between audiences and actors.[1] Meanwhile, in a domestic setting, the curtain, or blind, encloses and hides the inside from the outside, or, in what became the eleventh section of "Song of Myself," the unseen desirer from the objects of her desire: "She hides handsome and richly drest aft the blinds of the window" (*CP* 36). Whether covering a private window or a public stage, the curtain functions as Whitman's image of mediation, and he attaches to it the pejorative connotations of "originality," which to him implies mere newfangledness.

In a subsequent chapter, I shall turn to this passage again, as well as to the third of the famous self-descriptions, the one reported by Horace Traubel in a conversation dated Monday, July 2, 1888, and glossed by Traubel's marginal note "The Question of Form." In this passage, Whitman claims that the likeness of his poetry "is not the solid stately palace, nor the sculpture that adorns it, nor the paintings on its walls. Its analogy is *the Ocean*." Unlike the other two passages, this one does not emerge in the context of nationality, but like the first it contains an odd twist, as Whitman distances himself from poems that "are polished, rhymed regular, with all the elegance of fine conceits, carefully elaborated," but then carefully elaborates two fine conceits of his own, those of a metrically regular poem as a palace and of his own lines as "liquid, billowy waves."[2] Admittedly, these careful elaborations may owe something to Traubel, but if so, they correspond to many of Whitman's own inventions.

But at least once Whitman articulates his assumptions about poetic form and its relation to America in an uncharacteristically direct way. This passage, which is not as familiar as the other three, appears in "Ventures, on an Old Theme," included in the section of *Specimen Days and Collect* titled "Notes Left Over":

> In my opinion the time has arrived to essentially break down the barriers of form between prose and poetry. I say the latter is henceforth to win and maintain its character regardless of rhyme, and the measurement-rules of iambic, spondee, dactyl, &c., and that even if rhyme and those measurements continue to furnish the medium for inferior writers and themes, (especially for persiflage and the comic, as there seems henceforward, to the perfect taste, something inevitably comic in rhyme, merely in itself, and anyhow,) the truest and greatest *Poetry*, (while subtly and necessarily always rhythmic, and distinguishable easily enough,) can never again, in the English language, be express'd in arbitrary and rhyming metre, any more than the greatest eloquence, or the truest power and passion. While admitting that the venerable and heavenly forms of chiming versification have in their time play'd great and fitting parts—that the pensive complaint, the ballads, wars, amours, legends of Europe, &c., have, many of them, been inimitably render'd in rhyming verse—that there have been very illustrious poets whose shapes the mantle of such verse has beautifully and appropriately envelopt—and though the mantle has fallen, with perhaps added beauty, on some of our own age—it is, notwithstanding, certain to me, that

the day of such conventional rhyme is ended. In America, at any rate, and as a medium of highest aesthetic practical or spiritual expression, present or future, it palpably fails, and must fail, to serve. (*PW* 2:519–20)

Many feel that Whitman's writing fulfills the Emersonian prophecy of "The Poet"; even more explicitly this passage fulfills Tocqueville's prophecy about style in *Democracy in America*.[3] With unusual specificity, Whitman rejects the meter and rhyme of English verse as instances of what Tocqueville calls "an aspect of order, regularity, science, and art" that characterizes "periods of aristocracy." To Whitman, meter and rhyme stand for Europe, and Europe, throughout his writing, stands for the legacy of feudalism.

Its rejection of rhyme and meter places this passage in the tradition of Milton's note on the blank verse of *Paradise Lost* and Blake's metrical explanation of *Jerusalem*. Like these earlier poets, Whitman depends heavily on the Bible for authority and inspiration; yet he never connects his own rejection of rhyme and meter directly with Hebrew poetry, although in "The Bible as Poetry," first published in 1883 and later included in *November Boughs* (1888), he does cite an essay that argues that the great Hebrew poets used neither rhyme nor meter.[4] Instead, he personalizes his rejection with the call to break down the formal barriers between prose and verse, barriers he dissolves in the 1855 preface, where the variable ellipses, which contain anywhere from two to nine points, correspond to many of the line divisions in passages he recasts as verse in "By Blue Ontario's Shore" and "Song of Prudence." Of course, Whitman's verse contains hundreds of metrical lines, especially late in his career, and occasional rhymes. As for the barriers between verse and prose, the 1855 Preface turns out to be a rare instance of their blending. As in the passage above, the patterns established by most of his prose, although undeniably rhythmic, consistently differ from those of his verse.

What is original in this passage is the explicit link Whitman forges between his call for prosodic reform and America. He is not the first American poet to want prosodic reform; nor is he the first to meditate on a national poetry. In April 1825, the month before Whitman turned six, Bryant delivered his four "Lectures on Poetry" before the New York Athenaeum. The third of these lectures, "On Poetry in Its Relation to Our Age and Country," closes with a paragraph that anticipates the spirit of Whitman's 1855 preface: "I infer, then, that all the materials of poetry exist in our own country, with all the ordinary encouragements and opportunities for making a successful use of them. . . . If under these circumstances our poetry should finally fail of rivalling that of Europe, it will be because Genius sits idle in the midst of its treasures."[5] As for formal innovation, Bryant's essay "On Trisyllabic Feet in Iambic

Measure," partially published in 1819 but begun as early as 1811, argues for the variation of iambic monotony with trisyllabic substitutions: "For my part, when I meet with such passages, amid a dead waste of dissyllabic feet, their spirited irregularity refreshes and relieves me, like the sight of eminences and forests breaking the uniformity of a landscape" (*Prose Writings* 1:64–65).

Bryant's statement contains all the elements of an American fiction of form. Its figuration of verse as a natural landscape foreshadows the organicism of Emerson and Whitman, while its recognition of the "spirited irregularity" of trisyllabic feet in combination with disyllabic ones anticipates Whitman's exploitation of intermittent iambics alongside triple-meter variations.[6] If Bryant, whose name Whitman came to believe "ought to lead the list of American bards,"[7] were to identify this particular landscape, with its refreshing eminences and forests, as a distinctly American one and were then to argue that a distinctly American poetry demanded trisyllabic feet in iambic measure, he would construct the same kind of prescriptive fiction Whitman does in "Ventures, on an Old Theme."

But Bryant does not, and Whitman does. Many of the fictions invented by subsequent poets refrain from the same kind of prescriptive rhetoric Whitman employs, but Williams's late note "The American Idiom" (1960) shows that Whitman's pairing of prescription with nationalism still operates well into the twentieth century. In this piece, Williams opens by identifying the American idiom as "the language we speak in the United States" and distinguishing it from "the language used among cultured Englishmen," whom he associates with " 'the Establishment.' " After tracing the slippage of the American idiom into a secondary place, having "been driven" there "by our scholars," Williams recapitulates Whitman's move from national difference to formal prescription:

> We must go forward—uncertainly it may be, but courageously as we may. Be assured that measure in mathematics as in verse is inescapable; so in reply to the fixed foot of the ancient line, including the Elizabethans, we must have a reply: it is the variable foot which we are beginning to discover after Whitman's advent.
>
> "The Establishment," fixed in its commitments, has arrived at its last stand: the iambic pentameter, blank verse, the verse of Shakespeare and Marlowe which give it its prestige. A full stop. Until we go beyond that, "the Establishment" has an edge on us.[8]

Although the tone of this exhortation is unmistakably Williams's, the latent metaphors are typically American, as they doom "the Establishment" to making a "last stand," like Custer fighting the Cheyenne and

Sioux, and then represent it as a competitor who "has an edge on us." Williams gives "The American Idiom" an urgency missing from Whitman's more composed "Ventures, on an Old Theme"; yet, as Williams's reference to Whitman acknowledges, the link between the two is clear.

But what is the nature of Whitman's nationalism, the generating force behind not only his poems but also his formal prescriptions? As "Ventures, on an Old Theme" makes clear, Whitman's formalism operates within the context of his attitudes toward America, and it is to these that I want to turn briefly.[9] At times his nationalism degenerates into chauvinism, as in the sweeping statement of the 1855 preface that "the Americans of all nations at any time upon the earth have probably the fullest poetical nature" (*CRE* 709). Whitman's "probably" narrowly rescues this sentence from the constriction of its own parochialism. But although such moments, especially in the 1855 preface, are among the most famous in Whitman's writing, they are not, in fact, wholly representative. As a politically alert journalist, a wartime nurse, and traveler to the South (1848) and West (1879), he saw more of America than most, and much of what he saw left him disturbed and ambivalent. For example, in the early jeremiad "The Eighteenth Presidency!" (1856), in which he scorches Fillmore, Pierce, and the newly nominated Buchanan, he cries out in exasperation, "Where is the real America?":[10] "Where are the laboring persons, ploughmen, men with axes, spades, scythes, flails? Where are the carpenters, masons, machinists, drivers of horses, workmen in factories? Where is the spirit of the manliness and common-sense of These States? It does not appear in the government. It does not appear at all in the Presidency" (*CP* 1310).

Lincoln changed this last opinion, and the Civil War, called by Whitman "the Secession War," answered his question "Where is the real America?" in a harsh and humbling way: "I now doubt whether one can get a fair idea of what this war practically is, or what genuine America is, and her character, without some such experience as this I am having" (*PW* 1:63). This statement cannot help but strike readers of Whitman's wartime memoranda as profound, and even appalling, in its implications. Instead of identifying the real America with the automatic and idealized catalogue of "laboring persons," he now (1863) associates genuine America with the blood-storms at Fredericksburg, Chancellorsville, and Gettysburg, as presumably he will with the awful spring of 1864 and Wilderness, Spotsylvania, and Cold Harbor. Of course, those who would soften this vision of genuine America will point to the numerous portraits of comradeship, courage, faith, sympathy, and stoicism in the memoranda, and certainly these contribute to Whitman's national vision. But if he means what he says, then genuine America necessarily also includes the aggressiveness, brutality, inefficiency, and

waste he witnessed, both first- and secondhand, in many, many instances during the war years.[11]

By his own account, Whitman's service during the war broke him. If
this is true, his paralysis raises sobering questions about the cost of a
vision of genuine America. By the time of his trip west in 1879, his earlier vision of Americans as having the fullest poetical nature had yielded
to another set of superlatives: "By [the Mississippi's] demesnes, water'd
and welded by its branches, the Missouri, the Ohio, the Arkansas, the
Red, the Yazoo, the St. Francis and others, it already compacts twenty-
five millions of people, not merely the most peaceful and money-mak-
ing, but the most restless and warlike on earth" (*PW* 1:221–22). Here
the vision, although still stated in superlative terms, balances around the
"but," which suggests both the two-sidedness of America and Whitman's own divided feelings. These divided feelings may explain one of
the more puzzling revisions he made in "Song of Myself." In the editions of 1855, 1856, and 1860, the opening line of what became section
twenty-four reads, "Walt Whitman, an American, one of the roughs, a
kosmos." But in the 1867 edition of *Leaves of Grass*, the first after the
war, this line changes to "Walt Whitman am I, of mighty Manhattan the
son" before it subsequently settles, after the reinsertion of "a Kosmos"
in the 1871 edition, into its final form: "Walt Whitman, a kosmos, of
Manhattan the son."[12]

Why the deletion of "an American"? One could argue positively that
the revision personalizes Whitman's introduction of himself, binding
his identity to a particular locale, as in their different ways Dickinson,
Frost, and Williams would do after him. Certainly, any full discussion
of Whitman must consider the meaning of his ties to Long Island,
Brooklyn, and Manhattan. But Whitman's revision radically contracts
the national dimensions of the self he sets out to construct. One clue to
this puzzle lies in his wartime writings, for by naming his home, and
promoting the local over the national, he identifies himself in the same
way he identifies the soldiers of his memoranda: "D. S. G., bed 52,
wants a good book; has a sore, weak throat; would like some hore-
hound candy; is from New Jersey, 28th regiment. C. H. L., 145th Pennsylvania, lies in bed 6, with jaundice and erysipelas; also wounded;
stomach easily nauseated; bring him some oranges, also a little tart jelly;
hearty, full-blooded young fellow—(he got better in a few days, and is
now home on a furlough)" (*PW* 1:83). With the abstraction of an American union called into question, the local and regional assume new
prominence. "New Jersey" and "Pennsylvania" carry more concrete associations than the troubled abstraction "America." Before 1861, Whitman could be more confident, even glib, about the idea of America; after
1865, that idea becomes more tentative, provisional, and precious.
Whitman's qualification of his national identity reflects the profound

qualification that the Civil War forever imposes on the concept of nationhood. An identity rooted in place (Manhattan) is stable in a way that one based on political consensus (United States of America) is not.

But Whitman's revision may also reflect his desire to distance himself from the less savory aspects of America. In *Democratic Vistas*, he indicts postwar America in sweeping terms not restricted to the government and the president:

> With such advantages at present fully, or almost fully, possess'd—the Union just issued, victorious, from the struggle with the only foes it need ever fear, (namely, those within itself, the interior ones,) and with unprecedented materialistic advancement—society, in these States, is canker'd, crude, superstitious, and rotten. Political, or law-made society is, and private, or voluntary society, is also. In any vigor, the element of the moral conscience, the most important, the verteber to State or man, seems to me either entirely lacking, or seriously enfeebled or ungrown. (*PW* 2:369)

Whereas the 1856 piece "The Eighteenth Presidency!" idealizes laborers and lashes presidents, nominees, and convention delegates with invective rivaling that of Pound at his angriest ("The President eats dirt and excrement for his daily meals, likes it, and tries to force it on The States" [*CP* 1310]), the 1871 *Democratic Vistas* points an accusing finger at all parts of amoral, hypocritical, hollow-hearted, materialistic, infidel America. In his conviction that "at the core of democracy, finally, is the religious element" (*PW* 2:381), Whitman finds not only in the Washington government but in many of his own Manhattan haunts, "in shop, street, church, theatre, barroom" (*PW* 2:372), the symptoms of disease.

If the change from "an American" to "of Manhattan the son" helps defend Whitman against the indefensible aspects of America, he has other defenses as well. One is his version of Hegel, whom he knew through Joseph Gostwick's *German Literature* (1854).[13] In "Carlyle from American Points of View," included in *Specimen Days*, Whitman credits Gostwick's (spelled "Gostick's" by him) abstract of Hegel for his understanding, admitting that he is "recounting Hegel a little freely here" (*PW* 1:260). But the accuracy of Whitman's reading of Hegel, or of Gostwick's reading of Hegel, is not the primary issue. The primary issue is that Whitman found in Hegel "an essential and crowning justification of New World democracy in the creative realms of time and space," as well as a rebuttal to "Carlyle's ever-lurking pessimism and world-decadence" (*PW* 1:262), a pessimism that, according to Whitman, explains Carlyle's severe criticism of America. Specifically, Whitman dwells on his version of a Hegelian theodicy:

> In short (to put it in our own form, or summing up,) that thinker or analyzer or overlooker who by an inscrutable combination of train'd wisdom

and natural intuition most fully accepts in perfect faith the moral unity and sanity of the creative scheme, in history, science, and all life and time, present and future, is both the truest cosmical devotee or religioso, and the profoundest philosopher. While he who, by the spell of himself and his circumstance, sees darkness and despair in the sum of the workings of God's providence, and who, in that, denies or prevaricates, is, no matter how much piety plays on his lips, the most radical sinner and infidel. (*PW* 1:260)

"Carlyle from American Points of View" follows "Death of Thomas Carlyle" in *Specimen Days* and refers in its opening sentence to "that deceas'd author," who died early in 1881. Coming ten years after *Democratic Vistas*, Whitman's summation of Hegel eases him out of the bind into which parts of the earlier work get him. In the passage above, which ostensibly opposes Hegel to Carlyle, Whitman also articulates opposing sides of himself and examines two possible responses to the diseases he diagnoses in *Democratic Vistas*.[14] He could yield to darkness and despair, but to do so would be to succumb to the same sin with which he charges Americans of the Gilded Age, the sin of infidelism. If the core of democracy is the religious element, then infidelism begets the fall from democracy and Whitman's own national disenfranchisement. His conception of democracy assures that a loss of faith would render him a poet without a country. As a result, he has no choice but to take the path of "perfect faith" and affirm "the moral unity and sanity of the creative scheme," even when that scheme includes the questionably moral and not-so-sane aspects of American society and government during the administrations of Andrew Johnson and Ulysses Grant. Faced with comparable visions of America, Pound and Eliot would expatriate a few decades later. But for Whitman expatriation would mean a reconstruction of the poetic self beyond even his powers of transformation. For him, then, faith in the moral unity and sanity of American democracy provides the means of ideological repatriation.

Hegelian theodicy may have provided Whitman with a rational and religious defense of, and against, Reconstruction America, but his emotional defense was an idealization of the American West, which he visited for the first time between the publication of *Democratic Vistas* and "Carlyle from American Points of View." Of course, the West figures prominently in works written before the 1879 trip, as, for example, in the 1855 preface Whitman claims that an American bard incarnates the geography of states and rivers he has not yet seen and, in some cases, never did see. In "The Eighteenth Presidency!" published twenty-three years before his trip, Whitman's ideal man, and ideal president, comes from the West: "I would be much pleased to see some heroic, shrewd, fully-informed, healthy-bodied, middle-aged, beard-faced American blacksmith or boatman come down from the West across the Al-leghanies, and walk into the Presidency, dressed in a clean suit of work-ing attire, and with the tan all over his face, breast, and arms; I would certainly vote for that sort of man, possessing the due requirements, be-fore any other candidate" (*CP* 1308). This imaginative portrait of a mythic hero from the West combines elements of self-description, as that self is pictured on the frontispiece of the 1855 *Leaves of Grass*, with a prophecy of the coming of Abraham Lincoln from beyond the Alleghanies.[15]

Nine years later, in Whitman's wartime memoranda, the hero from the West appears in the avatar of the western soldier in Sherman's command. After the grand review of the armies in Washington during May 1865, Whitman recorded his impressions in a memorandum titled "Western Soldiers": "These Western soldiers are more slow in their movements, and in their intellectual quality also; have no extreme alert-ness. They are larger in size, have a more serious physiognomy, are con-tinually looking at you as they pass in the street. They are largely ani-mal, and handsomely so. . . . I always feel drawn toward the men, and like their personal contact when we are crowded close together, as fre-quently these days in the street-cars" (*PW* 1:106). Here the westerner has descended from mythic status into the flesh and blood of men Whit-man can see and touch on the streets. Described in animal, even bovine, terms, western men are now not so much the stuff of which presidents are made as the fulfillment of Whitman's *Calamus* vision. The crowding together of people in streetcars literalizes adhesiveness. As a concrete instance of Whitman's cherished abstraction, a crowded streetcar in a modern American city replaces the pastoral image of the calamus grow-ing along pond margins.

In *Democratic Vistas*, the West functions as an image of America's future, and so as an alternative to, even escape from, the darkening pres-ent. Predicting that in "a few years the dominion-heart of America will be far inland, toward the West" and conjecturing that his country's "fu-ture national capital may not be where the present one is" (*PW* 2:384–85), Whitman goes on to sketch the geographical ethos of a rejuvenated America:

> Those regions [along the Ohio, Missouri, and Mississippi rivers], with the group of powerful brothers toward the Pacific, . . . will compact and settle the traits of America, with all the old retain'd, but more expanded, grafted on newer, hardier, purely native stock. A giant growth, composite from the rest, getting their contribution, absorbing it, to make it more illustrious. From the north, intellect, the sun of things, also the idea of unswayable justice, anchor amid the last, the wildest tempests. From the south the liv-ing soul, the animus of good and bad, haughtily admitting no demonstra-

tion but its own. While from the west itself comes solid personality, with blood and brawn, and the deep quality of all-accepting fusion. (*PW* 2:385)

The characteristics of Sherman's western soldiers have now been mapped onto an entire region. The North will compensate for western intellectual slowness and, informed by the idea of unswayable justice, serve as something of a national superego; the South, the animated living soul consolidating and protecting itself, becomes the national ego, "haughtily" verging on egotism; and the West, identified with the physicality of "blood and brawn," corresponds to a national id, its unorganized desires and drives fulfilled by its "all-accepting fusion."

With so much positive feeling attached to his successive images of the West, it is not surprising that when he finally did make his "long jaunt" in the fall of 1879 at the age of sixty, Whitman fell in love: "Yes, I fell in love with Denver, and even felt a wish to spend my declining and dying days there" (*PW* 1:216). But his affections did not limit themselves to the men of urban Denver ("The Women of the West" reveals that Whitman was "not so well satisfied" with their female counterparts [*PW* 1:225–26]); they also extended to the landscape itself, which he describes in terms echoing Wordsworth, Coleridge, and Shelley:[16]

"I have found the law of my own poems," was the unspoken but more-and-more decided feeling that came to me as I pass'd, hour after hour, amid all this grim yet joyous elemental abandon—this plenitude of material, entire absence of art, untrammel'd play of primitive Nature—the chasm, the gorge, the crystal mountain stream, repeated scores, hundreds of miles—the broad handling and absolute uncrampedness—the fantastic forms, bathed in transparent browns, faint reds and grays, towering sometimes a thousand, sometimes two or three thousand feet high—at their tops now and then huge masses pois'd, and mixing with the clouds, with only their outlines, hazed in misty lilac, visible. (*PW* 1:210–11)

In this passage, from the aptly named "An Egotistical 'Find,'" the American poet of the egotistical sublime finally encounters a natural sublimity analogous to that projected by his poems. Whitman's rhapsody constitutes a retrospective *ars poetica*, one that rewrites Bryant's simile about eminences and forests breaking the uniformity of a landscape, as it identifies that landscape with a distinctly American terrain, the Platte Canyon of Colorado. But Whitman also rewrites himself, as the final image of mountains hazed in misty lilac recalls the earlier lilac of the 1855 preface, the carefully cultivated, ornamental bush that he makes an image of his formal schemes. Here that image has been replaced by "fantastic forms" that are much more appropriate emblems of the "entire absence of art."

The egotistical find in the Platte Canyon, in many ways the climax of his trip west, informs Whitman's fiction of a nationally appropriate form. Returning to "Ventures, on an Old Theme," one finds the remarks on formal schemes framed by references to the West. Whitman introduces the long passage about breaking down the barriers between prose and verse with the heading "NEW POETRY—*California, Canada, Texas*" (*PW* 2:519). Likewise, he follows his claim that in America conventional rhyme "palpably fails, and must fail, to serve" with an extended appeal to the muse of the prairies:

> The Muse of the Prairies, of California, Canada, Texas, and of the peaks of Colorado, dismissing the literary, as well as social etiquette of over-sea feudalism and caste, joyfully enlarging, adapting itself to comprehend the size of the whole people, with the free play, emotions, pride, passions, experiences, that belong to them, body and soul—to the general globe, and all its relations in astronomy, as the savans portray them to us—to the modern, the busy Nineteenth century, (as grandly poetic as any, only different,) with steamships, railroads, factories, electric telegraphs, cylinder presses—to the thought of the solidarity of nations, the brotherhood and sisterhood of the entire earth—to the dignity and heroism of the practical labor of farms, factories, foundries, workshops, mines, or on shipboard, or on lakes and rivers—resumes that other medium of expression, more flexible, more eligible—soars to the freer, vast, diviner heaven of prose. (*PW* 2:520)

Embodying some of the formal principles it celebrates, this carefully orchestrated sentence, with its strong rhythms and occasional metrical touches ("as grandly poetic as any": x/xx/xx/x), argues for an explicit connection between the "more flexible, more eligible" medium of unrhymed nonmetrical verse, which Whitman somewhat disingenuously calls "prose," and the social, emotional, psychological, technological, industrial, and economic aspects of an America invigorated by the West. The analogy between nineteenth-century America and "the freer, vast, diviner heaven of prose" surfaces in the parenthetical aside "as grandly poetic as any, only different," which refers ostensibly to Whitman's sense of America but also slyly to his sense of his own style.

But what about the entire absence of art in Whitman's art? Throughout his writing, he insists on the primary significance of political, historical, cultural, or social influences and on the secondary importance of formal or aesthetic concerns. In "A Backward Glance o'er Travel'd Roads" (1888), for example, he argues that "one needs only a little penetration to see, at more or less removes, the material facts of their country and radius, with the coloring of the moods of humanity at the time, and its gloomy or hopeful prospects, behind all poets and each poet, and forming their birth-marks" (*CRE* 566). Such a statement not only authorizes political, historical, cultural, and social studies of Whitman, but it also invites and promotes them.[17] Of course, such studies are often significant and meaningful, but they raise the question of whether or not the overtly, sometimes aggressively, political and historical side of Whitman's work masks something else.

In one of his long notes to the 1876 preface to the centennial edition of *Leaves of Grass*, Whitman shows this masking at work: "Besides, important as they are in my purpose as emotional expressions for humanity, the special meaning of the 'Calamus' cluster of 'Leaves of Grass,' (and more or less running through the book, and cropping out in 'Drum-Taps,') mainly resides in its political significance" (*PW* 2:471). Certainly, one can make a case for taking a poet's statements at face value, and Whitman's vision of an America "effectually welded together, intercalated, anneal'd into a living union" (*PW* 2:471) by means of adhesiveness has much to recommend it. But the "mainly" of "mainly resides in its political significance" has the same kind of false ring as the notorious letter of August 19, 1890, in which Whitman fends off John Addington Symonds's hints about the homosexual implications of *Calamus*: "Tho' always unmarried I have had six children— two are dead—One living southern grandchild, fine boy, who writes to me occasionally. Circumstances connected with their benefit and fortune have separated me from intimate relations."[18] At stake here is not the truth of Whitman's claim, doubtful as that may be. Nor is the issue whether or not the *Calamus* poems have any political significance; all sexuality has political significance at some level.[19] But Whitman's insistence that the significance of *Calamus* is *mainly* political, not personal, erotic, or confessional, shows him protesting too much, as he redefines his canon to accommodate the political significance of America's centennial and reshapes himself to fit the public role he plays sixteen years after the *Calamus* cluster appeared.

In other words, the political significance of America protects Whitman against aspects of his own work. In the 1876 preface, America defends him against homosexuality and its consequences. But elsewhere he looks to America to defend him against another aspect of his work, that which he calls "aestheticism": "No one will get at my verses who insists upon viewing them as a literary performance, or attempt at such performance, or as aiming mainly toward art or aestheticism" (*CRE* 574). This statement occurs in "A Backward Glance" and so within Whitman's general argument that "a sufficient Nationality . . . is often, if not always, the first element" in "estimating first-class song" (*CRE* 566). In "A Backward Glance," then, Whitman opposes nationality to aestheticism to diminish the importance of the latter, especially in his own poems: "And whether my friend[s] claim it for me or not, I know well enough, too, that in respect to pictorial talent, dramatic situations, and especially in verbal melody and all the conventional technique of poetry, not only the divine works that to-day stand ahead in the world's reading, but dozens more, transcend (some of them immeasurably transcend) all I have done, or could do" (*CRE* 566).[20] On the one hand, this passage reads simply as Whitman's humble acknowledgment that great poets have written great poems that overshadow his own. But on the other, it reveals a particular anxiousness about his own formalism, as he emphasizes "especially . . . verbal melody and all the conventional technique of poetry." This emphasis is misplaced, for it is especially in pictorial (i.e., descriptive) talent and dramatic situations that Whitman's verse is overshadowed by Homer, Dante, or Shakespeare; yet in verbal melody and technique his verse is, or aspires to be, in the phrasing of "Ventures, on an Old Theme," as grandly poetic as any, only different.

Whitman's promotion of nationality over formalism anticipates Stevens in significant ways, as Whitman would seem to concur with Stevens's distinction between poets who care about what they have to say and poets who care about the way they say it. The late statement in "An Old Man's Rejoinder," included in *Good-Bye My Fancy* (1891), that "I have not only not bother'd much about style, form, art, etc., but confess to more or less apathy (I believe I have sometimes caught myself in decided aversion) toward them throughout" (*PW* 2:656) would appear to associate Whitman unequivocally with the former. But as Stevens finds the distinction unraveling for him, so readers of Whitman cannot long maintain the separation of statement and style. Whitman's repeated claim that he succeeded at last in leaving stock poetical touches out of *Leaves of Grass*, although it cost him a great deal of trouble to do so (*PW* 1:22; 2:704), does not correspond to reality. Regular rhyme and meter may be gone, but, for example, alliteration, anaphora, assonance, apostrophe, parallelism, and personification are all stock poetical touches and all prominent features of Whitman's verse, many of which appear in the tale of a jetblack sunrise.

Two other small moments illustrate the complete fusion of statement and style in *Leaves of Grass*. The first is well known and appears in the 1855 "Song of Myself":

> The prostitute draggles her shawl, her bonnet bobs on her tipsy and
>   pimpled neck,
> The crowd laugh at her blackguard oaths, the men jeer and wink
>   to each other,
> (Miserable! I do not laugh at your oaths nor jeer you,)

The President holds a cabinet council, he is surrounded by the great
secretaries.

(CP 41)

The juxtaposition of "prostitute" and "President" appears ironic, as it
emphasizes the incongruity between two social, economic, or political
extremes. The alliteration of the two words, their other phonemic similarities (unvoiced /s/ and /t/ in *prostitute* become voiced /z/ and /d/ in
President, while medial /ə/ and terminal /t/ remain the same),[21] and their
accentual similarity (/xx) all seem to heighten the irony, as auditory
likeness contrasts with existential difference. Some see in Whitman's
pairing, and hear in his parenthetical apostrophe, an elevation or en-
nobling of the prostitute, who in an ideal democracy ranks the same as
the president.[22] Certainly, two other poems, "To a Common Prostitute"
(1860) and "The City Dead-House" (1867), could provide support for
this reading. But the poetical touches of auditory likeness tell another
story as well, one linked directly to political statement. In 1855 Pierce
was president, and Whitman's loathing of him and others surfaces in
"The Eighteenth Presidency!": "The berths, the Presidency included,
are bought, sold, electioneered for, prostituted, and filled with prostitutes" (CP 1309). If alliteration associates prostitutes with presidents to
elevate the former, it also does so to condemn the latter. In this reading,
irony evaporates, as auditory likeness underlines the deeper likeness
Whitman found unacceptable.

The second moment comes in the short poem "Cavalry Crossing a
Ford" (1865):

> A line in long array where they wind betwixt green islands,
> They take a serpentine course, their arms flash in the sun—hark to the
> musical clank,
> Behold the silvery river, in it the splashing horses loitering stop to drink,
> Behold the brown-faced men, each group, each person a picture, the
> negligent rest on the saddles,
> Some emerge on the opposite bank, others are just entering the ford—
> while,
> Scarlet and blue and snowy white,
> The guidon flags flutter gayly in the wind.

(CRE 300)

This little poem poses as a casual piece of reportage, a wartime sketch
from which stock poetical touches have been banished. Its concentration on visual detail and its relatively impersonal tone anticipate many
of the modernist experiments of fifty years later. In its apparent objec-

tivity and its temporal suspension of a single moment (enforced by the uncharacteristic enjambment "while, / Scarlet and blue and snowy white"), "Cavalry Crossing a Ford" achieves some of the same pictorial effects as a photograph by Mathew Brady, and the poem can be read as Whitman's reading of such a photograph.

But Whitman's poem is highly wrought, blending national history with aesthetics. From the first line, with its self-descriptive iambic opening "A line in long array," to the last, auditory effects enrich "the musical clank" of this picture. Particularly effective are the constant assonance or rhymes of *line-wind-islands, green-serpentine, arms-hark-Scarlet, course-horses-ford, flash-splashing, silvery-river,* and *clank-bank* in combination with the metrical touches, both iambic (especially the beginnings of the first four lines) and triple-meter ("hark to the musical clank"; "the negligent rest on the saddles"). But the best example of Whitman's close attention to style comes in the final line: "The guidon flags flutter gayly in the wind." The red-white-and-blue regimental pennants, though not necessarily the Stars and Stripes, certainly suggest the national flag, which Whitman describes and addresses on numerous occasions. Certainly, it is more likely that Whitman saw Union cavalry than Confederate. But red, white, and blue are also the colors of the Confederate flag, and the speaker of the poem does not explicitly identify the soldiers he sees, as though deliberately avoiding the taint of partisanship.[23]

What makes the final line remarkable is the phonemic chiasmus of "guidon flags flutter gayly" (/g/ . . . /fl/ . . . /fl/ . . . /g/). Although the word *chiasmus* comes from the crossing of Greek *chi*, it implies inversion, not the linear crossing of a ford, here the Virginia analogue of the Rubicon or Styx. One could argue for some sort of mimetic meaning in the figure, linking it, for example, to the reflections of riders crossing through water; yet the more significant link is that between this momentary intensification of auditory pattern and a rhetorical shift from apparent objectivity to the subjective comment "gayly." For a poet distrustful of stock poetical touches, Whitman shows himself surprisingly willing to risk the pathetic fallacy. In this case, however, the poem justifies the risk, for at one level it is a poem about aesthetics, specifically the aesthetics of the ordinary, here represented by the unheroic, matter-of-fact details of military maneuvers. The attribution of gaiety to the flags represents not a weakness in Whitman's treatment but a conscious displacement of aesthetic emotion, a displacement that shows that no matter how an observer may aim at photographic objectivity, his or her observations necessarily embed themselves in a subjectivity that cannot be wholly repressed. Whitman's chiasmus neatly represents this embedding, as the minimal observation "flags flutter" stands encased by words ("guidon" and "gayly") that implant that minimal observation into a larger context.

Like Stevens, Whitman may insist, however unconvincingly, that he believes in statement more than style, but, unlike Stevens, he sees America, with its politics, its history, the pressures of its reality, not simply as something to be evaded or resisted but also as a shield against the inescapable aestheticism of art. Whitman's aversion to aestheticism incorporates his belittling of "the smooth walks, trimm'd hedges, poseys and nightingales of the English poets"; yet he found the most disturbing embodiment of aesthetic tendencies not in any foreigner but in another American: "Poe's verses illustrate an intense faculty for technical and abstract beauty, with the rhyming art to excess, an incorrigible propensity toward nocturnal themes, a demoniac undertone behind every page" (*PW* 1:231). Dated January 1, 1880, "Edgar Poe's Significance" immediately follows the last of the memoranda devoted to Whitman's trip west. This placement in *Specimen Days* dramatizes the real significance of Poe as the antithesis of the sublimity Whitman finds in the Platte Canyon: "The lush and the weird that have taken such extraordinary possession of Nineteenth century verse-lovers—what mean they? The inevitable tendency of poetic culture to morbidity, abnormal beauty—the sickliness of all technical thought or refinement in itself—the abnegation of the perennial and democratic concretes at first hand, the body, the earth and sea, sex and the like—and the substitution of something for them at second or third hand—what bearings have they on current pathological study?" (*PW* 1:232–33).

As "Carlyle from American Points of View" attempts to exorcise his pessimistic side, the side that sees only darkness and despair in current America, so "Edgar Poe's Significance" attempts to exorcise the unhealthy aspects of Whitman's own aesthetic tendency. No reader of Whitman's early fiction, particularly such strange pieces as "Death in the School-Room," "One Wicked Impulse!" "The Last Loyalist," "Wild Frank's Return," or "The Boy Lover," can doubt the young Whitman's attraction to what he condemns here as pathological. In his critique of Poe, whose example he obviously finds threatening, Whitman identifies the earlier poet with "an intense faculty for technical and abstract beauty, with the rhyming art to excess," or with an aesthetic formalism that causes Poe and others like him to abnegate "the perennial and democratic concretes at first hand." The language here points to an alienation from human life, particularly human life in America, which Whitman distrusts, even fears.

In Whitman's view, the path of aesthetic formalism leads directly to disconnection from America. That a poet could follow Poe and still retain a nourishing sense of nationality does not appear to be an option. Given such a view of aestheticism, Whitman has no choice but to renounce it:

> Spirit that form'd this scene,
> These tumbled rock-piles grim and red,
> These reckless heaven-ambitious peaks,
> These gorges, turbulent-clear streams, this naked freshness,
> These formless wild arrays, for reasons of their own,
> I know thee, savage spirit—we have communed together,
> Mine too such wild arrays, for reasons of their own;
> Was't charged against my chants they had forgotten art?
> To fuse within themselves its rules precise and delicatesse?
> The lyrist's measur'd beat, the wrought-out temple's grace—column
>   and polish'd arch forgot?
> But thou that revelest here—spirit that form'd this scene,
> They have remember'd thee.
>
> (*CRE* 486)

Bearing the headnote "Written in the Platte Cañon, Colorado," this poem, first published in 1881, is a paradox, for it defends the absence of art, of rules, and of meter in artful iambic verse. Whitman may be demonstrating that he can toss off metrical verse as easily as anyone in order to suggest that technical achievement without spirit is bankrupt. Certainly, his many comments on form reveal that he holds this belief.

But to argue this way is to reduce "Spirit That Form'd This Scene" to little more than a joke in which Whitman has the last laugh, a joke he would be unlikely to make in the significant context of his experience in the Platte Canyon. The power, even pathos, of the poem derives from Whitman's acknowledgment that, whatever his critics and detractors think, he has not been able to forget art altogether, an acknowledgment that for him amounts to a confession. Confessing his artfulness to the spirit that formed the canyon, he insists that his own aestheticism has not caused him to forget that spirit or its original act of *poiesis*, an instance of one of the "concretes" from which he fears separation. At once defensive and repentant, Whitman both seeks and performs his own absolution for what he sees as the sin of formalism, a sin his prescriptions exhort American poets to avoid but also one that his example shows them how to fictionalize.

THREE

THE BROKEN MATHEMATICS OF
EMILY DICKINSON

W HAT APPEARS to be missing from Dickinson's poems and letters, which is not missing from the work of Whitman and so many other American poets, is some statement about her own forms.[1] She often speaks of poets and poetry, both explicitly and implicitly by means of figure. Cynthia Griffin Wolff has examined what she calls Dickinson's "metapoetic" tropes, arguing that the poet "customarily referred to her poetry as a 'veil' or 'flowers' or 'snow.'" In addition, she confirms what others, such as Robert Sherwood, have noticed before her, namely that Dickinson often employs the conventional figure of the bird to represent the poet.[2] To these figures must be added Dickinson's many images of song, singers, or singing, which derive from the traditional association of poem with "song," an association behind the earliest occurrences of this word in English.

But all these are figures of poems, poets, and poetry, not of the formal structures of verse, which clearly meant so much to Dickinson. Like Stevens, she wrote several poems about *poiesis*, the maker's act of creating a world out of formally patterned language, but even more than he, she remained silent about the formal patterns themselves.[3] A rare exception, her remark defending her use of rhyme to Higginson (June 7, 1862), has attracted the notice of many: "I thanked you for your justice—but could not drop the Bells whose jingling cooled my Tramp."[4]

Tantalizing for both its rarity and its figurative suggestiveness, this statement contains a little fiction not only about rhyme but also about Dickinson's sense of herself as a poet. Although it appears to trivialize rhyme as mere "jingling," the image casts Dickinson in the role of a horse, a domesticated beast of burden. Representing herself in harness, she suggests to Higginson that rhyme functions not as a simple adornment of that harness but as a necessary relief from the mental and physical overheating caused by her work, either her domestic exertions in the Dickinson Homestead, her poetic exertions in solitude, or both. The appearance of the verb "cool" in this context is especially striking, since it echoes another well-known image of temperature quoted from her: "'If

I read a book [and] it makes my whole body so cold no fire ever can warm me I know *that* is poetry' " (Higginson to his first wife, Mary, August 16, 1870; *L* 2:473–74). Here the therapeutic cooling of rhyme has intensified into an extreme state, one that blurs great pleasure with great pain and recalls the shocked numbness experienced by "Freezing persons" who "recollect the Snow—" (poem 341, c. 1862). Most interesting about the fiction of jingling bells, however, is its synesthesia; the bell-like sound of rhyme produces a tactile sensation of coolness. To suggest, even figuratively, that rhyme has this dramatic physiological effect is to rescue that device from the realm of the conventionally ornamental, to which Higginson apparently has condemned it, and to insist on its inescapable physical immediacy as an auditory phenomenon, something capable of being experienced acutely by the body through the ears. Dickinson attempts to remind Higginson that the formal patterns of verse both reflect and stimulate the most basic rhythms known to physical beings in a physical world.

In the absence of bald, denotative statements, one must turn to such elliptical, connotative figures to discover Dickinson's attitudes toward poetic form. As Wolff points out, one of these involves the pun on "foot" or "feet."[5] Of course, this pun does not originate with Dickinson; it bears a long history of conventional usage. Younger than the pun on feet but, by the time Dickinson began making fair copies of her poems, no less conventional is the Emersonian fiction that the forms of verse pair themselves with the forms of nature.[6] Admittedly, Dickinson never projects this fiction as nakedly as Whitman does in his famous analogy between his lines and the ocean: "Its verses are the liquid, billowy waves, ever rising and falling, perhaps sunny and smooth, perhaps wild with storm, always moving, always alike in their nature as rolling waves, but hardly any two exactly alike in size or measure (meter), never having the sense of something finished and fixed, always suggesting something beyond."[7] The directness with which Whitman insists that his lines *are* waves, not that they are *like* waves, has no counterpart in Dickinson's prose, except perhaps the one-sentence letter to Higginson (1876) that reads, "Nature is a Haunted House—but Art—a House that tries to be haunted" (*L* 2:554). But even this statement remains oblique compared with Whitman's, since it says nothing about poetic form. Furthermore, unlike Whitman, whose lines "are" waves, Dickinson admits that her art "tries to be" what nature is already. The difference here is more than rhetorical, more than a difference in confidence; it reflects an important difference in attitude toward the Emersonian myth of form.

Enclosed in Dickinson's second letter to Higginson, postmarked April 25, 1862, poem 321 later received from him the title "The Wind":

Of all the Sounds despatched abroad,
There's not a Charge to me
Like that old measure in the Boughs—
That phraseless Melody—
The Wind does—working like a Hand,
Whose fingers Comb the Sky—
Then quiver down—with tufts of Tune—
Permitted Gods, and me—.

In these lines, both the Emersonian myth of natural form and its precursor, the Romantic figure of the Aeolian harp, operate without irony. Dickinson's wind bears a family resemblance to both Shelley's west wind and Emerson's north wind, "the fierce artificer" indifferent to "number or proportion," which sculpts the snow in his metapoetic fable "The Snow-Storm" (1841). But Dickinson's wind works more calmly than they do, preferring combing and quivering to the more energetically sublime activities of Shelley's or Emerson's, both described as "wild." The only hint of sublimity resides in the possible meanings of "Charge."

Webster's dictionary identifies two strains of meaning appropriate to the context of "There's not a Charge to me / Like that old measure in the Boughs."[8] The first involves the general sense of an "order, injunction, mandate, command" or "a trust," as, for example, "the people of a parish are called the minister's *charge*." The second pertains to electricity: "In *electrical experiments*, a quantity of electrical fluid, communicated to a coated jar, vial, or pane of glass." This doubleness reflects Dickinson's simultaneous commitment both to the semiology of New England Congregationalism and to the most recent discoveries of natural science. The charge the wind brings to the speaker could be an order or command, entrusting her with a special commission as a poet, as God commands his prophets to speak, or it could be the physical excitement of sheer perception, recalling the jingling bells of rhyme that, passing through the ear, register as tactile sensation. Either way, the old measure of the wind in the boughs realizes itself in Dickinson's poem as the old measure of common meter, the hymn form associated with a congregational charge to worship and, in the revivalist atmosphere so common in Amherst, with the emotional charge experienced in conversion.

In Whitman's idiom, then, the old measure of common meter *is* the old measure in the Boughs "Permitted Gods, and me." This particular poem appears to embrace without hesitation the Emersonian fiction that natural forms replicate themselves as poetic ones. A variant reading of one word confirms that Dickinson is indeed meditating here on the role of nature in determining the formal structures of *poiesis*. In a second fair copy of the poem sent to Susan Dickinson, "Pattern" substitutes for "fashion" in the lines "And even in the Urn—/ I cannot vouch the merry Dust / Do not arise and play, / In some odd Pattern of it's own—" (P 1:247).[9] The gist of these lines is that the "fleshless Chant" of the wind affects not only the living; it may stir up even the dust of the dead. Because the copies sent to Higginson and Sue are otherwise identical, this single difference between them stands out. *Pattern* and *fashion* are related on two levels. According to Webster's, both can imply ornamentation: the third definition of *pattern* is "figure or style of ornamental execution" and the fourth definition of *fashion* is "the prevailing mode of dress or ornament." But it is at another level that they are more significantly synonymous. The primary meaning of *pattern* is "an original or model proposed for imitation; the archetype" and the second meaning of *fashion* is "form; model to be imitated; pattern." For Dickinson's speaker, the pattern of the wind's "phraseless Melody" is so deeply ingrained ("Inheritance, it is, to us—/ . . . inner than the Bone—") that it continues to replicate itself in our physical remains even after our bodies disintegrate. In the wind, nature presents an archetype to be imitated by the figures, styles, or ornaments of art.

Considered in isolation, "Of all the Sounds despatched abroad" would suggest that Dickinson follows Emerson's lead, and other poems readily support this judgment. In poem 1670, a strange poem undated by Johnson, Dickinson resorts to the conventions of the dream poem as she describes her vision of a worm in her room that turns to a snake and speaks. Like his more famous counterpart in poem 986, "A narrow Fellow in the Grass" (c. 1865), this snake elicits " 'No cordiality' " from Dickinson's speaker:

> He fathomed me—
> Then to a Rhythm *Slim*
> Secreted in his Form
> As Patterns swim
> Projected him.

In this erotic nightmare, Dickinson extends the Emersonian myth from the inanimate realm of the wind to the animate one of the male snake and his projecting "Patterns." His "slim" rhythm becomes the natural archetype of the verse that replicates it here in a narrow column of dimeter and trimeter lines.

But the fiction of natural form does not operate in this important poem:

> Four Trees—upon a solitary Acre—
> Without Design

Or Order, or Apparent Action—
Maintain—

The Sun—upon a Morning meets them—
The Wind—
No nearer Neighbor—have they—
But God—

The Acre gives them—Place—
They—Him—Attention of Passer by—
Of Shadow, or of Squirrel, haply—
Or Boy—

What Deed is Their's unto the General Nature—
What Plan
They severally—retard—or further—
Unknown—.

(poem 742, c. 1863)

Inevitably, this richly self-descriptive poem calls to mind Frost's "De-sign," as both lyrics meditate on the presence or absence of a larger in-tention in nature. Dickinson's poem signals its self-descriptive status with its first word, "Four," which points to both the number of lines in her quatrains and the number of quatrains in her poem. The adjective "solitary" resonates oddly, since in nature solitary acres do not exist; the land lies continuous, not broken into isolated units. Only with the coming of humans do acres emerge, as land gets cleared and fenced, bought and sold. The arrangement of the four trees in relation to one another may not exhibit any apparent design, but their framing upon a solitary acre reveals the presence of human intention. After all, these particular trees have not been cut down. Furthermore, the speaker care-fully identifies the place as an acre, which means someone has taken the trouble to measure it.

Design, then, is not solely a matter of patterning parts within a com-position; it also involves the initial selection and framing of those parts. As the boundaries of a solitary acre suggest some ordering intention op-erating behind this arrangement, so the boundaries of a solitary page attest to a framing impulse, the impulse in which order and design origi-nate. The adjective "Apparent" hints that the absence of design, order, or significant action may be illusory. Even more striking is the bare predicate "Maintain," the final one-word line of the first stanza, which frames the poem by anticipating the only other such line, "Unknown," the final one of the last. Webster's gives only one definition of *maintain* as an intransitive verb: "To affirm a position; to assert." But even this definition borders on transitivity, since in affirming a position, one must maintain something. Nothing in her lexicon accounts for Dickinson's singular use of this verb, which, unlike its more active and definite variant "Do reign—" suggests that the trees barely "are." With "Maintain," the speaker not only denies the trees "Apparent Action," she also qualifies their very existence.

Like the best Imagist poems, the first stanza orders and designs while striving to erase obvious signs of order and design. As Dickinson's poem continues, however, this self-erasure, which has already rubbed out narrative with the use of the static "Maintain" and the presence of a first-person speaker with the avoidance of "I," begins to work on the formal design of the verse itself. Not only do the four lines of any given quatrain actively disorder its metrical or rhyming symmetry, but each quatrain also dissociates itself from the other three. Dickinson's target here is pattern itself. An archetypal quatrain of pentameter-dimeter-pentameter-dimeter, rhyming *xaya*, has all but disintegrated, as no single quatrain follows this model. In fact, the model itself cannot be clearly defined, since the first and second stanzas link the supposedly nonrhyming lines with alliteration; the third stanza gestures at both an internal couplet ("by" and "haply") and the triple rhyme of its second, third, and fourth lines (/aI/, /i/, /ɔI/); and the fourth stanza rhymes *abab*.

Four quatrains on a solitary page, without definite design or order, maintain. Nevertheless, despite the absence of definiteness, a form-giving consciousness, analogous to the one that measures land in acres, displays itself throughout. That a plan is unknown does not necessarily mean that it does not exist. For all the speaker knows, the four trees may be acting in accordance with a design of "the General Nature." But the point is that the General Nature, as represented in this poem, does not fulfill the fiction of natural form. It does not make apparent to the poet any formal pattern or archetype that a poem can replicate. Significantly, the wind appears in this poem, as it does in the more Emersonian "Of all the Sounds despatched abroad." Here, however, it does not move through the four trees combing out "that old measure in the Boughs—." In fact, in the second stanza of "Four Trees—" the wind is stripped of its predicate and exiled to a line of its own. Its function is ambiguous. Does it parallel the sun in meeting the trees each morning, or is it the nearest neighbor of the trees, except for God? Dickinson's wind claims closer kinship with the ambiguous wind of Stevens's "The Snow Man" than with the wind of Shelley or Emerson.

In the absence of natural archetype, then, another myth of design must cohere. This alternative myth does not necessarily replace the Emersonian one. Dickinson's figurative uses of the word "meter," for example, show that the myth of natural form still informs some of her metaphors for design, as in "The Days—to Mighty Metres stept—" (poem 593, c. 1862), "They have a little Odor—that to me / Is metre—nay—'tis melody—" (poem 785, c. 1863), and "The lower metres of the Year / When Nature's laugh is done" (poem 1115, c. 1868). But a counterfiction evolves to challenge nature when nature fails to makes its designs clear. According to it, the origin of order, design, pattern, or form lies in the mind of the poet herself. Where she does not recognize or acknowledge design in the relation of various phenomena to one another, as in "Four Trees—," she imposes that design.

A good place to see this counterfiction at work is in Dickinson's mathematical images:

> The Days that we can spare
> Are those a Function die
> Or Friend or Nature—stranded then
> In our Economy
>
> Our Estimates a Scheme—
> Our Ultimates a Sham—
> We let go all of Time without
> Arithmetic of him—.
>
> (poem 1184, c. 1871)

Arranged in short meter (6–6–8–6), this poem examines the phenomenology of anniversaries, specifically anniversaries of loss. Although *function* does have mathematical meaning ("In *mathematics*, the *function* of a variable quantity, is any algebraic expression into which that quantity enters"), Webster's most appropriate definition of the word for this context is the fifth: "power; faculty, animal or intellectual." For the speaker, the losses of power, the deaths of friends, or the annual vanishings in nature all correspond to particular days that detach themselves from the temporal continuum and become "stranded then / In our Economy." *Economy* has a range of possible meanings, but they all involve management, regulation, law, rule, system, arrangement, or order. An anniversary "strands" a day by isolating it within our sense of time, causing us to manage, regulate, arrange, or order that sense in an altered way.

Furthermore, if the emergence of new anniversaries can keep revising our perceptions of time, then we find "Our Ultimates a Sham—." About thirty-five years before Einstein's postulation of his theory of relativity (1905), Dickinson arrives at a vision of the conditional, relative nature of time and perception. Against the background of this relativity, human "Estimates," those tentative judgments that involve numerical reckoning or measurement, become "Schemes" in the double sense of plans or designs and plots or intrigues. In the absence of ultimates, estimates become the only designs. "The Days that we can spare" denies the fiction of natural form and its ultimate archetypes. The only designs its speaker acknowledges originate in the vicissitudes of human perception and experience.

As relativity replaces ultimates, estimates replace the verifiable computations of arithmetic, the "science of numbers," according to Webster's. In a formal image of the letting "go all of Time without / Arithmetic of him—," Dickinson roughens the penultimate line, metrically and syntactically, before she ends it with what for her is not a common enjambment, that between preposition and object. A momentary ambiguity allows *without* to function as an adverb meaning "not within," creating the fleeting impression that, according to the speaker, we let go of any notion that time exists outside the mind. The archetypes of prosody, time's arithmetic, now lie within.[10]

As a student at Amherst Academy, Dickinson had access to various texts in arithmetic and algebra,[11] as well as to the pervasive ideas of Edward Hitchcock, president of Amherst College, who argues that "Mathematics . . . forms the very framework of nature's harmonies, and is essential to the argument for a God."[12] In this context, the relinquishing of time's arithmetic would suggest a weakening of the mind's confidence in "the framework of nature's harmonies." It also suggests a deepening commitment to arrangements and structures that do not fit into that framework:

> If I could tell how glad I was
> I should not be so glad—
> But when I cannot make the Force,
> Nor mould it into Word,
> I know it is a sign
> That new Dilemma be
> From mathematics further off
> Than from Eternity.

(poem 1668, undated)

Built of four lines of common meter followed by four of short, this poem takes *poiesis* as its explicit subject. How does a poet "make the Force" of emotion and "mould it into Word" without violating the essential ineffability of that emotion? This is the poet's dilemma, but in Dickinson's particular case, it is also a sign that the structures of *poiesis* do not locate themselves within the harmoniously mathematical framework of nature. In fact, this poem suggests that such structures can more easily accommodate the difficult notion of a supernatural Eternity than they can that of mathematical harmony in nature.

About twenty-two years before she made a fair copy of "The Days that we can spare," Dickinson wrote out a short poem in common meter that anticipates the association of loss with mathematical estimation found in the later poem:

> As by the dead we love to sit,
> Become so wondrous dear—
> As for the lost we grapple
> Tho' all the rest are here—
>
> In broken mathematics
> We estimate our prize
> Vast—in it's fading ratio
> To our penurious eyes!

(poem 88, c. 1859)

Among the many metaphors for Dickinson's choice of metrical mode, none so neatly encapsulates her critique of the fiction of natural form as the image of "broken mathematics." In it, the framework of nature's harmonies, asserted so confidently by Hitchcock, disintegrates. Faced with death and loss, Dickinson's speaker cannot sustain her vision of an ultimate "prize" or its vast ratio to her present condition. In nature, ratios tend to come in whole numbers, but whole numbers have no place in the fractional world of broken mathematics. In the formal structures of verse, the guiding archetype often reflects this brokenness.

The absence of bald statements describing her own poetic forms has not prevented later poets and critics from enlisting Dickinson in support of various aesthetic ideologies. Amy Lowell, for example, transforms her into a patron saint of modernist revolt: "Thirty years after her death the flag under which she fought had become a great banner, the symbol of militant revolt."[13] In his early examination of Dickinson's prosody (1935), made before readers had an "adequate text for a study of her method," Gay Wilson Allen comments that her formal techniques, particularly her "irregular line divisions," were accepted by later poets, "especially the *vers librists*." Robert Weisbuch associates Dickinson with Charles Olson's campaign against what he termed the "closed" verse of Eliot and others. Finally, in her poem "'I Am in Danger—Sir—'" (1964), Adrienne Rich calls Dickinson's "hoard of dazzling scraps a battlefield" on which a woman, "masculine / in single-mindedness," chose "to have it out at last."[14]

Protomodernist, proto-*vers librist*, protoprojectivist, protofeminist, Dickinson invites these retroactive categorizations by articulating fully no guiding principles, beliefs, or ideologies. At least in matters of religion, such articulation ran counter to her nature. Although some have argued that Dickinson's early religious defiance yielded later in her life to a quiet faith, she never enunciated a creed or doctrine. As she declared to Mary Emerson Haven in a letter of February 13, 1859, "Mr. S. preached in our church last Sabbath upon 'predestination,' but I do not respect 'doctrines,' and did not listen to him, so I can neither praise, nor blame" (L 2:346). But in fairness to those who think they recognize in Dickinson's "hoard of scraps" affinities with a particular religious, aesthetic, or existential outlook, she did choose to "dwell in Possibility" (poem 657, c. 1862), the endless possibilities of figuration, ellipsis, and connotation that, in turn, invite endless readings and interpretations. A poet of less powerful possibilities, one more committed to the "Prose" of creeds, doctrines, and explanations, would not elicit so many different attempts to enlist her as an ally.

If there is a hovering principle that informs Dickinson's work and invites the retroactive categorizations above, it is a principle of seeing the world in terms of fragments rather than of wholes. A letter from early September 1880 to her cousin, Louise Norcross, opens with a meditation on the power of writing, a power "to impel shapes to eyes at a distance, which for them have the whole area of life or of death." Describing it is an "awful" power, possessed by any "pencil in the street," Dickinson then turns to an image of an "earnest letter" able to make "each instant" a gun, "harmless because 'unloaded,' but that touched 'goes off.'" After intervening chat, the letter closes with this sentence: "This is but a fragment, but wholes are not below" (L 3:670–71). For all the power of writing to create life or death for a reader, the power of *poiesis* in its most basic form, no pencil in the street, or in the garret, has the power to make anything but fragments, since, according to Dickinson, wholes do not exist. All our arithmetic must be done in broken mathematics.

That Dickinson's utterances are irregular, discontinuous, and fragmented is a commonplace among her critics.[15] In the next section, however, I would like to examine three formal features of her writing to demonstrate that although Dickinson assumes "wholes are not below," her supposedly fragmented structures actually tend toward likeness and congruity, not necessarily toward unity, but toward a pluralistic harmony among fragments.

2

The first formal feature of Dickinson's writing is metricality itself, not as it manifests itself in her uses of hymnody, of which so many discussions already exist, but as it challenges the fundamental distinction between verse and prose:

They shut me up in Prose—
As when a little Girl
They put me in the Closet—
Because they liked me "still"—

Still! Could themself have peeped—
And seen my Brain—go round—
They might as wise have lodged a Bird
For Treason—in the Pound—

Himself has but to will
And easy as a Star
Look down upon Captivity—
And laugh—No more have I—.

(poem 613, c. 1862)

The first line of this poem endows "Prose" with figurative possibilities; it could function as a metaphor for some dreary domestic or familial situation, a "Captivity" imposed on the speaker. But the comparison with a bird, one of Dickinson's familiar images for the poet, suggests that the speaker is also using "Prose" to mean a mode of writing. "They" have attempted, unsuccessfully, to confine her attention to prose. The final stanza could mean that the speaker can escape from prose into verse as easily as a bird can fly from the pound. As soon as her captors turn their backs, she can read or write poetry. But the lines "Still! Could themself have peeped— / And seen my Brain—go round—" show that the speaker's liberation is an interior one, a liberation managed within the limits of her captivity. In other words, as shutting a child in a closet will not necessarily "still" that child, so confinement to prose will not necessarily shut out the structures of verse.

Pointing to Dickinson's mannerism of turning her prose "abruptly into metered expression" in her early letters to Higginson, Porter comments that she seems to be trying to demonstrate to him that the rhythms of verse "so pervade her consciousness that she cannot make the distinction between them and unmetered prose." Discussing the three "Master" letters, Gelpi remarks that their "diction and imagery are so much an extension of the poetry that these letters are best read (as are many of Dickinson's letters) as prose poems or free verse." Often, however, not only the diction and imagery of her letters but also their formal structures overlap with those of her verse. Some letters are far too metrical to be considered prose poems or free verse. For Dickinson, writing cannot be broken down into two separate modes, the unmetered language of prose and the metered language of verse. Instead, the metricality of her prose insists on the continuity and likeness of the two modes.[16]

Examples of this continuity abound. In a letter of October 17, 1851, to her brother, Dickinson arranges the poem "There is another sky" (poem 2) as prose (*L* 1:149). In his edition, Johnson arranges the text as verse, admitting that because Dickinson did not indicate line division, the "line arrangement and capitalization of first letters in the lines are here arbitrarily established" (*P* 1:3). Conversely, in a letter of January 1874 to Higginson, she arranges six lines of prose as verse, sandwiching them between two other passages of verse (excerpts from poems 1249 and 1259, both c. 1873; *L* 2:518). In a letter of January 2, 1885, to Mr. and Mrs. E. J. Loomis, she arranges poem 1639 as verse ("A Letter is a joy of Earth—/ It is denied the Gods—"), but in a letter written the same month to Charles H. Clark, the poem appears as prose: "Had we but one assenting word, but a Letter is a joy of Earth—it is denied the Gods" (*L* 3:855, 857). In addition to individual metrical lines that appear in both poems and letters, there are a host of metrical sentences that appear only in the prose: "There are no Dead, dear Katie, the Grave is but our moan for them" (*L* 2:469); "To shut our eyes is Travel" (*L* 2:482); "What Miracles the News is!" (*L* 2:483); "The stimulus of Loss makes most Possession mean" (*L* 2:489). This sampling from twenty pages demonstrates the density of such sentences.

But the most powerfully sustained example of the metrical continuity between prose and verse is this letter to Sue, written early in October 1883 after the death of her son Gilbert:[17]

Dear Sue—
    The Vision of Immortal Life has been fulfilled—
    How simply at the last the Fathom comes! The Passenger and not the Sea, we find surprises us—
    Gilbert rejoiced in Secrets—
    His Life was panting with them—With what menace of Light he cried "Dont tell, Aunt Emily"! Now my ascended Playmate must instruct *me*. Show us, prattling Preceptor, but the way to thee!
    He knew no niggard moment—His Life was full of Boon—The Playthings of the Dervish were not so wild as his—
    No crescent was this Creature—He traveled from the Full—
    Such soar, but never set—
    I see him in the Star, and meet his sweet velocity in everything that flies— His Life was like the Bugle, which winds itself away, his Elegy an echo—his Requiem ecstasy—
    Dawn and Meridian in one.
    Wherefore would he wait, wronged only of Night, which he left for us—
    Without a speculation, our little Ajax spans the whole—

          Pass to thy Rendezvous of Light,
          Pangless except for us—

Who slowly ford the Mystery
Which thou hast leaped across!

Emily. (*L* 3:799)

The first three sentences scan iambically without variation, reserving the first trochaic substitution, "Gilbert," for the sudden naming of the dead. Then the longest paragraph, beginning "His Life was panting with them—," moves away from the iambic norm as the letter turns to anecdote, only to return again with the final phrase of the apostrophe to the "prattling Preceptor." The following paragraph, beginning "He knew no niggard moment—," consists of four iambic trimeter lines, the first and third with feminine endings, and constitutes a concealed quatrain. The next line ("No crescent . . .") echoes its pairing of trimeter lines, feminine and masculine. Throughout its remainder, the letter moves in and out of the iambic norm, as now its auditory structure becomes dense with rhyme, assonance, and alliteration. Dickinson's closing poem, 1564, fulfills the impulse toward verse, suggested but not realized by the concealed quatrain.[18]

Writing her brother early in June of 1854, Dickinson excuses herself with this disclaimer: "I'm so tired now, that I write just as it happens, so you must'nt expect any style." She then restates her artlessness in the next paragraph: "This is truly extempore, Austin—I have no notes in my pocket" (*L* 1:296). These statements imply that the pressures of reality, in this case fatigue, obviate the ornaments of style. Pushed to her limits, Dickinson can only "write just as it happens." But nearly thirty years later, the remarkable letter to Sue demonstrates that style actually coincides with the pressures of an extreme situation. Writing one of the women closest to her about the death of a child she loved deeply, Dickinson does not observe the formulaic conventions of the condolence letter; yet, neither does she plead the privilege of artlessness. Instead, the letter she composes traces the evolution of prose into verse and the birth of a poem.

Casting Gilbert as Preceptor, she makes him her heavenly Muse: "Now my ascended Playmate must instruct *me*." Many echoes resonate here, among them the self-descriptive poem beginning "I cannot dance upon my Toes—/ No Man instructed me—" (poem 326, c. 1862), included in a letter written to Higginson in August 1862 and often read as Dickinson's apologia to him for what he called her "spasmodic" gait. In addition, she often uses the term "Preceptor" in reference to Higginson himself, having asked him in her letter of June 7, 1862, "But, will you be my Preceptor, Mr Higginson?" (*L* 2:409). But Higginson remained an earthly instructor, and Gilbert, now ascended, has larger knowledge to impart. The letter to Sue enacts his instruction, as the language begins in prose, establishing a metricality that falters but recovers, and culminates in verse. Behind the immediate expression of her loss, Dickinson constructs a model of writing in which the formal structures of prose and verse are continuous. Her model revises the history of literature in which verse, the product of oral tradition, precedes prose, the product of literacy and writing. Dickinson shows here how the former grows out of the latter, as language becomes refined and condensed by the pressures of loss.

The wholeness of the logos may have splintered into the fragments of Babel, but for Dickinson metricality prevents her own language from breaking down even further into a polarity of separate modes. If the fiction implicit in this metrical bridging is that letters are like poems, then for her the converse is also true. In poem 441 (c. 1862), Dickinson states explicitly the congruence of the two genres: "This is my letter to the World / That never wrote to Me—." Poem 494 (c. 1862) apostrophizes a "Happy Letter" on its way to a male, or in a second version a female, correspondent and instructs the letter itself to apologize for the speaker's inadequacies as a writer. Poem 1035 (c. 1865) is whimsically epistolary, as the speaker, addressing "Bee," signs himself "Yours, Fly." In poem 1320 (c. 1874), an unnamed speaker tells "Dear March," "I got your Letter, and the Birds—." As the formal features of verse pervade Dickinson's letters, so the epistolary style surfaces in many of her poems. Some argue, for example, that the dash, discussed more fully below, enters Dickinson's prosody from the standard epistolary usage of the period. The point is that although Dickinson may do her figuring in broken mathematics, her formal structures piece together the shards she inherits.

Certainly, this last statement holds true for her use of rhyme, the second formal feature to consider and the one that, unlike meter or the dash, belongs almost solely to verse. Most previous discussions of Dickinson's rhymes concentrate on inventorying their various types.[19] Such inventories demonstrate that Dickinson was not a mere primitive whose irregularities indicate technical roughness and lack of polish; she was a conscious innovator, especially as a rhymer, one who has few equals in English and none in American poetry. Furthermore, as "Four Trees—" demonstrates, her triumphs often include breaking patterns.

Those who argue that Dickinson's full rhymes can be associated with an ideal or a standard of artfulness that she questioned are correct, but their association of her partial rhymes with worldliness or informality errs by failing to recognize how variations on the artificial and conventional necessarily extend, even intensify, the artificial and conventional. Full rhyme affords a basic, primitive pleasure to the literate and illiterate alike; partial rhyme directs itself not only toward the literate but also toward a sophisticated portion of the literate, those readers steeped deeply enough in poetry to appreciate its rarefied formal touches. More substantial are arguments that locate partial rhyme within the figurative realm of broken mathematics, claiming, for example, that the broken aspect of partial rhyme expresses an inner fragmentation or that it mimes the outer shape of a fractured universe; yet, even though such arguments attribute to rhyme appropriate figurative significance, they often misread the function of rhyme in a world in pieces.

Since its publication in 1944, W. K. Wimsatt's essay "One Relation of Rhyme to Reason" has directed many subsequent theoretical discussions of rhyme.[20] Wimsatt's main point is that rhyme is not merely a matter of the likeness of word sounds; it is also a matter of likeness in word meanings, a likeness that the likeness in sound momentarily enforces. Many of the taxonomists of Dickinson's partial rhymes, before and after Wimsatt, fail to recognize this crucial aspect of her practice. Just as important as the auditory texture of partial rhymes is the semantic texture, the momentary fiction that the pairing of two words generates:

> For each extatic instant
> We must an anguish pay
> In keen and quivering ratio
> To the extasy.
>
> For each beloved hour
> Sharp pittances of years—
> Bitter contested farthings—
> And Coffers heaped with Tears!
>
> (poem 125, c. 1859)

Bearing the Emersonian title "Compensation" in *Poems* (1891), this poem echoes 88, with its image of the ultimate "prize / Vast—in its fading ratio" that loss forces us to estimate in broken mathematics. The poem contains two rhymes, the first a partial (vowel) rhyme (*pay-extasy*), the second a full rhyme (*years-Tears*). Here the progression from partial to full rhyme supports the objection that no consistent correlation exists between rhyme and mood. In this case, Dickinson reserves full rhyme for the relentless closure of fate. As full rhyme matches sound to sound unequivocally, so the law of compensation matches ecstasy to anguish.

Of the two rhymes, Wimsatt would consider the first "daring," the second "tame." The first pairs a monosyllabic verb with a trisyllabic noun, direct object of that verb, whereas the second merely pairs two monosyllabic nouns, both functioning as objects of prepositions. The first rhyme matches the phoneme /e/ with the phoneme /i/, or "long" *a* with "long" *e*, recalling that the former is actually a diphthong comprised of /e/ and /i/. On the semantic level, the rhyming of *years* with *Tears* merely underlines the obvious, inevitable truth that the years will bring tears. The rhyme is a cliché and appears in many poems that have nothing to do with compensation. Far more interesting is the rhyming of *pay* with *extasy*, as this pairing encapsulates the difficult psychological truth looming behind so much of Dickinson's life and work: ecstasy costs. The fiction generated by this rhyme assumes the same economic model of the mind that informs, for example, poem 1184 and its meditation on anniversaries "stranded then / In our Economy."

Other examples of Dickinson's rhyming powers clamor for attention. One could return, for example, to "Four Trees—upon a solitary Acre—" to savor the semantic richness of the pairings *Design-Maintain*, *Wind-God*, or *Plan-Unknown*, three rhymes that sketch the meaning of the entire poem. Full treatment of Dickinson's rhyming must include exploration of the semantic territory Wimsatt charts. But Wimsatt concerns himself primarily with Chaucer and Pope, and hence with full rhyme. Likewise, Hollander's modifications and extensions of Wimsatt do the same. When he asserts that "the question should not be whether two elements rhyme or not, but how close they are" in lexical form, morphophonemic construction, meaning, or conceptual category, he does not consider the many variables introduced by partial rhyming.[21] In contrast, the taxonomists of Dickinson's rhymes focus exclusively on an auditory spectrum of likeness or difference in sound.

It would appear that these spectra might be aligned to provide a full description of Dickinson's technique. Parallel to Wimsatt's tame-daring spectrum or Hollander's close-distant one would lie another describing an auditory range from identical to nonrhyme. Do these spectra correspond to one another in such a way that a certain degree of auditory likeness corresponds to a similar degree of semantic or other likeness? In other words, is a partial rhyme likely to be what Wimsatt would consider daring or a full rhyme tame? Although the example of "For each extatic instant" suggests this may be the case, in fact the answer is no, not necessarily. In "Four Trees—," for example, the rhyme *Wind-God* represents what Small calls semiconsonance. With nothing but the final phoneme /d/ in common, this pairing lies well toward the nonrhyme end of the auditory spectrum; yet in Wimsatt's terms, it lies closer to the tame end of the semantic one, since it matches two monosyllabic nouns, one of which (*Wind*) functions ambiguously.

Wimsatt's analysis of Pope demonstrates how his rhymes produce irony by rhyming words that differ in length, part of speech, grammatical function, and, ultimately, meaning. For Wimsatt, cleverness lies in matching auditory likeness with semantic difference; for Hollander, it lies in matching auditory likeness with more general differences. Obviously, partial rhyme has no place in their schemes. The matching of auditory difference with semantic difference does not beget irony and so is not particularly clever. As for Dickinson's critics, they, too, are preoccupied with differences, specifically, with descriptions and interpretations of difference.

But for Dickinson rhyme is a trope of likeness. Any likeness in word sounds joins words, and the joining of words in striking, resonant combinations is an act of mending, a way of reassembling the broken pieces of Babel. Nonrhyme is silence. Our habit of calling blank verse "blank" registers a perception of absence. As identical rhyme (for example, *seke-seeke* in the opening lines of the General Prologue) is in Chaucer what Hollander calls "an occasion of plenitude," although it falls flat in modern English, so partial rhyme is an occasion of plenitude in Dickinson, although twentieth-century readers may consider it dissonant, fragmented, and "modern." When Donald Wesling asserts that the "off-key consonant rhymes of Dickinson, Owen, Auden, and the later Yeats are clearly deliberate dishevelments," he groups her with later poets whose attitudes toward rhyme were revised by modernism, attitudes she could not share.[22] To consider a partial rhyme broken or incomplete is to measure it against full rhyme. When measured against silence or blankness, however, partial rhyme brims with resonance. At the time Dickinson told Higginson that she could not abandon her jingling Bells, only half her rhymes were full.[23] But her metaphor does not distinguish between full and partial, and presumably she found the latter, which comprised the other half of her rhymes, no less vital and soothing.

The association of partial rhyme with disillusion, dissonance, or dishevelment finds no support in this poem, which varies its trochaic norm with frequent dactyllic substitutions:

> Better—than Music! For I—who heard it—
> I was used—to the Birds—before—
> This—was different—'Twas Translation—
> Of all tunes I knew—and more—
>
> 'Twasn't contained—like other stanza—
> No one could play it—the second time—
> But the Composer—perfect Mozart—
> Perish with him—that Keyless Rhyme!
>
> So—Children—told how Brooks in Eden—
> Bubbled a better—Melody—
> Quaintly infer—Eve's great surrender—
> Urging the feet—that would—not—fly—

Children—matured—are wiser—mostly—
Eden—a legend—dimly told—
Eve—and the Anguish—Grandame's story—
But—I was telling a tune—I heard—

Not such a strain—the Church—baptizes
When the last Saint—goes up the Aisles—
Not such a stanza splits the silence—
When the Redemption strikes her Bells—

Let me not spill—its smallest cadence—
Humming—for promise—when alone—
Humming—until my faint Rehearsal—
Drop into tune—around the Throne—.

(poem 503, c. 1862)

Full and partial rhyme are represented equally here: *before-more*, *time-Rhyme*, *Melody-fly*, *told-heard*, *Aisles-Bells*, *alone-throne*. Although this sequence defines a pattern of *xxyyyx* (where *x* stands for full rhymes, *y* for partial), enclosing the poem in instances of full rhyme and thereby providing definite closure, any attempt to tie the partial rhymes to a mood of defeat or failure must be limited. One could argue that the rhyme *Melody-fly* reflects the Fall brought about by "Eve's great surrender," but no such explanation explains *told-heard* or *Aisles-Bells*. Furthermore, the general tone of the poem is one of joy and exultation, which its three partial rhymes do nothing to undermine.

This poem celebrates religious vision using the terms of poetry and music. The "tune" the speaker hears inside herself brings "Translation," both in the sense that it translates her from earth to heaven and in the sense that it renders into another figurative language all the other kinds of music she has heard. As the poem moves through its images of the Fall "—and the Anguish—," it becomes clear that the vision is one of paradise regained. Most significant, however, are the suggestions in the final two stanzas that this inner tune surpasses anything heard in "the Church" and that it is a tune the speaker will keep inside herself, rehearsing it until she lets it out in heaven. This last suggestion hints that the speaker refers self-descriptively to her own tunes or verses, which she describes as "my faint Rehearsal" of the divine tune.

In the mind of this speaker, a vision of paradise regained realizes itself as "that Keyless Rhyme!" According to Webster's, a musical key "is the fundamental note or tone to which the whole piece is accommodated." A key implies a tonal system, so that "Keyless" rhyme would be rhyme (or, by synecdoche, verse) that does not define itself systematically against any fundamental note or tone, rhyme that refers to no particular system or scale.[24] Those who hear only dissonant minor chords in Dickinson's partial rhymes assume that her poems are written in the major key of full rhyme. They are not, however, as the large share of partial rhymes indicates. Poets who use full rhymes most of the time may use occasional partial ones to dishevel; against a matrix of programmatic sameness, difference jars. But a poet who favors neither full nor partial rhymes will soothe or jar inconsistently. The only consistent effect of her partial rhymes will be the honing of the ear. By making the forty or so phonemes of English each do the work of rhyming, Dickinson multiplies the types of rhyme. By multiplying types of rhyme, she multiplies the opportunities for hearing likenesses among the sounds of words. The more one hears likenesses among words, the more one hears the tunes of language. The more one hears the tunes of language, the less broken the world sounds.

If Dickinson's critics have labored to perfect a descriptive taxonomy of her rhymes, then of her dashes, the third formal feature to consider, they have struggled to discover an etiology. Somewhat uncharitably, Waggoner dismisses the "foolishness" that has been written about Dickinson's use of this mark.[25] He himself follows Porter in identifying her dashes with Samuel Worcester's edition of Watts's *Psalms, Hymns, and Spiritual Songs* (1827), available to Dickinson both at church and at home. The passage both critics cite appears in Worcester's introduction: "In the *punctuation* regard has been had to musical expression. In some instances, therefore, different points or pauses are inserted, from what would have been used, had the grammatical construction, only, been regarded. The *dash* is intended to denote an expressive suspension."[26] With its invocations of "musical expression," "expressive suspension," and "judicious observance of the pauses," this passage would not sound out of place in a modernist manifesto written eighty-five or ninety years later. Pound, Williams, and Olson all made claims about the schemes of verse that echo Worcester's explanations. But whereas Worcester was talking about how he used print, specifically punctuation, to direct the musical performance of hymns, Pound, Williams, and Olson adopted the fiction of musical performance to describe the writing of poems. If Dickinson herself had written the passage above, there would be much to discuss, but she did not, and the hymn theory remains one among others.

Sewall rejects what he calls "the elocutionary theory," first advanced by Edith Perry Stamm in 1963, that the dashes in Dickinson's manuscripts slant upward or downward to indicate rising or falling inflection. He then quotes approvingly Richard Green Parker's *Aids to English Composition*: "The proper use of the dash is to express a sudden stop, or change of the subject; but, by modern writers, it is employed as a substitute for all of the other marks."[27] Significantly, this explanation does not square with that offered by the hymn theory, for according to the latter, a dash denotes suspension, whereas according to Parker, it denotes a sudden stopping or changing. One is left with two mutually exclusive propositions: If the dash originates in Watts's hymnal, it stands for prolongation; if in the rhetoric of composition, for cessation or transition. Then again, according to Parker, it may stand for any of the other marks and, hence, for any one of a number of different functions. Used instead of a semicolon, for example, a dash, according to Webster, would stand for "a pause to be observed in reading or speaking, of less duration than the colon, double the duration of the comma, or half the duration of the period." But, of course, a writer who also uses dashes for all these other marks is generating another "keyless" system, an unstable, self-referential code without a determined basis for signification.

If liberal use of the dash characterizes the midnineteenth-century rhetoric of prose, then Weisbuch may be justified in linking it to the prevailing epistolary style.[28] Dashes end lines of verse in Dickinson's first poem (1850), but they do not appear within a line until poem 6 (c. 1858), where they function rather unremarkably as commas: "And the Earth—they tell me—." Meanwhile, however, dashes punctuate her earliest letter, written to her brother on April 18, 1842, although not until a letter of March 28, 1846, does her usage foreshadow what is to come. Writing to Abiah Root, Dickinson is describing the death of Sophia Holland: "There she lay mild & beautiful as in health & her pale features lit up with an unearthly—smile" (L 1:32). The junction between a single adjective and the noun it modifies admits no punctuation. Dickinson cannot be using the mark in place of any other, since none would be appropriate. Furthermore, Parker's explanation of a sudden stop or change would not account for this particular dash, since no real stop or change occurs. Ironically, Worcester's musical notion of "expressive suspension" is far more appropriate to this unmusical context. A letter from Sue Dickinson to her sister-in-law discussing the second stanza of "Safe in their Alabaster Chambers" demonstrates that the dash did not belong solely to the poet (L 2:379–80), but no dash in Sue's letter functions in this same odd way. In short, the epistolary theory does not explain Dickinson's punctuation of "unearthly—smile," a written sign for the uncanny threshold her friend is crossing as she passes from living to dead.

Attempts to trace the etiology of something as effective and idiosyncratic as Dickinson's dashes cannot fairly be called "foolish." Waggoner's preemptive dismissal of rival theories assumes that the origin of the dash is obvious, which it is not. Dashes that may denote suspension appear in the same letter or poem as those that denote a stop or change. Still other dashes may denote both or neither. Less uncertain are attempts to describe the phenomenology of the dash, of which there are many.[29] Either explicitly or implicitly, they often point to the breaking up of time and certainty projected in "As by the dead we love to sit" (poem 88) and "The Days that we can spare" (poem 1184). Various descriptions may emphasize different aspects of the dash, so that in a particular instance one description may be more useful than another, but most associate it with the broken mathematics of time's arithmetic. What needs further consideration is how the phenomenology of the dash, of its breaking functions or broken aspects, cooperates with and affects the phenomenology of Dickinson's lineation.

A survey of theories leaves one unable to decide whether the dash comes from hymns and denotes suspension or from letters and denotes stopping. Such indecision is itself telling, for it reflects the dual nature of Dickinson's dashes. In the musical context of Watts's hymns, Worcester uses a dash to mark the cooperation of verbal text and music. In the prose context of midnineteenth-century letters, a dash marks the coordination of grammatical phrases into sentences. But in the verse context of her poems, Dickinson's dashes mediate between the modulations of syntax and the overall contours of lineation, a mediation between the discontinuous and the continuous. If the dash appears to serve the contradictory functions of prolongation and termination, that is because it does, expressing the possibilities of disintegration within the subsuming integrity of the line.

Her poems demonstrate that the integrity of her lines, both auditory and visual, meant a great deal to Dickinson. In addition to the painstaking care with which she made fair copies of her poems and stitched them into fascicles, a care no poet would take who was indifferent to the visual aspects of her poems, there is the example of her reaction to the misprinting of "A narrow Fellow in the Grass" (poem 986) in the *Springfield Daily Republican* (February 1866).[30] In the fair copy written about 1865, the third and fourth lines read: "You may have met Him—did you not / His notice sudden is—" (P 2:711). In another fair copy sent to Sue and written about 1872, Dickinson changes one word and makes her intentions even clearer: "You may have met him? Did you not / His notice instant is—" (P 2:712). The *Republican* printed these lines as "You may have met him—did you not, / His notice instant is" (P 2:714). The mere insertion of the comma after "not" elicited this response from Dickinson, writing to Higginson in a letter postmarked March 17, 1866: "Lest you meet my Snake and suppose I deceive it was robbed of me—defeated too of the third line by the punctuation. The third and fourth were one—I had told you I did not print—I feared you might think me ostensible" (*L* 2:450). In her last two statements, Dickinson sounds as though she is saying to Higginson, I told you so; the reason I refuse to publish is that editors and printers make such egregious mistakes. But since the error makes no audible difference (even without terminal punctuation, the syntax prevents the third and fourth lines from being "one"), Dickinson's complaint borders on the overly fastidious and fussy. Furthermore, it demonstrates that she cared very much, perhaps too much, about the visual aspects of her poems, particularly the integrity of her lines.

Without the benefit of a definitive text before him, Allen argues that, along with rhyme, Dickinson's "irregular line division is one of the two most important innovations in her verse technique," especially to many of the *vers librists*.[31] Since the texts available to him in 1935 were even more regularized than those of the Johnson edition, this is an odd claim, as, even in the later edition, most of her line divisions are comparatively tame. If Allen means that occasionally Dickinson breaks a line in a quatrain so that it has five lines, this is hardly an important innovation. If he means that she uses enjambment in original ways, the earlier examples of Donne, Milton, Shakespeare, and Keats suggest that he overstates that originality. Bold enjambments of the kind that Williams would later exploit are relatively rare in Dickinson. When they occur, they stand out sharply, as in "Signed away / What portion of me be / Assignable" (poem 465, c. 1862) or this remarkable example:

> This Consciousness that is aware
> Of Neighbors and the Sun
> Will be the one aware of Death
> And that itself alone
>
> Is traversing the interval
> Experience between
> And most profound experiment
> Appointed unto Men—.
>
> (poem 822, c. 1864)

The enjambment between "itself alone" and "is" not only mimes ultimate isolation by splitting subject from predicate, here the all-important verb of being itself; it also straddles a boundary between stanzas, forcing syntax to traverse "the interval" along with consciousness.

But the relative scarcity of such examples suggests that although her verse is not as end-stopped as Whitman's, Dickinson generally protects the alignment of syntax and line. She may have sensed fragmentation and dissonance as keenly as her modernist successors, perhaps even more keenly, but she chose to enclose formal images of fragmentation and dissonance within continuous structures, such as metrical, syntactically independent lines. This is why the dash became so crucial to her. On the one hand, she wanted to maintain the integrity of her lines, but on the other, she wanted to explore and exploit the possibilities for framing bits of language that later poets, such as Williams, would realize with enjambment.

In her revisions of "Safe in their Alabaster Chambers" (poem 216), for example, the dash joins into one line what Dickinson first arranges as two. In the version of 1859, the final lines of the first stanza read "Rafter of satin, / And Roof of stone." In the version of 1861, the "frostier" one prompted by Sue's criticism, these lines are one: "Rafter of Satin—and Roof of Stone!" (P 1:151). From this single example one cannot argue that the dash always joins what might have been broken, as in the version of the second stanza that Dickinson sent to Higginson she divides two long lines ("Grand go the Years—in the Crescent—above them—" and "Diadems—drop—and Doges—surrender—") at the points marked respectively by the first and second dashes; yet even in these examples, the dashes mark off the joints of syntax, the places at which a poet such as Williams might opt for enjambment and at which Dickinson, most of the time, does not.

One way to read many of Dickinson's dash-peppered lines is to think of them historically as blueprints for the systematic enjambment so common only thirty or forty years after her death. In "Four Trees—upon a solitary Acre—," for example, dashes in the final lines could translate easily into further line divisions: "What Plan / They severally—retard—or further— / Unknown—." The same could be said for many of the lines in "Better—than Music!": "So—Children—told how Brooks in Eden— / Bubbled a better—Melody— / Quaintly infer—Eve's great surrender— / Urging the feet—that would—not—fly—." If Dickinson's enjambments tend to be tame, her dashes often break syntax in daring ways, as in this second example in which they divide subject from predicate, adjective from noun, verb from object, and adverb from auxiliary and main verbs.

Much of what could be and has been said about the effects of enjambment also could be said about the effects of these dashes.[32] But the largest difference between the lineations of Dickinson and those of, say, Williams is that even though both poets work closely with fragments of syntax, Williams maps those fragments onto the page as lines that pull more strongly down the page rather than across, and Dickinson does not. Williams sacrifices much of the horizontality of verse to dramatize the segmental nature of language, but Dickinson does not. The dual function of the dash, as instrument of both prolongation and termination, now makes sense. It allows the momentary termination of syntactic movement as it prolongs the horizontal movement of the verse line. At least in relation to lineation, Dickinson wanted things both ways. She sought to combine the linear integrity sanctioned by English metrical tradition with the syntactic ruptures encouraged by American radical experimentalism. In her success, she shows herself a genuine and triumphant innovator.

3

Despite the absence of baldly self-descriptive statements, Dickinson's poems demonstrate her involvement with, and revision of, the fiction of natural form. She generates a counterfiction that challenges the notion that nature represents a mathematically harmonious framework to engage, both formally and thematically, instances of brokenness. But this engagement does not beget so much a poetics of brokenness, especially in comparison to Dickinson's modernist successors, as it does a poetics of mending, of piecing together. She does not fuse the fragments she encounters into a seamless whole; her versions of metricality, rhyme, and punctuation make the seams all too plain. Instead, Dickinson's rigorous formalism dramatizes the effort to salvage some continuity, congruence, likeness, or integrity in a world that endangers each and all of these. For her, the intense absorption in the formal structures of verse merges with a strategy for restoration.

If the absence of self-descriptive statements corresponds in Dickinson's case to an acute formalism, then to what does her apparent absence of political, historical, or national interest correspond? If she poses to Higginson as a neophyte, flatly lying when she claims, "I made no verse—but one or two—until this winter—Sir—" (L 2:404), how can she be trusted not to dissemble in such letters as this one to Elizabeth Holland in the late autumn of 1884:

> The Leaves are flying high away, and the Heart flies with them, though where that wondrous Firm alight, is not "an open secret—" What a curious Lie that phrase is! I see it of Politicians—Before I write to you again, we shall have had a new Czar—Is the Sister a Patriot?
> "George Washington was the Father of his Country"—"George Who?"
> That sums all Politics to me—but then I love the Drums, and they are busy now—. (L 3:849)

Election day is at hand, Grover Cleveland is about to be elected "Czar" for the first time by the American people, and yet this keenly intelligent, well-read daughter of a politically active man, who served as both state and national representative, feigns indifference to all but the superficial pageantry of American politics. Here she constructs an opposition between the natural world of autumn and the rhetorical world of politicians, but the image of the flying leaves, an image that Homer, Dante, Milton, and Shelley have made inseparable from poetic tradition itself, suggests that the opposition is also between poetry and politics.

Johnson points to this letter in support of his claim that Dickinson "did not live in history and held no view of it, past or current" (*L* 1:xx). Although he appears to take her declaration of political disengagement at face value, other commentators argue differently. Quoting Jay Leyda's insight that "quiet Amherst had its quota of violence," Sewall warns that "it is not right to think of her as detached from the affairs of the nation and the world." Even more explicitly, Wolosky contends that "Dickinson's indifference to all worldly affairs . . . was neither as complete nor as straightforward as has been traditionally assumed." Arguing that the coincidence between the outbreak of the Civil War and the surge in Dickinson's own creativity has never been properly assessed, Wolosky continues that the poet's work should "be placed, not only within the intellectual and literary currents of her period, but also into the realm of concrete historical events."[33]

Although her poems pose more interpretive problems, certainly Dickinson's letters make one wonder how their editor could reach the conclusion he does. From her first half-serious reference to her "Whig feelings" in a letter written to Abiah Root on February 23, 1845 (*L* 1:12), to a late reference to local murders in a letter written a month before her death (*L* 3:902), Dickinson's correspondence bristles with evidence of her knowledge of history, politics, current events, and the pressures of what Stevens calls "life in a state of violence." References to the Civil War, the capture of Jefferson Davis, the attempt to place the Modoc Indians of Oregon on a reservation, the panic of 1873, the passage of the silver bill in 1878, the Molly Maguires, and the assassination of Garfield in 1881 represent only a part of Dickinson's annotations of American history in the second half of the nineteenth century. Meanwhile, allusions to Bismarck and the Franco-Prussian War, the movement by Great Britain of Indian troops into Malta, and the mission of General Gordon to relieve the British garrison at Khartoum reveal that she absorbed much about international events from her devoted study of the newspapers, retaining more than sensational accounts of local accidents and disasters.

But what is Dickinson's idea of America itself? At times she invokes an image of national identity in humorous, even flippant, contexts, as in a Valentine letter of 1850, perhaps written to George Gould: "We will be David and Jonathan, or Damon and Pythias, or what is better than either, the United States of America" (*L* 1:92). After two examples of male friendship, one from the Hebrew Bible and one from the classical world, Dickinson shifts not only to the present but also to a political abstraction; united states are "better" than close friends because their union produces a single entity, a country. Similarly, chatting to her brother in a letter of March 7, 1852, she associates the upcoming wedding of Catherine Hitchcock and Henry Storrs with America: "Dont know whether they will have a wedding, or not, presume the *faculty* will be present in robes. I am more and more convinced, that this is a great country!" (*L* 1:188). Is Dickinson simply being facetious when she cites as an instance of American greatness the pomp and circumstance of a wedding between the daughter of a college president and a young man whom, according to Johnson, Henry Ward Beecher considered "one of the foremost men in the American pulpit" (*L* 3:955)? Does she assume her brother will share her sense of irony, noting the likeness between an academic faculty in robes and the self-important pageantry that characterizes other public occasions in America? Perhaps she does, but the breathless, exhilarated, slightly manic tone of the letter ("It's a glorious afternoon—the sky is blue and warm") suggests that Dickinson may be venting a touch of youthful enthusiasm, enthusiasm that extends here to her sense of a nation in which such people as Kate Hitchcock and Henry Storrs can become united states.

Still, other references reveal that Dickinson sometimes chafes under the burden of American self-consciousness. Writing again to Austin (March 24, 1853), she savors a particular episode in the intrigue of the courtship between her brother and Sue: "Sue's outwitted them all—ha-ha! just imagine me giving three cheers for American Independence!" (*L* 1:233). Another ambiguous moment, this could mean that Sue's ingenuity does credit to the American myth of self-determined autonomy; yet the rhetorical pressure of these remarks, with their self-dramatizing "ha-ha!" suggests that Dickinson may also mean "just imagine *me* giving three cheers," as though she expects Austin to recognize the incongruity of his heterodox sister's honoring a national abstraction.

An even plainer hint of discontent appears at the end of a letter to Sue (June 11, 1852): "Why cant *I* be a Delegate to the great Whig Convention?—dont I know all about Daniel Webster, and the Tariff, and the Law? Then, Susie I could see you during a pause in the session—but I dont like this country at all, and I shant stay here any longer! 'Delenda est' America, Massachusetts and all!" (*L* 1:212). Wolff reads this passage as an expression of Dickinson's rage against "the unbroken front of male faces that constituted any political gathering." In turn, this reading joins others in Wolff's larger, persuasive argument that Dickinson envied her brother his many worldly opportunities for success and fame.[34] But although the immediate occasion for her rage may be the male domination of American politics, its hyperbolic expression is tailored for the absent Sue. The converse of the 1850 Valentine, in which the United States constitutes a metaphor for the union of friends, this letter to Sue rails against America for enforcing a geographical separation. Coming only three months after the statement "I am more and more convinced, that this is a great country," the revision of Cato's *Delenda est Carthago* ("Carthage must be destroyed") suggests a potentially troublesome ambivalence toward America.

Dickinson's ambivalence toward America originates in her ambivalence toward the world, which surfaces first in her early struggles with Christianity and the problem of conversion. In an early letter to Abiah Root (March 28, 1846), the struggle defines itself plainly: "It was then my greatest pleasure to commune alone with the great God & to feel that he would listen to my prayers. I determined to devote my whole life to his service & desired that all might taste of the stream of living water from which I cooled my thirst. But the world allured me & in an unguarded moment I listened to her syren voice" (*L* 1:30). The image of the world as alluring, destructive siren reveals Dickinson's divided attitude, and this division repeats itself in subsequent letters. In another letter to Abiah (May 16, 1848), she confesses that "it is hard for me to give up the world" (*L* 1:67). To Jane Humphrey (January 23, 1850) she admits that despite "an opportunity rare for cultivating meekness—and patience—and submission—and for turning my back to this very sinful, and wicked world," she inclines "to other things" (*L* 1:82). After narrating her pilgrimage to Mount Vernon and "the tomb of General George Washington" to Elizabeth Holland (March 18, 1855), the same correspondent to whom she writes "George Who?" Dickinson exclaims, "Thank God there is a world" (*L* 2:319); yet writing to the Hollands three years later (about November 6, 1858), she echoes the statement to Sue, "I dont like this country at all, and I shant stay here any longer!": "I can't stay any longer in a world of death" (*L* 2:341).

Ambivalence toward the world involves both attraction and repulsion. As long as the objects of her love flourish, Dickinson finds it hard to give up the world, but when separation or death threatens, she longs to escape it. Her ambivalence toward America results from a similar mixture of attraction and repulsion. As long as friendship and love enlarge themselves against a background of national myth or abstraction, America attracts, but when its image of ideal union or independence falters in the face of actual separation or limitation, it repels. The geographical vastness of America, which Whitman celebrates so rhapsodically, is for Dickinson a reality to be feared and hated, for it makes possible the loss of people such as Austin and Sue, who considered moving to Michigan before they succumbed to pressures to remain in Amherst. The most striking example of Dickinson's own fiction of America comes in a letter to Mabel Loomis Todd, then sojourning in Europe (summer 1885):

Brother and Sister's Friend—

"Sweet Land of Liberty" is a superfluous Carol till it concern ourselves—then it outrealms the Birds.

I saw the American Flag last Night in the shutting West, and I felt for every Exile.

I trust you are homesick. That is the sweetest courtesy we pay an absent friend. (*L* 3:882)

After attempting to recall lines from Emerson's "The Humble-Bee" and instructing Todd to "Touch Shakespeare for me," Dickinson signs this letter "America."

In his 1855 preface, Whitman projects his version of the identification of an American poet with the country: "His spirit responds to his country's spirit. . . . he incarnates its geography and natural life and rivers and lakes" (*CRE* 711). But Dickinson is not at all interested in the incarnation of America Whitman envisions. She does not identify herself with Oregon or Texas or Maine. When she signs herself "America," she attempts to embody that which her correspondent has left behind, the home from which Todd, in Dickinson's view, is exiled. "Home is the definition of God," she tells Perez Cowan in late October 1870 (*L* 2:483), but she could as easily have written, Home is the definition of America. For Dickinson, home and the inner peace home provides constitute the "Sweet Land of Liberty"; the idea of America has no reality "till it concern ourselves."

This intensely personalized, even internalized, fiction of America emerges in the signature, which actually recalls Shakespeare, whom Todd is supposed to "touch" on Dickinson's behalf. Of Shakespeare's plays, as Sewall points out, "*Antony and Cleopatra* was a favorite, and most intimately quoted."[35] Among those quotations is this three-word letter to Sue (about 1874): " 'Egypt—thou knew'st'—" (*L* 2:533). Dickinson's source is Antony's speech beginning "Egypt, thou knew'st too well / My heart was to thy rudder tied by the strings, / And thou shouldst tow me after" (3.11.56–58). Borrowing Antony's political and geographical metonymy for Cleopatra, "Egypt," Dickinson expresses her deep emotional connection to Sue. With the signature "America," she designates herself with a similar metonymy, one that denotes an emotional connection with an absent friend rather than a political or geographical reality.

America serves Dickinson most fully, then, as a set of figurative images for inner states and experiences. Just as she internalizes the topography of the Bible when she calls Gethsemane "but a Province—in the
Being's Centre—" (poem 553, c. 1862), so she internalizes her national
identity when she asks Higginson (late May 1874), "Is it Intellect that
the Patriot means when he speaks of his 'Native Land'?" (L 2:525).
Similarly, writing to her Norcross cousins in mid-April of 1875, one
hundred years after the start of the Revolution, Dickinson personalizes
Emerson's version of the Minute Man at Concord, appropriating his
historical image for her own expressive purposes: "I have only a butter-
cup to offer for the centennial, as an 'embattled farmer' has but little
time" (L 2:539). In a letter to Abigail Cooper, written about 1877, the
revision of the America myth anticipates the letter to Mabel Loomis
Todd quoted above: " 'My Country, 'tis of thee,' has always meant the
Woods—to me—'Sweet Land of Liberty,' I trust is your own—" (L
2:586). This last example recalls Dickinson's treatment of Congrega-
tionalist orthodoxy in such poems as 324 (c. 1860): "Some keep the
Sabbath going to Church— / I keep it, staying at Home—." In the separate but analogous rhetorics of patriotism and faith, she recognizes multiple opportunities for minting new metaphors out of verbal signs already rich with association.

The internalization of American history, politics, myth, and rhetoric
undoubtedly parallels a current of indirect criticism comparable to that
implicit in "Some keep the Sabbath going to Church—." But Dickinson's repeated uses of the secular material of Americanness, like her
many uses of the sacred material of Congregational Christianity, suggest that she found such material too nourishing to be neglected. What
she criticizes she also depends on: "My Country is Truth. . . . I like
Truth—it . . . is a free Democracy."[36] On the surface, these statements
may appear to mean that Dickinson considers herself bound to a moral
reality rather than to a national one; yet such statements also depend for
their figurative force on an assumption that the idea of "a free Democracy" is meaningful and attractive. In other words, it would be a mistake to conclude that because Dickinson says less than Emerson or
Whitman about specific political, historical, or national concerns, the
myths and realities of life in America necessarily mean any less to her
than to them.

Evidence from the poems confirms that the principles behind Dickinson's prose also operate in her verse. Although her poems make far
more obvious use of biblical, Christian, and Congregational material
than they do of America, it would be hard to miss the implications of
such a poem as this:

My country need not change her gown,
Her triple suit as sweet
As when 'twas cut at Lexington,
And first pronounced "a fit."

Great Britain disapproves, "the stars";
Disparagement discreet,—
There's something in their attitude
That taunts her bayonet.

                              (poem 1511, c. 1881)

Apparently written to commemorate Independence Day and referred to by Dickinson as "My Country's Wardrobe" in a letter to Higginson (November 1880; L 3:681), this poem radiates a nationalism that rivals that of Emerson's "American Scholar" or Whitman's 1855 preface. Anthologizers and critics have passed over this poem,[37] apparently relegating it to minor status, but it is not merely an ephemeral piece of patriotic occasional verse. The menacing final line, with its deliberately flattened rhyme, underscores the likeness, and confrontation, of the points of American stars and the points of British bayonets. "There's something in their attitude" amounts to an admission that it is not merely American independence that galls Great Britain as much as it is the feisty, even insolent, American posture of aggressive defiance. Most important, however, is the identification of each country as "her" and the figurative transformation of the flag into a woman's gown. For a poet who took to wearing nothing but white, the symbolic significance of dress cannot be overstated, nor, for someone who kept to her father's house and saw few visitors, can the significance of a deliberately cultivated "attitude" that others disparage. Dickinson could have expected Higginson to make these associations himself. The poem does not depend for its meanings on such biographical elements; yet they enhance the self-descriptive tones already present. The identification of America's independent attitude with the speaker's own remains unmistakable.

Dickinson's national consciousness also surfaces vividly in a poem written about twenty years earlier, one that ends with lines that have received much more critical attention: "Because I see—New Englandly— / The Queen, discerns like me— / Provincially—" (poem 285, c. 1861). The subject of this poem, which begins "The Robin's my Criterion for Tune— / Because I grow—where Robins do—," is the inevitability of a national poetry. Geography determines vision, a limitation from which not even the queen of England is free. But beyond this general truth lies a more original observation about the nature of a specifically American poetry, an observation Frost and Williams embraced but Pound and Eliot fled. Within the geographical limitations of the country, American poets often seek further self-definition by identifying themselves with local place and region. Both the sectional nature and the demographic diversity of the United States force American poets to choose from among, or to combine aspects of, three options: follow Whitman's example of a poetry that attempts to be all-inclusive; follow Pound's and Eliot's examples of a poetry that avoids the burden of nationality by attempting to be international and cosmopolitan; or follow Dickinson's, Frost's, and Williams's examples of a poetry intimately connected with the particular sensibility of a particular place. The insight of Dickinson's poem, then, is that the most important difference for her as a poet is not simply the one between England and America but rather that between England and New England.

Other national references in the poems have their counterparts in the letters. For example, the rhetoric of " 'Sic transit gloria mundi' " (poem 3), written for Valentine's Day in 1852, constitutes a more innocent, less bitter version of the letter written four months later to Sue announcing " 'Delenda est' America, Massachusetts and all!" Like the letter, the poem projects a national role for its speaker: "Unto the Legislature / My country bids me go; / I'll take my *india rubbers*, / In case the *wind* should blow!" Although the light tone differs markedly from that of the letter to Sue, behind its clever incorporation of such figures from American history as Columbus, Daniel Boone, and "Our Fathers" on Bunker Hill lies the same association of nationality with friendship or love that informs not only that letter but also the other examples above: "Good bye, Sir, I am going; / My country calleth me; / . . . Then, farewell, Tuscarora, / And farewell, Sir, to thee!" Whereas attending the legislature would allow Dickinson to see the absent Sue, here the legislature calls the speaker away from her valentine, presumably so that he may miss her. Trivial as the situation may appear, it signals a deeper opposition in Dickinson's thinking, an opposition between a public, national involvement and a private, emotional one.

To personalize and internalize the categories of American experience is to absorb the public and national into the private and emotional. A psychological reading of such absorption might see it as Dickinson's response to, or defense against, a father who buried himself in public and political activities. A feminist reading might interpret it as her inevitable reaction to a public or a nation that made no place for her. But the main question here is another one: If the absence of self-descriptive statements corresponds in Dickinson's case to a fully developed formalism, then to what does her apparent absence of political, historical, or national interest correspond? One immediate answer is negative: It does not correspond to a strategy for evasion, such as Stevens's. Whereas he sees poetic style as one means by which poets engage their imaginative powers of *poiesis* to resist the pressures exerted by reality on Americans, Dickinson does not. Admittedly, her sense of style and form does not explicitly link itself to the public program, as described by Emerson or Whitman, of forging a unique national poetry; yet neither does it seal itself away in an imagined isolation. If she does not appear to many readers to be nationalist, or even national, this does not mean she has no sense of nationality, any more than her refusal to comment on her own forms means she has no sense of formality. If Emerson or Whitman would not have written this poem, neither would Stevens:

> Soto! Explore thyself!
> Therein thyself shalt find
> The "Undiscovered Continent"—
> No Settler had the Mind.

(poem 832, c. 1864)

A revision of both Christ's "Physician, heal thyself" and the inscription at the Delphic oracle, "Know thyself," this injunction addresses the Spanish explorer, Hernando de Soto, as though he were Hamlet. The "Undiscovered Continent," either a misquotation or a deliberate modification of Hamlet's "The undiscover'd country from whose bourn / No traveller returns" (3.1.78–79), is death, the erasure of the self. In the opposition between settlers and explorers, the speaker, like Dickinson herself, identifies with the latter. That de Soto himself died during his explorations of what became the American southeast makes this fable all the more significant. As so many of Dickinson's poems demonstrate, the exploration of the self must include the exploration of the self's demise. What is more, one of the conditions of such exploration, which here revises both its classical and Christian precedents, is that the explorer is certain to meet death during it. This much would make the quatrain a model of allusion and compression; yet by mapping internal geography onto an American landscape, Dickinson adds another dimension. Making figurative use of de Soto, as Williams and Crane would later make figurative use of Columbus in more explicit treatments of America, she fashions an emblem for human experience as it is realized in the New World. That that experience is essentially private is undeniable; that its emblem comes from a poet with a firm sense of nationality is, too.

Nowhere does Dickinson say that her formalism results from an attempt to distinguish American poetry from British or to reflect the realities of contemporary America. Since other poets do say such things, one assumes that they mean what they say and that since she does not, she does not. But in her internalization of America, Dickinson demonstrates a nationalism distinct from that of more aggressive apologists. As she tells Higginson, her "I" stands for "a supposed person"; yet in such poems as the following, that supposed person has definite traits:

> Between My Country—and the Others—
> There is a Sea—
> But Flowers—negotiate between us—
> As Ministry.

> (poem 905, c. 1864)

Printed as a six-line stanza in *Unpublished Poems* (1935), the poem carries the editorial notation "In the old grave-yard." Read with this in mind, it functions as simple metaphor: The speaker's country is the land of the living, separated from the undiscovered country of death by an unbridgeable gulf. Like foreign ministers representing their countries, flowers represent the dead to us, as they reappear each spring after the death of winter, and represent us to the dead, as we lay them on graves.

To this extent, Dickinson's "I" could represent any person who feels the distance between the living and the dead. Even without the editorial notation, the poem could stand as a representation of any person who feels separated from others. Read this way, it becomes an image of the isolated self, connected with other selves only as countries on different continents are connected by water. But if that person happens to be American, as the opening lines suggest, the statement "Between My Country—and the Others—/ There is a Sea—" acquires a particular resonance. Then Dickinson's achievement becomes the alignment of a national experience of geography, a geography that has determined the history of American attitudes and policies toward other countries, with a personal sense of isolation. As an American, the speaker is doubly isolated, and that isolation lies at the heart of both Dickinson's writing and her fiction of America. Her unique, uncompromising formalism reflects this isolation. It originates in private vision and asserts its differences from tradition; it functions as a sign of inwardness, a token of the self that modifies the public conventions of form for its own uses. But at the same time it also represents her attempt to cross the sea between living and dead, as in its ministry it negotiates between herself and the readers she never knew.

FOUR

EZRA POUND AND THE TERRIFYIN'
VOICE OF CIVILIZATION

DICKINSON meant little, if anything, to Pound. Her name appears nowhere in his shorter poems, *Cantos*, *Literary Essays*, *Selected Prose*, World War II radio broadcasts, or 1950 collection of letters. Even Stevens, about whom Pound had almost nothing to say, crops up in a radio broadcast (November 6, 1941) and in at least one unpublished letter.[1] One explanation of Pound's indifference to Dickinson, whose poems emerged in a scholarly edition during his confinement at St. Elizabeths and letters the year of his release, is that in his eyes Whitman eclipsed her. Certainly, he has much to say about Whitman, and a good deal of criticism traces Pound's genealogy to the author of *Leaves of Grass*. Pound himself makes this tracing inevitable, as on more than one occasion he adopts the metaphor of paternity to describe his relation to Whitman. In his 1909 prose note "What I Feel about Walt Whitman," he confesses, "Personally I might be very glad to conceal my relationship to my spiritual father and brag about my more congenial ancestry—Dante, Shakespeare, Theocritus, Villon, but the descent is a bit difficult to establish."[2] Likewise, in the familiar poem "A Pact," first published in the April 1913 issue of *Poetry*, Pound apostrophizes Whitman in explicitly filial terms: "I come to you as a grown child / Who has had a pig-headed father."[3]

Such obvious language lends itself to the analysis of influence theory, though Bloom himself finds "Whitman quite unrecognizable in nearly every reference Pound makes to him."[4] Other critical assessments of this lineage tend to depend on how commentators feel toward either Whitman or Pound, as well as on how they balance the love against the hate in this love-hate relationship.[5] The variable nature of critical judgment reveals itself in the indexes of the many books on Pound. Some list numerous references to Whitman, some few, some none. The index of Hugh Kenner's *Poetry of Ezra Pound* (1951), for example, contains no entries on Whitman, while that of his *Pound Era* (1971) includes one. Meanwhile, both books pay considerable attention to the members of Pound's "more congenial ancestry."

Reviewing the vicissitudes of Pound's treatment of Whitman between, say, 1909 and the allusions to "Out of the Cradle Endlessly

Rocking" in canto 82 (1948) would confirm Hugh Witemeyer's judgment that "Pound's attitude toward Whitman was highly ambivalent."[6] Inevitably, Pound's ambivalence toward Whitman associates itself with his ambivalence toward America, to which I shall return. For now I want to consider two different critical assessments of Pound's Whitmanian ancestry, since they lead directly into a discussion of poetic technique.

In his survey of American poetry, Pearce argues that the "principal [sic] of form and technique in the *Cantos* is so deliberately opposed to that in Whitman's poetry that the one is vitalized by the other, if only by virtue of a certain resistance." Pearce goes on to explain that the "crux of the opposition" between Whitman and Pound "lies in two conceptions of style," illustrating these two conceptions by quoting two passages: first, the famous one from the preface to the 1855 *Leaves of Grass* in which Whitman announces that he will not have in his writing "any elegance or effect or originality" to hang between him and his readers "like curtains" and, second, one from Pound's *Guide to Kulchur* (1938) that claims "the attainment of a style consists in so knowing words that one will communicate the various parts of what one says with the various degrees and weights of importance which one wishes."[7]

In the passages Pearce quotes, Whitman promises that his language will be transparent, whereas Pound contends that a writer's language must be so finely calibrated that it expresses exactly what he or she intends. On the surface, this opposition appears to be one between no mediation and considerable mediation. Whitman's dream of a transparent language belongs to the fiction of Romantic organicism. Pound's dream of a perfectly controlled language suggests a Neoclassical commitment to rhetorical stability, appropriateness, and precision. To Pearce's mind, this opposition derives not simply from a difference between two temperaments but specifically from Pound's negative reaction to Whitman. In other words, Pound's attitude toward style reflects, at least in part, his troublesome ambivalence toward his poetic father. But attractively concise as it is, this formulation needs reconsideration.

Although many real differences between the style of *Leaves of Grass* and that of the *Cantos* force themselves immediately on a reader's attention, the two statements quoted by Pearce, one explicitly self-descriptive and one implicitly so, do not exclude one another. In fact, they do not even differ radically, for they share the assumption that style must not interfere. In Whitman's view, his writing must not prevent his readers from seeing what he sees, or at least from seeing in the same self-reflexive way he does ("You shall stand by my side and look in the mirror with me" [*CRE* 717]); in Pound's view, his writing must not prevent his communication of what he wishes to say. Both views envision a poetic language purged of whatever will thwart direct access to a reader's understanding, such as the distracting static of dead metaphor, dead rhyme, or dead meter. Furthermore, both views project theoretical ideals that neither poet observes in practice. As the tale of a jetblack sunrise demonstrates, the rich linguistic and formal features of Whitman's verse characterize writing that is hardly without "elegance or effect or originality." Likewise, as any page of the *Cantos* demonstrates, the shifting, indeterminate play of possible meanings suggests that the ideal of a perfectly controlled, stable, precise language has dissolved into writing that makes the authorial intention of what "one wishes" impossible to fix, if not altogether irrelevant.

If the two views do oppose one another, opposition lies in strategic emphasis, as each poet indicates the way he wants to be read. Anticipating the objection that he celebrates himself to the exclusion of all else, Whitman attempts to shift attention away from his role as craftsman. A reader who is too aware of his stylistic control may begin to feel manipulated into agreeing with the disarmingly innocent proposition "For every atom belonging to me as good belongs to you" (*CP* 27) and become too suspicious to grant the identification between writer and reader without which "Song of Myself" collapses. Conversely, anticipating the objection that the verse of the *Cantos* juxtaposes snatches and fragments to the exclusion of wholeness and coherence, Pound attempts to recall attention to his role as craftsman. If he can reassure his readers that his writing communicates what he wants to say, those readers may be more inclined to grant that Pound's long poem must amount to more than the sum of its parts, since it fulfills his intention, even if what it amounts to remains obscure to some.

If Pearce overestimates the differences between Whitman's and Pound's conceptions of style, Blasing, writing twenty-six years later, underestimates them. In her mapping of American poetry, she groups Whitman and Pound, along with Frank O'Hara, as "anagogic poets," that is, poets whose writing "proposes a coincidence of textual and existential experience, figurative and literal language, poetic and natural form." In proposing these coincidences, anagogic poetry "rejects all ordained, hierarchical forms," prefers free verse, breaks down the distinction between form and content, uses the collage method and epic forms, and employs synecdoche in "a compositional method where relationships of contiguity and those of similarity coincide, so that prose and poetry are points on a continuum rather than opposites."[8]

Again, the symmetrical neatness of Blasing's taxonomy attracts and compels. Certainly, the formal features of the *Cantos* resemble those of "Song of Myself" more than they do anything by Poe, Emerson, or Dickinson, whom Blasing places at the heads of three other categories.

But in urging this resemblance, Blasing neglects significant differences. Although Whitman, at least early in his career, usually does prefer free verse and reject inherited forms, the same cannot be said so easily of Pound, who also values the metrical and the inherited. Although Whitman and Pound often treat prose and verse as points on a continuum, this habit does not distinguish them from Dickinson, as we have seen. As for breaking down the distinction between form and content, Whitman and Pound are doing what any good writer does, as Christine Brook-Rose argues in her spirited attempt to kill what she calls the "monster" of the division between form and content.[9] In fairness to Blasing, however, one must distinguish between the persistence of this division in criticism and the mythologizing of it by poets. But even here Whitman and Pound differ, as Whitman's figure of curtains hanging between him and his reader implies a fiction of form that differs from Pound's. This difference emerges most strikingly in the latter's attitude toward the supposed coincidence of poetic and natural form, a coincidence Whitman's verse asserts.

Some of Pound's earliest prose statements about poetic form and technique appear in "I Gather the Limbs of Osiris," originally a series of articles in the *New Age* (1911–12). Commenting on Pound's title, Kenner turns to the *Oxford Companion to Classical Literature* to learn that "it was Osiris, 'the male productive principle in nature,' who became when his scattered limbs had been regathered the god of the dead (of Homer, of the Seafarer poet, of Arnaut Daniel), but also 'the source . . . of renewed life.'"[10] More expansive treatment of Osiris lies in the *Golden Bough* of Frazer, whom Pound, in one of several scattered references, calls "essential to contemporary clear thinking."[11] Having narrated the myth of Osiris, which "is told in a connected form only by Plutarch," Frazer locates the origin of Egyptian ceremonies for the dead in the Osiris myth. His broken body converted into the first mummy by the spells and manipulations of his relatives and friends, Osiris serves as the prototype of all the mummified dead. Then Frazer explains that "from the Middle Kingdom onwards it was the regular practice to address the deceased as 'Osiris So-and-So,' as if he were the god himself, and to add the standing epithet 'true of speech,' because true speech was characteristic of Osiris."[12]

In the myth of Osiris, then, Pound finds not only an image of his own gathering of scattered literature to recover the immediacy of dead poets but also an image of "true speech," an ideal that informs his many comments on style, technique, and form, as well as his remarks on culture, history, and economics. Early in "I Gather the Limbs of Osiris," Pound describes "style" in relation to Arnaut Daniel: "At a time when both prose and poetry were loose-jointed, prolix, barbaric, he, to all intents and virtually, rediscovered 'style'. He conceived, that is, a manner of writing in which each word should bear some burden, should make some special contribution to the effect of the whole. The poem is an organism in which each part functions, gives to sound or to sense something—preferably to sound *and* sense gives something" (*SP* 27). For Pound, Daniel's style represents true speech, which consists of "so knowing words," as he puts it in *Guide to Kulchur*, that not one is wasted. This early formulation anticipates the second plank of the Imagist platform of 1913, to which on more than one occasion Pound refers as the most important of the three principles: "To use absolutely no word that does not contribute to the presentation."[13]

But particularly interesting here is the assertion that the "poem is an organism." What clearer evidence of Pound's organicism could one ask for? And yet, despite the word "organism," this statement does not assume the same interchangeability of natural and poetic forms assumed by Emerson and Whitman. In claiming that each part of a poem "functions," Pound could just as easily have described a poem as a machine, anticipating Williams's formulation that a poem is a machine made out of words. Nothing in the context of Pound's statement demonstrates an interest in associating a poem with the growth of a tree or the breaking of waves. Admittedly, in the "Credo" section of "A Retrospect" (1918), he makes the following avowal: "*Form.*—I think there is a 'fluid' as well as a 'solid' content, that some poems may have form as a tree has form, some as water poured into a vase. That most symmetrical forms have certain uses. That a vast number of subjects cannot be precisely, and therefore not properly rendered in symmetrical forms" (*LE* 9). But here the organicist's tree receives no more attention than the predetermined forms that Coleridge, borrowing from Schlegel, calls "mechanic . . . as when to a mass of wet clay we give whatever shape we wish it to retain when hardened."[14] Significantly, Pound does not maintain the parallelism of his own formal credo. In the first part of his first sentence, fluidity precedes solidity, but in the second part the tree precedes the water poured into a vase. This chiastic crossing suggests a convergence of supposed opposites, a convergence Pound underlines two sentences later when he declares that "the artist should master all known forms and systems of metric."

Representations of Pound as an organicist like Whitman, or as a patron saint of later poets who write in free verse, inevitably misrepresent. In both theory and practice, he demonstrates his ultimate indifference to, and impatience with, the distinction between metrical and free verse. In a section of "I Gather the Limbs of Osiris" headed "On Technique," for example, he takes both camps to task: "Likewise you will hear the people, one set of them, raging against form—by which they mean external symmetry—and another set against free verse. And it is quite certain that none of these people have any exact, effable concept of what they do mean; or if they have a definite dislike of something properly dislikable, they only succeeded in expressing a dislike for something not quite it and not quite not it" (SP 31). Similarly, statements throughout his letters reveal Pound's conviction that polemic on behalf of either metrical or free verse does not reflect true speech. In 1915 he exhorts Harriet Monroe: "Keep on moving, remember that poetry is more important than verse free or otherwise" (L 67). In 1916 he lectures Iris Barry: "No one can do good free verse who hasn't struggled with the regular; at least I don't know anyone who has" (L 79). In 1918, again writing to Harriet Monroe, he vents his exasperation with readers who limit themselves to one kind of verse: "Simply the vers libre public are probably by now as stone blind to the vocal or oral properties of a poem as the 'sonnet' public was five or seven years ago to the actual language, i.e. all that has made my stuff interesting since 'Contemporania'" (L 127).

In his exasperation, Pound violates his own rule against the use of synesthesia, as he rails against readers who are "stone blind" to the auditory properties that make the "stuff" he wrote after the publication of twelve poems in the April 1913 issue of *Poetry* so much more than interesting. If he is angry, he has good reason to be, for he casts his poems before readers he expects to be skilled and flexible enough to hear, for example, the meter, and hence the complexity, behind the famous line of canto 81, "(To break the pentameter, that was the first heave)," a parenthetical statement that associates prosodic innovation with American politics, as it follows an allusion to Adams and Jefferson. But too often, at least for Pound's taste, those readers remain deaf, as those who read in this line a slogan promoting free verse have failed to hear and to appreciate the symmetry of its triple meter: x/xx/xx/xx/x.[15] In other words, the line does not authorize the replacement of iambic pentameter by free verse; it simply calls for a verse that makes meaningful use of the full range of prosodic forms, both metrical and nonmetrical. If it projects an opposition, that opposition is not one between iambic pentameter and free verse but between the monopoly of iambic pentameter and a prosodic pluralism that also includes iambic pentameter.[16]

Confirmation of this reading comes only two pages later in the famous passage beginning "What thou lovest well remains" (C 520–21). Kenner sees in this section of canto 81 Pound's "attainment of his honorable truce" with the past masters of English tradition.[17] As such, its importance derives not simply from its beauty but also from the attitude it reflects. More than thirty years earlier, Pound announced his pact with the maverick Whitman in a tone still feisty and defiant. At Pisa he makes another, quieter pact, this one not with a maverick poet but with the many poets of meter and symmetrical form, including Milton, whom Pound tends to undervalue.[18] But it is *Paradise Lost* that prepares Pound's reader, in more ways than one, to appreciate the forceful structure of "First came the seen, then thus the palpable / Elysium, though it were in the halls of hell" (C 521). In this enjambment, "the palpable" passes from nominal to adjectival status, as abstractions such as "the seen" and "the palpable" suddenly ground themselves in a specific place, a cage at Pisa transformed by vision into the classical realm of the blessed. The language may be pagan, but the psychological truth of these lines resonates clearly with that of Satan's "The mind is its own place, and in itself / Can make a Heav'n of Hell, a Hell of Heav'n."

Brooke-Rose chides Pound's adverse critics for quoting from canto 81 "for the wrong reasons."[19] It is wrong, or at least misreading, to quote from canto 81 as an example of what Pound can do when he cleans up the mess of the *Cantos* and gets down to writing real lyric poetry, complete with rhyme, archaism, and the telltale syncope ("lov'st") that signifies the dominance of metrical regularity. But it is also misreading for even a sympathetic critic to quote from canto 81 as an example of Pound's Whitmanian organicism. Blasing, who understands that the passage beginning "What thou lovest well remains" represents "an extended homage to the scaled music of the English lyric tradition," which "scales the very climax of its 'awakening' to the pentameter," still insists that Pound's invocation of "the green world" reflects his knowledge that "organicism rewrites the tradition." Consciously or unconsciously aware of the difficulty here, she adds in a note, "Pound's use of the English meter in canto 81 compares with Whitman's occasional allusions to the same rhythm: it both invokes the authority of the English lyric tradition and justifies his deviation from it."[20] But Pound's homage to, or truce with, the history of English versification has little, if anything, in common with Whitman's use of iambic meter. The former corresponds to a fully self-conscious acknowledgment, and affirmation, of exactly the aspect of poetic tradition Pound first admired Whitman for rebelling against ("Like Dante he wrote in the 'vulgar tongue', in a new metric" [*SP* 146]), whereas the latter, especially in Whitman's later poems, implies a retreat from an earlier radicalism.

Because canto 81 celebrates the old metric, not a new one, it implies a difference from Whitman, rather than a similarity to him. Of course, the conflicting feelings Pound holds toward Whitman make it inevitable that the implicit critique of canto 81 will be followed quickly by the implicit homage of canto 82. But still he has established his distance from Whitman: to him the old metric is as vital as the new; it forms part of the true heritage and, consequently, of the true speech. One need only consider the monotony of Whitman's "O Captain! My Captain!" to understand the difference between metrical homage and metrical capitulation. Whitman's poem collapses before the authority of English lyric tradition, forgetting all about meaningful deviation from it. A poet who believes, as Whitman appears to in his 1855 preface, that "the poems distilled from other poems will probably pass away" (CRE 728) thinks of poetic tradition in a way altogether different from the way Pound does.[21] In renouncing the past, Whitman grants to himself an authority that enables him to make his greatest poems and to define the terms on which his readers read them; yet at the same time he forfeits the authority and enabling powers that only the tradition can grant, as "O Captain! My Captain!" makes painfully clear. For Whitman "what is past is past" (CRE 713), including the old metric, now supplanted by "the free growth of metrical laws." As liberating and exhilarating as Pound found Whitman's fiction of form, it could never be wholly his.

2

What is Pound's own fiction of form? Although in the passage about Daniel's style the word "organism" misleads, the word "functions" does not. Whenever Pound turns to matters of style, form, or technique, he usually ends up discussing function, effect, and response.[22] Returning to the "On Technique" section of "I Gather the Limbs of Osiris," for example, we find this definition: "As for the arts and their technique— technique is the means of conveying an exact impression of exactly what one means in such a way as to exhilarate" (SP 33). Anticipating by a quarter century the similar formulation about style in Guide to Kulchur, this statement precedes a paragraph devoted wholly to a survey of different prosodic systems: "When it comes to poetry, I hold no brief for any particular system of metric." Pound's immediate transition from exhilaration to prosody implies a move from effect to cause, one that evaluates verse structure not in terms of genre, convention, decorum, or appropriateness but in terms of how it makes a reader feel.

Later in the same series of articles, a similar emphasis characterizes Pound's discussion of form: "I mean . . . that one must call a spade a spade in form so exactly adjusted, in a metric in itself so seductive, that the statement will not bore the auditor" (SP 41). He then considers the dignity of simple and direct utterance, arguing that "it must be conveyed by art, and by the art of the verse structure, by something that exalts the reader, making him feel that he is in contact with something arranged more finely than the commonplace." A last example of this attention to the nature of form and technique appears in a letter of 1913, written to Harriet Monroe: "There's no use in a strong impulse if it is all or nearly all lost in bungling transmission and technique. This obnoxious word that I'm always brandishing about means nothing but a transmission of the impulse intact. It means that you not only get the thing off your own chest, but that you get it into some one else's" (*L* 23). To exhilarate the reader, to seduce the reader, not to bore the reader, to exalt the reader, to get a thing into the reader's chest: a common thread stitches these ideas together.

For a poet so often accused of snubbing or bullying his readers, Pound projects a fiction of form that is anxiously concerned with those readers. Pound's is a fiction of function and effect, and its uniqueness becomes apparent in relation to other poetic fictions of form. Although both Emerson and Whitman want to move and change their readers, their organicism concentrates on the analogy between verse structure and natural phenomena, not on a reader's response. Although Dickinson's statement about knowing poetry by the feeling of having the top of her head taken off shows she associates poetry with powerful response, that response is her own, like the cooling she experiences upon hearing the jingling bells of rhyme, not her readers'. Opposed to the myth of natural form, Dickinson's fiction of restoration also works by analogy, as it links poetic structures of likeness to gestures of rebuilding in a world of splinters. Even Williams's fiction of a measure made for the American idiom is analogical, for it assumes a correspondence between new formal structures and spoken language.

In describing poetic form in terms of both function (its role in transmitting to a reader what the poet wishes to say) and effect (how it makes that reader feel), Pound combines pragmatism with phenomenology. In itself the combination should not surprise. After all, advertisements make profitable use of precisely the same combination. But what does surprise is that in Pound's case all the scholarship and erudition should produce a myth of form so fundamentally practical, accessible, and free of mystification. In this sense Pound's case exactly reverses that of Williams, who lacked scholarship and erudition, a lack that Pound, among others, made him feel keenly and that caused him to generate an elaborate fiction of poetic form. As Williams's fiction of measure attempts on some level to compensate for too little learning, even though, as Pound reminds us, "a good poet is not always an educated man" (*SP* 113), so Pound's attempts on some level to compensate for too much.

Of course, to say that Pound's fiction of form is fundamentally pragmatic is not to say that he never makes obscure or mystifying statements about his own practices. In tracing the successive theories of the Luminous Detail, Imagism, Vorticism, and the Ideogrammic Method, as well as such apparently self-descriptive figures as "the rose in the steel dust" (*C* 449), one encounters numerous ambiguities, inconsistencies, and lacunae. But these are really beside the point, or at least beside the point that for Pound poetic form must justify itself primarily in terms of function and effect. The Luminous Detail, for example, originates in Pound's comments about a "New Method in Scholarship" (*SP* 21), so that even though it suggests analogies with the "hard light, clear edges" Pound associated with Imagism (*L* 38), initially it implies a critical method as much as a poetic technique. Likewise, the Ideogrammic Method, which derives from the Luminous Detail, recognizes no generic boundaries in its having "a good deal to do with the efficiency of verbal manifestation, and with the transmittibility of a conviction."[23] Although this statement echoes Pound's other assertions about the function of technique, it pertains equally, at least in his mind, to the construction of a canto, a critical essay, or a radio broadcast. Accordingly, it does not describe any essential aspect of verse as verse. The same can be said of Vorticism, which not only includes several kinds of writing but also several kinds of art. Invigorating as it may be to link poetry to painting, sculpture, or photography, statements large enough to include all these media cannot be made specific enough to illuminate the formal details of any one. As for Imagism, Eliot's comment in "Reflections on *Vers Libre*" (1917) that it "is a theory about the use of material," not a theory of verse form, might make Brooke-Rose and others nervous, as the critical monster of form-divided-from-content threatens to rear its head, especially since Eliot's assertion forgets or ignores the third plank of the Imagist platform, which refers explicitly to prosody ("to compose in the sequence of the musical phrase, not in sequence of a metronome"). But Pound's brief affiliation with the Imagist school, not to mention his subsequent dissatisfaction with it, suggests that its relevance to his conception of poetic form must be qualified.

If one wanted to challenge the pragmatism of that conception, Pound's comments on quantity in English verse would offer a more appropriate target.[24] But Pound's refusal to extrapolate from occasional remarks about quantity to a larger mythology distinguishes him from Williams. Lacking Pound's firsthand knowledge of quantitative meter, Williams literalized Pound's admittedly imperfect analogies and from that literalization generated the fiction of a new time-based measure suited to the American idiom. Similarly, Pound's occasional remarks about the use of typographic patterning in verse distinguish him from Olson, who literalized the analogy between typewritten inscription and spoken utterance, generating the fiction of Projective Verse. Although one can trace several assertions in Olson's 1950 essay to offhand statements made by Pound in various letters, larger differences remain between the two poets. Writing to Laurence Binyon in 1938, for example, Pound declares, "I think one has right to all sorts of printing dodges to clarify or make easy the reader's path" (*L* 313); or writing Hubert Creekmore the following year, he maintains that "ALL typographic disposition, placing of words *on* the page, is intended to facilitate the reader's intonation" (*L* 322). Such relatively modest, limited, and uncontroversial claims stop well short of Olson's full-blown fiction: "It is the advantage of the typewriter that, due to its rigidity and its space precisions, it can, for a poet, indicate exactly the breath, the pauses, the suspensions even of syllables, the juxtapositions even of parts of phrases, which he intends. . . . It is time we picked the fruits of the experiments of Cummings, Pound, Williams, each of whom has, after his way, already used the machine as a scoring to his composing, as a script to its vocalization."[25] Typically, Pound views the typewriter and its "dodges" as an aid to communication, to the transmission of what he wishes a reader to hear or understand, whereas Olson views it as the precise representation of the poet's speaking voice that the reader must reproduce. Behind Olson's fiction lies the dream that the graphic surface of a poem will dissolve into the reader's unmediated hearing and vocalization. Behind Pound's remarks lies a canny sense of how graphic arrangements manipulate reading patterns and consequently generate rhythmic effects.

Pound's sophistication protects him from the exaggeration of his own figurative statements. In a famous letter to his father (April 11, 1927; *L* 210) or in a remark reported by Yeats in "A Packet for Ezra Pound" (1929), Pound can compare his *Cantos* to a fugue, the same term Hart Crane uses to describe the "Cutty Sark" section of his *Bridge* to Otto Kahn. But, unlike Crane, Pound shows that he knows too well the limitations of such self-description, sympathizing "with those who cry out against the describing of work in any particular art by a terminology borrowed from all the others" because such description is "a make-shift, a laziness" (*SP* 35). In a letter of April 1937 to John Lackay Brown, he acknowledges specifically the limits of his fugue analogy: "Take a fugue: theme, response, contrasujet. *Not* that I mean to make an exact analogy of structure" (*L* 294). Such pragmatism guards against self-deception, as it contains the germ of a healthy skepticism. Free to roam among various prosodic systems, to recognize analogies between verse forms and the technical aspects of other arts, to experiment with the typewriter, and even to echo, in a faint and qualified way, other poets' myths, such as the myth of organicism, Pound approaches the building of poems as something of a formal nomad. Refusing allegiance to any one mode or method, he opts for an eclecticism that guarantees his freedom. Underlying his eclecticism is a belief in the relatively simple fiction of function and effect, which insists that technique must help the poet communicate to the reader, who in turn must experience powerful feeling.

Although Pound's formal eclecticism prevents the construction of a subsuming personal myth such as Whitman's or Hopkins's or Williams's or Olson's, his formalism is not casual. In his case, eclecticism represents not the defense of the dilettante but the preoccupation with form characteristic of so many American poets. Consequently, despite his sophistication and learning, he can also sound too trusting, even naive, in his overestimation of technique, as in the often-quoted statement from his "Credo," "I believe in technique as the test of a man's sincerity" (*LE* 9), or in an earlier, more expansive passage from "I Gather the Limbs of Osiris" that anticipates it:

> There is the slighter "technique of manner", a thing reducible almost to rules, a matter of "j's" and "d's", of order and sequence, a thing attenuable, a thing verging off until it degenerates into rhetoric; and this slighter technique is also a thing of price, notwithstanding that all the qualities which differentiate poetry from prose are things born before syntax; this technique of surface is valuable above its smoother virtues simply because it is technique, and because technique is the only gauge and test of a man's lasting sincerity. (*SP* 34)

Pound considers the "technique of manner" or "of surface" slighter than what he calls in the previous paragraph the "Technique of Content," which controls the "peculiar energy which . . . is the power of tradition, of centuries of race consciousness, of agreement, of association," and which he admits "nothing short of genius understands."

This passage reveals much about the young Pound and prefigures more to come. The statement that technique is the only test of a poet's sincerity is in many ways a winning one, as it implies a craftsman "who cares and believes really in the pint of truth that is in him" and who "will work, year in and year out, to find the perfect expression," a heroic figure oblivious to time and fashion and the marketplace, like Thoreau's idealized artist of Kouroo, who presides over the last chapter of *Walden* as he labors to make a perfect staff. But considered from another angle, the affirmation of a technique of surface defends the young poet against Content, with a capital C, not necessarily because he has nothing to say but because Content belongs to a land ruled by gigantic geniuses, dead gods such as Homer, Dante, Chaucer, and Shakespeare, who appear in "I Gather the Limbs of Osiris" as "four distinct phases of consciousness" (*SP* 29).

Pound's high estimation of technique stamps him in the eyes of both his adverse and sympathetic critics. Whatever the value of distinguishing between technique, or form, and content, the fact remains that he showed considerable anxiety about the relation between them, an anxiety that associates itself in different ways at different points in his career with his notions of an audience. Pound objected to the appearance on the cover of *Poetry* of "that infamous remark of Whitman's about poets needing an audience" (*L* 107; see also 147) implicitly because such a need compromises the artistic integrity of the poet, but many remarks reveal Pound's own preoccupation with his audience.[26] In *Personae*, for example, he addresses many poems to his own poems, creating a subgenre Witemeyer has dubbed "the Whitmanian envoi."[27] No matter how aggressively defiant or insouciant such poems as "The Condolence," "Salutation the Second," "Commission," "Further Instructions," "Salvationists," "Ancora," and "Epilogue" ("O chansons foregoing") may sound, they manifest Pound's obsession with an imagined readership. In turn, this preoccupation with an imagined readership parallels his preoccupation with Content, that power that abides in the land of genius. Both preoccupations intensified during Pound's career, precipitating what some would consider the discovery of, others the fall into, Content.

Pound's determined formalism informs his long letter to Williams (October 21, 1908), written soon after he arrived in London. Presenting Williams with an eight-item "list of facts on which I and 9,000,000 poets have spieled endlessly," he effectively preempts a discussion of content by implying that originality lies not so much in a poet's choice of subject, although he or she may treat that subject more frankly and openly than other poets, as in formal technique: "Sometimes I use rules of Spanish, Anglo-Saxon and Greek metric that are not common in the English of Milton's or Miss Austen's day. I doubt, however, if you are sufficiently au courant to know just what the poets and musicians *and* painters are doing with a good deal of convention that has masqueraded as law" (*L* 4). Smacking of that unmistakable tone that helped propel him quickly into prominence, this passage manages to define poetic sophistication (what is "au courant") in formal terms, not coincidentally the terms that best describe the well-read Pound's own expertise. To formal convention masquerading as law he opposes alternative "rules" gleaned from his reading, rules of which Williams, who has yet to publish the conventional accentual-syllabic verse of his privately printed *Poems* (1909), has little idea. Significantly, the implicit snub of Williams's technical understanding follows a paragraph deriding Pound's imagined audience, here represented by the generalized epithet "the public": "As for the 'eyes of too ruthless public': damn their eyes. No art ever yet grew by looking into the eyes of the public, ruthless or otherwise."

This early letter represents an extreme phase of Pound's attitude toward both poetic form and readers of poetry. Technique is all, and readers who can't appreciate technique be damned. Still to come is the fiction of function and effect developed in "I Gather the Limbs of Osiris" three or four years later. Of course, it would be a mistake to argue that Pound softened steadily toward his readership, abandoning all hostility for an empathic solicitousness. At any point in his career he can lash out angrily at his audience. But this letter of 1908 does testify to a stage before Pound's fiction of form emerged. He did not bring it with him from Venice.

By the time he was writing the various installments of "I Gather the Limbs of Osiris," Pound was also struggling to decide how much weight he should attribute to content. In addition to the pairing of the Technique of Content and the technique of surface, he arrives at this formulation: "Beyond its external symmetry, every formal poem should have its internal thought-form, or, at least, thought progress. This form can, of course, be as well displayed in a prose version as in a metrical one" (*SP* 40). For a poet for whom, as Brook-Rose argues, technique is "*not* separated from the paraphrasable 'plot' or 'subject' or 'theme' or 'content,'"[28] this statement swerves perilously close to the heresy of paraphrase. In context, Pound is attempting to demonstrate the style of Daniel's language by giving a prose translation of "En Breu Brisaral Temps Braus," so that one might dismiss his statement as arising from a purely heuristic gambit. But the statement about the Technique of Content does not appear in such a qualified context, nor does this unexpectedly naked confession to Iris Barry in 1916: "My present feeling is that 'nothing is worth while save desire' and I am sick of verse without it" (*L* 78). Since Pound devoted much of his correspondence with Barry to guiding her through prosodic exercises, such as writing Sapphics in English, this frank admission that he values the emotional component in verse becomes all the more striking. Significantly, in affirming emotional content (desire) over all else, presumably including technique, Pound casts himself as a reader of others' verses, one who wants poets to get something off their chests and into his.

Between "I Gather the Limbs of Osiris" and this letter to Iris Barry, Pound assumed numerous editorial duties, working for magazines and assembling anthologies, duties that must have modified his earlier public-be-damned attitude. In the statement to Barry, one hears the weariness of a man who has sifted through thousands of poems, good, bad, and indifferent, burying himself in the role of a reader to discover a handful of verses to be forwarded to Chicago or elsewhere. In the process, apparently, his uncompromising emphasis on the technique of surface yielded to, or at least made room for, his hunger for content. An important moment in Pound's growing acknowledgment of content appears three years after the letter to Barry, in the tenth section of "Homage to Sextus Propertius," first published as part of the complete poem in *Quia Pauper Amavi* (1919):

> We were coming near to the house,
> > and they gave another yank to my cloak,
> And it was morning, and I wanted to see if she was alone, and resting,
> And Cynthia was alone in her bed.
> > > > I was stupefied.
> I had never seen her looking so beautiful,
> > No, not when she was tunick'd in purple.
>
> Such aspect was presented to me, me recently emerged from my visions,
> You will observe that pure form has its value.
>
> > > > > (*P* 225)

K. K. Ruthven comments that here Pound brings Propertius, who has been kidnapped and taken to Cynthia's bedroom, "up-to-date by attributing to him a fundamental tenet of modern abstract art," a tenet held by Kandinsky, whose thinking Pound valued enough to recommend to his readers for application to verse writing.[29] But even though Pound may have admired Kandinsky, in its context the final line of this passage, which flirts throughout with a triple-meter norm, tingles with irony. After all, Propertius is standing by the bed of his mistress, who is wearing little more than "a new Sidonian night cap," entranced with admiration and, presumably, desire. Under the circumstances, the aside "You will observe that pure form has its value" is ludicrously inappropriate, first because it suddenly exposes the reader as voyeur, a "you" whose presence has been only implicit until Propertius lapses into untimely didacticism, and second because, as the end of the tenth section confirms, the value of pure form, even the beautiful form of Cynthia's naked body, is radically diminished if possession of that form does not follow. Having failed to keep his rendezvous with her, Propertius loses Cynthia and comments laconically, "Since that day I have had no pleasant nights." Pure form may have value in a theory of painting or verse, but perhaps not in the realm of human desire.

The year before *Quia Pauper Amavi* appeared, Pound met Major C. H. Douglas in the *New Age* office, and the course of his poetic career changed.[30] With that meeting, and the study of Social Credit to which it led, Pound gradually began to see the relation of form to content in new ways and to reassess his ties to the public. As early as his essay "Patria

Mia" (first published 1912; revised 1913), he recognized that a "work of art need not contain any statement of a political or of a social or of a philosophical conviction, but it nearly always implies one" (*SP* 130). But those latent political, social, and philosophical convictions moved sharply into the foreground of Pound's thinking. With that move came a new attitude toward his earlier aestheticism and its preoccupation with technique. Pound's new attitude troubled Ford Madox Ford, who traces the change to his friend's boredom (September 9, 1920): "You are in fact bored with civilisation here—very properly; and so you get bored with the *rendering* of that civilisation. It is not a good frame of mind to get into—this preoccupation with Subject rather than with rendering; it amounts really to your barring out of artistic treatment everything and everyone with whom you have not had personal—and agreeable—contacts."[31]

Despite Ford's admonishment, and despite his own later denial that his concern shifted wholly from form to ideas, Pound consciously distances himself from his earlier aestheticism.[32] This distancing begins in *Hugh Selwyn Mauberley* (1920), with its admiring portrait of the "stylist" (*P* 195) usually assumed to be Ford, but since in this poem the aesthete Mauberly appears to triumph over the pragmatic E. P., Pound's exorcism of his aesthetic tendencies remains unresolved. More explicit is a letter to Mencken, written in 1928, in which Pound refers to Oswald Garrison Villard as someone who "still thinks I'm a lily-carrying aeeesthete with green hair and blue whiskers" (*L* 219). This caricature of some Oscar Wilde–like figure from the nineties aims at comedy, but the force of Pound's "still" in "still thinks" also directs itself toward self-caricature, as it suggests that at an earlier time in his life he may have resembled the stereotype more closely. Fourteen years later, the critique of his own early aestheticism surfaces again in a radio broadcast entitled "McArthur" (March 26, 1942): "The aesthetic angle, that the whole of my generation grew up in, all LOOKING harmless, so HARMLESS" (*EPS* 75). Similarly, in a speech broadcast the same year (July 10, 1942), he redefines his educational training, which he used to intimidate Williams in the letter of 1908, from this alternative point of view: "Now in spite of lean years, and how, I have always enjoyed a large share of privilege. Got stocked up with University advantages. [Great?] deal of mental pleasure. Always could bask in the best of what had been written and thought. That was nice for me, and it delayed my public utility for a decade. I had a nice time, but I contributed singularly little to curin' the world's diseases" (*EPS* 195). This autobiographical account completely revises the image of himself Pound projects in the 1908 letter. Not only does the study of Spanish or Anglo-Saxon or Greek poetry yield little more than "mental pleasure," as opposed to the crucial tech-

nical knowledge of what is au courant, but the public-be-damned attitude has dissolved into a commitment to "public utility."

In the name of public utility, the older Pound promotes content. In
the broadcast of March 25, 1943, he puts the matter quite bluntly: "My
talks on the radio will eventually have to be judged by their content.
Neither the medium of diffusion nor the merits or defects of my exposition can be the final basis of judgment. The contents will have to serve
as that basis. I have taken up one point after another, one bit of evidence
after another, trying to explain the facts in the simplest possible terms,
trying to catch and hold the attention of individual hearers" (*EPS* 261).
One might argue quite reasonably that what holds true for judging a
radio broadcast does not necessarily hold true for judging a work of art;
yet the same emphasis on content appears in Pound's critical judgments
of literature. In the broadcast of May 11, 1942, for example, he recommends the work of Céline "not only for the force of his prosody, but for
the content" (*EPS* 129). Likewise, in the broadcast of May 21, 1942, he
singles out Joyce's *Ulysses* not for its overwhelming stylistic achievement but its content: "*Ulysses* dishes up the capitalist situation, the
HELL made in great cities by the usury system" (*EPS* 141). In this reappraisal of the novel he himself was instrumental in bringing to the
world's attention, Pound reduces its significance to the political, social,
and philosophical convictions that its subject matter implies, at least in
his mind.

In other words, for the older Pound content is no longer inaccessible
as Content, the daunting synthesis of culture that the younger Pound
believed only genius understands. Instead, "CONTENT, the INSIDES, the
subject matter" is the "old man's road," as he tells the young poet T. C.
Wilson (October 30, 1933), whereas "music," or the sound of verse,
belongs to the country of young poets (*L* 248). For the older Pound all
writing, all art, and all artifacts of civilization are bursting with content,
specifically with the content of economic revelation.[33] If, for example,
one combines Pound's familiar claim that an epic includes history with
another of his claims, "history without econ. is just gibberish" (*L* 263),
one hears the implied formulation that an epic necessarily includes economics. In this context, a statement in a letter to Basil Bunting (December 1936) becomes particularly striking: "The poet's job is to *define* and
yet again define till the detail of surface is in accord with the root in
justice" (*L* 277). This sentence revises the formulation, made twenty-
five years earlier, that the technique of surface is slighter than the
Technique of Content, as it directly relates the two, identifying content
(justice) as the "root" of stylistic technique.

Pound's most concise poetic treatment of the rooting of stylistic technique in the content of political, social, and philosophical convictions

comes in canto 45: "with usura the line grows thick / with usura is no clear demarcation / and no man can find site for his dwelling" (*C* 229). In a letter of January 8, 1938, he explains to Carlo Izzo that the line thickening with usury "means the *line* in painting and design" (*L* 303). Although this much should be clear to most readers from the context, Pound adds an extra dimension to this reading: "I can tell the bank-rate and component of tolerance for usury in any epoch by the quality of *line* in painting." Apparently, this ability to read in art the economic conditions of a particular time meant a good deal to him, for he repeats the formulation almost four years later in the broadcast of July 6, 1942: "I affirm that future art criticism will be able to tell the component of usury tolerance. How far the TOLERANCE of usury prevailed, or did not prevail when a given picture was painted. Sense of design, precision of LINE, will give way to interest in detail" (*EPS* 193). It is one thing to make the relatively modest claim that any work of art implies political, social, or philosophical convictions; it is quite another to read the technical aspects of art, say the width of a line in a painting or the meter of a line in a poem, as windows on economic reality. The former position implies that in addition to its other meanings (abstract, mimetic, expressive) form also yields historical, which for Pound is to say economic, meaning. But the latter subordinates all other meanings of form to its historical significance, so that in effect, for Pound, form becomes an allegory of economics, as its technical aspects cease to be polysemous signifiers and reduce themselves instead to monosemous ones.

Whereas the younger Pound values formal technique because it tests a poet's sincerity, because it communicates what a poet intends to say to a reader, and because it causes the reader to feel something he or she would not otherwise feel, the older Pound values formal technique as a clue to solving the historical puzzle of how money got the world into trouble. In so literalizing the relation of form to content, he pushes his pragmatic fiction of function and effect to its extreme. What formal technique helps the poet communicate to readers, or the radio broadcaster to "individual hearers," is the machination of usury, and the effect that this communication is supposed to generate is "the rich man's panic, the bourgeois panic," which "starts when he begins not to KNOW" (*EPS* 195–96). Pound ascribes to himself the power to panic others, to terrify them with knowledge, in a late letter to Harriet Monroe (December 27, 1931): "Keep on remindin 'em that we ain't bolcheviks, but only the terrifyin' voice of civilization, kulchuh, refinement, aesthetic perception" (*L* 237). In other words, at last his own voice has become the daunting voice of Content, charged with the "peculiar energy" of "the power of tradition, of centuries of race consciousness, of agreement, of association." As for the " 'em" Monroe is to keep reminding, they are the readers of *Poetry*, associated in Pound's mind with the ultimate reader whose image he keeps always before him, America itself.

3

In the criticism of poetry, "voice" remains a figurative term, that elusive construct combining aspects of what Pound calls "melopoeia," "phanopoeia," and "logopoeia." But in the case of Pound's radio broadcasts, most of which he directed toward a specifically American audience, "voice" signifies a literal presence.[34] In his early references to radio, made before he himself began broadcasting, he describes the presence as an infernal one: "God damn destructive and dispersive devil of an invention. . . . If anyone is a purrfekk HERRRRkules, he may survive, and *may* clarify his style in *resistance* to the devil box" (to Ronald Duncan, March 31, 1940; *L* 342–43). Even though the radio antagonizes Pound, he recognizes in it an adversarial presence whose intrusiveness he can turn to his advantage, defining his own written style (interestingly enough, at this early stage not his content) in opposition to its spoken words.

His hostile feelings make Pound's accession to the microphone of Rome Radio the following year ironic; yet by his own account he turned to the spoken presence of the radio because of a new absence in his writing life: "Result [of the reduction in postal service to the Western Hemisphere], so far as my private life is concerned, is that not bein' able to continue private correspondence by letter with the more lively American youth, gentry and professoriate, I had to stir round and git onto the air, only line [left] me" (*EPS* 97). Of course, his use of radio as a substitute for written correspondence suggests that much of that correspondence involved one-way lecturing, as it did. But behind the reshuffling of presences and absences lies Pound's familiar pragmatic concern with reaching an audience. In fact, the imagined presence or absence of his audience haunts Pound throughout his broadcasts: "When I talk into [the] microphone, I have to think of at least one or more people who might conceivably understand what I am saying" (*EPS* 215).

In more ways than one, Pound's radio broadcasts were his letter to the world that never wrote to him. The Dickinsonian echo is no empty coincidence, for the wartime Pound found himself disconnected, as the earlier poet had, from both an audience he could identify and a country he could identify with. In this context the broadcast entitled "Continuity" (July 6, 1942) becomes especially compelling. It opens with a statement revealing Pound's anxiety about his own power to communicate and his listeners' ability to understand: "Had I the tongue of men and angels I should be unable to make sure that even the most faithful listeners would be able to hear and grasp the whole of a series of my talks" (*EPS* 191). Pound's antipathy to both the Bible and Christianity coats the Pauline echo (1 Cor. 13:1) with strangeness. Speaking with the tongues of men and angels would represent the apotheosis of style, but for Paul that apotheosis would be as meaningless as "sounding brass, or a tinkling cymbal" without the content of charity or love. Pound's odd appropriation of Paul's figure twists it into meaning that even if his own speaking (and, because he read from typescripts, writing) underwent stylistic apotheosis, he still could not be sure his reader-listener would understand him.

In this important moment, Pound confesses the limits of style, form, and technique, admitting that even if he perfects these, he cannot guarantee their effectiveness. Immediately, he turns in the next sentence to consider "the disadvantage of the radio form," as opposed to printed texts "available to the American and English public." With a book, a "reader CAN, when he wishes, look back, take up the statement of the preface, see where Chapter X hitches onto Chapter I." Since a reader can reread but a listener without a tape-recorder cannot relisten, Pound tries to blame the failure of communication on the radio "form." But this rationalization is not altogether convincing, especially in light of his assessment of his own most important book years later in canto 116: "And I am not a demigod, / I cannot make it cohere" (*C* 796).

Nevertheless, Pound continues to deplore the limitations of form:

> I am held up, enraged, by the delay needed to change a typing ribbon, so much is there that OUGHT to be put into the young American head. Don't know which, what to put down, can't write two scripts at once. NECESSARY facts, ideas, come in pell-mell. I try to get too much into ten minutes. Condensed form O.K. in book, saves eyesight, reader can turn back, can look at a summary. Mebbe if I had more sense of form, legal training, God knows what, could get the matter across the Atlantic, or the bally old channel. (*EPS* 192)

In his exasperation, Pound lets drop the illusion of impromptu speaking and rails about the typewriter, a mechanism for writing. The Projectivist dream of typing as a transparent representation of speaking and breathing disintegrates before the practical reality of changing a ribbon. But most important here is Pound's association of his own formal shortcomings ("Mebbe if I had more sense of form") with talking to America and Americans. Although some might feel Pound's radio broadcasts deserve his own criticisms, as his pell-mell rattle of facts and ideas pummels the reader-listener, the real force, even pathos, of this passage resides in the fiction behind it, not so much the fiction of function and effect, though it is there too, but the even grander fiction that with the right form he can make himself understood by his country.

This fiction underlies not only the radio broadcasts made during World War II but also the poems Pound had been writing for more than thirty years. In the 1912 poem "Epilogue," the association of poetic form with America is explicit:

> I bring you the spoils, my nation,
> I, who went out in exile,
>   Am returned to thee with gifts.
>
> I, who have laboured long in the tombs,
>   Am come back therefrom with riches.
>
> Behold my spices and robes, my nation,
> My gifts of Tyre.
>
> Here are my rimes of the south;
> Here are strange fashions of music;
> Here is my knowledge.
>
> Behold, I am come with patterns;
> Behold, I return with devices,
> Cunning the craft, cunning the work, the fashion.[35]

Writing to Harriet Monroe (October 13, 1912), who at Pound's request did not print "Epilogue," he glosses the poem this way:

> "The Epilogue" refers to *The Spirit of Romance* to the experiments and paradigms of form and metre—quantities, alliteration, polyphonic rimes in *Canzoni* and *Ripostes*, and to the translations of *The Sonnets and Ballate of Guido Cavalcanti*, and *The Canzoni of Arnaut Daniel* (now in publisher's hands). It has been my hope that this work will help to break the surface of convention and that the raw matter, and analysis of primitive systems may be of use in building the new art of metrics and of words.
>
> The "Yawp" is respected from Denmark to Bengal, but we can't stop with the "Yawp." We have no longer any excuse for not taking up the complete art. (*L* 11)

Pound's early emphasis on prosody and his related ambivalence toward Whitman (the "Yawp") both make themselves felt here. But the real significance of the poem he renounced two months later as "probably very bad" (*L* 13), aside from its variation of the triple-meter norm ("Behold, I return with devices") that he would use later in his major poems, lies in the relationship he defines between himself and America.[36]

Pound imagines himself as a prodigal son returning not in disgrace but in triumph. Leaving home, he has gone into exile not so much to escape home as to make his fortune and demonstrate to those at home that he is no failure. Like the departing youth told by his parents to write when he finds work, Pound defines his subsequent achievements, here explicitly the achievement of formal discovery, in terms of fulfilled parental expectations. To press this reading into the realm of biography by arguing that for Pound America functioned as a metonymy for his own parents, Homer and Isabel, who always made much of their only child's literary accomplishments, is tempting, especially since it might account for his hostility to Freud, but unnecessary. In the poems, essays, and letters, the pattern shows clearly enough.

According to the pattern, Pound seeks eagerly to fulfill America's expectations by performance and production, but then turns to anger or bitterness when performance and production go unnoticed or unappreciated. The pattern breeds intense ambivalence, characterized in Pound's case by attraction to and repulsion from his audience, as well as by recurring motifs of wandering, exile, and loneliness. As a defense against his own troublesome feelings, he often asserts his indifference to nationality, projecting an ideal of international appreciation of the arts. In a letter to Harriet Monroe (November 7, 1913), for example, he urges the transcendence of nationality quite emphatically: "Until 'we' accept what I've been insisting on for a decade, i.e., a universal standard which pays no attention to time or country—a Weltlitteratur standard—there is no hope. . . . The *gods* do not care about lines of political geography" (*L* 24–25). Here Pound neatly dissolves national identity into the perspective of eternity, although he does so a bit too easily, since in fact the gods, at least as Homer and Virgil represent them, care deeply about "lines of political geography," for old kingdoms fall and new ones rise only with their blessings and curses. But Pound strikes a characteristic note in this statement, one that echoes in statements from later letters, such as this one to Williams (September 11, 1920): "Not that I care a curse for ANY nation as such or that, so far as I know, I have ever suggested that I was trying to write U.S. poetry" (*L* 157).

Such statements contribute to the image of Pound as the worldly, urbane, well-educated man of letters, one whose aesthetic tastes and judgments range far too widely to be limited by any principle so mundane as nationality. Certainly, Williams, among others, saw Pound this way and attacked him for his internationalism. But far too many other statements confirm that this internationalism masks other feelings and belongs to the ranks of Pound's many carefully cultivated personae. In a letter of February 1, 1919, to Marianne Moore, he interrupts his own remarks comparing the status of American painters and sculptors to that of American writers with this aside: "Must let it alone (I must). Must return to the unconcern with U.S.A. that I had before 1911–12" (*L* 148).

The 1909 piece "What I Feel about Walt Whitman" shows clearly that Pound's pre-1911 "unconcern" with America is more imagined than real. Furthermore, his repeated "must" implies a sense of urgency that the immediate context does not merit. One cannot help inferring that the attraction of unconcern lies in an escape from conflicting feelings toward America, an inference strengthened by the portrait of Maude Gonne that Pound draws in a letter to John Quinn written less than three months earlier (November 15, 1918): "It is a great pity, with all her charm, that the mind twists everything that goes into it, on this particular subject (just like Yeats on his ghosts)" (*L* 141). In context, Pound is describing the effects of Gonne's own fervid Irish nationalism, but his portrait of political monomania also has serious implications for himself, as he knows all too well: "Heaven knows, I may have a touch of it myself re Xtianity, but I try to control it." Anticipating his own absorption in economics, anti-Semitism, and the politics of wartime America, Pound's portrait of fixation blurs into self-description.

Reexamination of claims for his own indifference to nationality reveals the lining of patriotic feeling, where *patriotic* retains its radical sense of an action or attitude that acknowledges the *patria* or fatherland. Writing Harriet Monroe about the possibility of *Poetry* selecting six volumes of verse a year, he turns to lecture her: "And get a jury with at least one member who has heard of an international standard of values, who don't think pathriotism consists in protecting the inferior product but in bringing it up to top level and making it bite on the nail" (March 23, 1927; *L* 209). Despite the apparent echo of his call for a "Weltlitteratur standard" and the intentional misspelling "pathriotism," Pound closes his exhortation with an idealized version of American poetry, one that on its surface exactly reverses Melville's exhortation in "Hawthorne and His Mosses" (1850) that America should "first praise mediocrity even, in her own children, before she praises . . . the best excellence in the children of any other land." Although more than once Pound argues explicitly against praising mediocre American poetry simply because it is American, he shares with Melville, who after all recommends this praise only as a first step, an ultimate vision of a national literature that will inspire more than a merely patronizing or condescending response.

As Melville's vision in "Hawthorne and His Mosses" derives from Emerson's "American Scholar" (1837), so Pound's vision of an improved American poetry appears to reverse Emerson's grand annunciation in that essay: "Our day of dependence, our long apprenticeship to the learning of other lands, draws to a close." In Pound's view, America's apprenticeship to the learning of other lands has not even begun, let alone drawn to a close, and the ignorance and laziness of American writers continually aggravate him, as he shows in a letter to Simon Guggenheim, written shortly after the announcement of the new foundation for the support of American letters (February 24, 1925): "The whole of our literature suffers from ignorance" (*L* 196). In Emerson's view, American poets imitate European models too much, in Pound's, too little, as the latter suggests in "Cantico del Sole" (1918), a poem that envisions a well-educated America: "The thought of what America would be like / If the Classics had a wide circulation / Troubles my sleep" (*P* 183).

The image of Pound's troubled sleep is not necessarily figurative. His self-appointed role as reformer of American poetry placed him in a difficult, if not impossible, position, and his divided feelings toward his task are unmistakable. In a letter to R. P. Blackmur (March 26, 1925), he states his position bluntly: "As to establishing any sort of milieu in America: it is not my job" (*L* 199). This statement affects the unconcern he wishes for in the letter to Moore, but it does not square with this assertion made seventeen years later: "My job, as I see it, is to save what's left of America, and keep up some sort of civilization somewhere or other" (*EPS* 49–50). Typically, Pound defines his relationship to America in terms of a job, of a task he will or will not perform or a product he will or will not produce. Of course, dogging a poet with his own inconsistencies can mean little in itself and inevitably recalls Emerson on the subject of foolish hobgoblins or Whitman on self-contradiction. But in Pound's case, the swings from one extreme to the other are so drastic and self-canceling that one cannot help suspecting they arise from a deeper issue.

Pound's love-hate feelings for America express themselves dramatically in his writing. In considering first his expressions of positive feelings, one finds numerous instances of his love of, identification with, or pride in America. A clear example appears in the poem "To Whistler, American" (1912):

> You had your searches, your uncertainties,
> And this is good to know—for us, I mean,
> Who bear the brunt of our America
> And try to wrench her impulse into art.
>
> (*P* 235)

In a letter to Harriet Monroe accompanying this poem (August 18, 1912), Pound moves quickly from his hope that American poetry will absorb "the same sort of life and intensity" Whistler brought American painting to Pound's larger vision of an American Renaissance: "Any agonizing that tends to hurry what I believe in the end to be inevitable, our American Risorgimento, is dear to me" (*L* 10). This heralding of an American Renaissance anticipates the essay "Patria Mia," first published later the same year, in which Pound makes the significance of Whistler's example even clearer: "What Whistler has proved once and for all, is that being born an American does not eternally damn a man or prevent him from the ultimate and highest achievement in the arts" (*SP* 117).

Whistler's example gives Pound "more courage for living" than any other manifestation of American energy (*SP* 116), but of course such an enthusiastic celebration suggests that his own Americanness left Pound badly in need of such encouragement. After all, of all the words for a young man to choose to describe his own sense of poetic election, "brunt" suggests that his country, or at least his national consciousness, sometimes burdens him with excessive force. Even the statement of positive feeling cannot free itself wholly from ambiguity, as the rest of "Patria Mia" demonstrates. Although Pound feathers the essay with such unembarrassed testimonies as "We are, I believe, the most generous people in the world, or, at least, the most catholic in our generosity" (*SP* 119), his "We" does not come easily to him. Significantly, he shifts to the first person plural soon after his comments on Whistler, yet he does so only after he has established a comfortable distance for himself by means of the third person: "One returns from Europe and one takes note of the size and vigour of this new strange people. They are not Anglo-Saxon; their gods are not the gods whom one was reared to reverence. And one wonders what they have to do with lyric measures and the nature of 'quantity'" (*SP* 104). For some the transition from the American character to prosody will constitute a non sequitur, but for a young poet intent on wrenching America's impulse into art, the two could not be more closely associated. Pound's use of "they" to describe Americans and "one" to describe himself aims at an objectivity he never really felt, as the later shift to "we" makes clear.

Equally important, however, is the shift from "we" to "you": "And if you have any vital interest in art and letters, and happen to like talking about them, you sooner or later leave the country" (*SP* 122). Here the second person masks the first, as Pound describes his own situation upon discovering that in America he was "simply so much farther removed from the sources, from the few dynamic people who really know good from bad" (*SP* 122). Although Pound sets out to defend the thesis that "America has a chance for Renaissance" (*SP* 102), he ends up justifying his own exile by suggesting that he has to leave his country because he wants so badly to improve its art. To those who might, or to Williams who did, take issue with this logic, Pound offers another defense of his own expatriation: "If a man's work require him to live in exile, let him suffer, or enjoy, his exile gladly. But it would be about as easy for an American to become a Chinaman or a Hindoo as for him to acquire an Englishness, or a Frenchness, or a European-ness that is more than half a skin deep" (*SP* 124). To those who argue that in exile he becomes a man without a country, Pound answers in language that suggests that his Americanness is not so much an identity he cherishes fondly as an undeniable aspect of his character that Emerson would include under the category "fate."

It is another of the large ironies of Pound's career that he visited America only twice between 1908, when he departed for Italy, and 1945, when he returned to stand trial for treason, and yet he staunchly, even angrily, asserted his Americanness to those who challenged it. In contrast, Eliot combined his new British citizenship with several lengthy sojourns in America, although Pound expressed his doubts about the significance of Eliot's new nationality: "It can't be said that an alteration on Mr. Eliot's passport has altered the essential Americanness of his work" (*SP* 163). Defending his own Americanness in an angry mood, Pound snaps at Hubert Creekmore, "I don't have to *try* to be American" (*L* 322). Coming in a letter of February 1939, written two months before his second return to America, Pound's assertion of his nationality combines with the criticism that led to him to seek out politicians in Washington in an effort to avert war: "Am I American? Yes, and buggar the present state of the country, the utter betrayal of the American Constitution. . . . And as to "am I American": wait for Cantos 62/71 now here in rough typescript." The final reference to the *Cantos*, specifically to the group devoted to John Adams, casts a certain light on Pound's researches into American history. When, for example, in canto 66 he has Adams assert, "So there is no drop not American in me" (*C* 380), the second president speaks for Pound himself.

But much more than Eliot or anyone else, Williams managed to goad Pound into defending his Americanness. After Williams published in the *Little Review* (October 1917) the first three sections of what later became *Kora in Hell* (1920), Pound wrote him "one of his hurried letters in which he urged me to give some hint by which the reader of good will might come at my intention," as Williams narrates in the "Prologue" to *Kora*.[37] Even through the screen of indirect discourse, Pound's emphasis on the reader's reception of an author's intention speaks loudly. Williams later quoted about two-thirds of Pound's "hurried" letter (November 10, 1917) in his "Prologue"; yet his quotation omits all references in Pound's letter to one Williams must have written him. Among the parts of Pound's letter Williams does not include is the following: "I had no ulterior or hidden meaning in calling you or the imaginary correspondent an 'American' author. Still, what the hell else are you? I mean apart from being a citizen, a good fellow (in your better moments), a grouch, a slightly hypersensitized animal, etc.?? Wot bloody kind of author are you save Amurkun (same as me)?" (*L* 123). As this excerpt suggests, Williams has fictionalized the genesis of Pound's letter. Pound may have been responding to the first publication of Williams's "Improvisations," but obviously he is also responding to Williams's touchiness about being called "American." Attempting to deny any pejorative meaning in his use of the label "American" by identifying himself as such, Pound then moves to the heart of the matter: "If you had any confidence in America you wouldn't be so touchy about it. I thought the —— —— —— —— millenium that we all idiotically look for and work for was to be the day when an American artist could stay at home without being dragged into civic campaigns, dilutations of controversy, etc., when he could stay in America without growing propagandist." Williams begins quoting here, after Pound offers another version of the American Renaissance he envisions, but among Williams's subsequent omissions is the final sentence of this passage: "You have the naive credulity of a Co. Claire immigrant. But I (der grosse Ich) have the virus, the bacillus of the land in my blood, for nearly three bleating centuries. (Bloody snob. 'Eave a brick at 'im!!!!) You (read your Freud) have a Vaterersatz, you have a paternal image at your fireside, and you call it John Bull" (L 124).

Williams suppresses Pound's psychoanalytic diagnosis, along with the other material above, no doubt because it threatens him with an unattractive truth and complicates his image of "the best enemy United States verse has," as he calls Pound in the "Prologue" to Kora. But the omitted sentences and paragraphs also implicate Pound, whose analysis of Williams contains an element of projection. Although Pound turns the tables on Williams by casting himself as the indigenous American and the Rutherford doctor as an immigrant, the statement that touchiness about America implies a lack of confidence in the country aptly describes the attitudes reflected in his own writing, such as "Patria Mia." Even more significant, however, is the reference to Freud, who usually attracts only negative commentary in Pound's writing. Vaterersatz means "father-surrogate" and could have come to Pound's attention from any number of pre-1917 sources, such as Totem und Tabu (1913). Pound's generally negative view of Freud, as well as his tendency on occasion to read superficially, necessarily qualifies any linking of a specific Freudian term to a larger complex of ideas, which Pound may or may not have accepted or understood fully. Nevertheless, in his amateur diagnosis of Williams he makes clear his belief that a country can be a father-surrogate, although in Williams's case that country is England (John Bull).

Using psychoanalytic terminology loosely, Pound is doing what many amateur readers of Freud do; he is borrowing figurative language with little or no sense of its clinical genesis. He probably does not mean to assert that in Williams's mental life England substitutes for William George Williams, an Englishman, although such an interpretation has possibilities, as, for example, in his "Prologue" Williams associates the letter he quotes with an anecdote about his father meeting Pound. Similarly, in drawing the conclusion that Pound's own *Vaterersatz* is America, one must be careful not to tie that conclusion too closely to the actual relationship between Homer Pound and his son. Pound's reference to Freud demonstrates simply that in his mind *patriotism* retains the etymological force of the root *pater*, which is to say that for him national consciousness assumed the volatile energies of the family romance.

Although Pound's designation of America as "her" in the poem "To Whistler, American" ("And try to wrench her impulse into art") suggests that his father-surrogate may be a male-female composite, the language he uses to describe America is usually either masculine or neutral.[38] In the context of "What I Feel about Walt Whitman," for example, Whitman, America, paternity, and ambivalence blend and blur in a revealing way: "And, to be frank, Whitman is to my fatherland (*Patriam quam odi et amo* for no uncertain reasons) what Dante is to Italy and I at my best can only be a strife for a renaissance in America of all the lost or temporarily mislaid beauty, truth, valour, glory of Greece, Italy, England and all the rest of it" (*SP* 146). Pound's paternal metaphors for Whitman ("my spiritual father"; "pig-headed father") gather significance in light of an earlier statement about him in the same essay: "He *is* America" (*SP* 145). For Pound the chain of substitutions ultimately forms a circle. America functions as a father-surrogate, attracting the ambivalent feelings a son feels toward his father, but Whitman also represents a country-surrogate, so that the national identity becomes embodied and personalized in a single individual. Ambivalence toward Whitman substitutes for ambivalence toward America, which substitutes for ambivalence toward a father, which is what Pound called Whitman.

For Dickinson, circularity or circumference implies expansiveness and transcendence, but for Pound the circling from Whitman to America to father to Whitman describes a pattern of entrapment and constriction. The parenthetical statement *Patriam quam odi et amo* illustrates the understandable complexity of Pound's attitude. Although the Latin carries the irony that the word for "fatherland" is feminine, the description of America as "the fatherland which I hate and I love" is not necessarily remarkable in itself, as many might share Pound's divided feeling. But the Latin does more than veil a confession he may have felt reluctant to make so baldly, despite his intention "to be frank" in his voicing of emotion generated in him "for no uncertain reasons." It also echoes the *locus classicus* of ambivalence, this two-line poem from the *Carmina* of Catullus: "Odi et amo. quare id faciam, fortasse requiris. / nescio, sed fieri sentio et excrucior." (I hate and love. Why do I do it? perhaps you ask. I don't know; but I feel it and I'm tortured.)[39]

In light of Catullus's "nescio," Pound's double negative, "for no un-certain reasons," as well as his relegation of the whole statement to parenthetical status, represents a less than convincing attempt at self-persuasion. For a poet whose Americanness emerges clearly in what he himself calls "the American habit of quotation" (*L* 124), which consists of Americans wrapping "themselves about a formula of words instead of about their own centres" (*SP* 102), the allusion to Catullus amounts to an evasion of his own center, of the core feeling he found excruciating in the full etymological sense *excrucior* bears, that of torment by cruci-fixion. Although some might argue that Pound's casual aside cannot sustain the large weight of such a reading, his subsequent progress from London to Paris, to Rapallo, to the echo chamber of Rome Radio, to the cage at Pisa, to the confinement at St. Elizabeths, and back to Italy cor-responds to the itinerary of a man driven by conflicting feelings that he himself can neither control nor explain.

Certainly, the charged ambivalence of Catullus, whom Pound praises as the "most hard-edged and intense of the Latin poets" (*L* 69), hangs over his expressions of negative feelings toward America. Like *Vater-ersatz, Ambivalenz* also comes from Freud, bearing associations to the clinical setting of a patient smuggling emotion past an internal censor.[40] In the context of Pound's radio broadcasts, for example, such associa-tions are hard to avoid. Arguments about Pound's fascism, treason, anti-Semitism, and sanity have raged for almost fifty years, at least since his indictment for treason by a federal grand jury on July 26, 1943.[41] As a result, it may be impossible to approach the broadcasts with neutrality or objectivity, but many readers will notice two characteristics im-mediately. First, ambivalence toward America underlies the talks, as Pound reviles American leadership and foreign policy while he identifies himself with "AMERICAN heritage" (*EPS* 387–88). Second, their most sensational rhetorical feature is invective. Although Pound's broadcasts, like his poems, letters, and essays, have unique features that stamp them as distinctly his, the linking of ambivalence to invective recalls both Whitman in "The Eighteenth Presidency!" (1856) and, beyond him, Catullus, as many passages from his *Carmina* demonstrate clearly. Pound's more vituperative moments look tame beside the attacks in the *Carmina* against Lesbia, Catullus's notorious lover, or the obscenities of the Gellius sequence.

The point is not to explain away the real difficulties posed by writing like that found in the radio broadcasts. After all, it would mean little to a lawyer or a psychiatrist, not to mention someone appalled by Pound's anti-Semitism, to say that Catullus offers a stylistic and rhetorical precedent for much of what appears in "The Poor Man's Cantos," as Doob refers to the radio broadcasts (*EPS* 437). Instead, the point is to show by analogy with a poet whom he read closely that Pound's contradictory attitude toward America tormented him, leading to a language, a style, and a set of rhetorical techniques that arise from the national *Vaterersatz*, the paternal image at his fireside, which nothing he learned from Whitman, so closely associated with that image, could help him escape.

One useful way to reread Pound's early poems about America, such as "From Chebar," "Redondillas, or Something of That Sort," "Pax Saturni," or "L'Homme Moyen Sensuel," is to consider them as dialogues, or shouting matches, between the voice of Whitman, at his most celebratory, and the voice of Catullus. In "From Chebar," for example, the title of which alludes to the first verse of Ezekiel, Pound implicitly identifies himself with the prophet during the Babylonian exile. Parallelism and anaphora mark the style as Whitmanian, as do the apostrophizing of America and the oracular tone. But the import of Pound's address to his country differs wholly from that of *Leaves of Grass*:

> Before you were, America!
>
> I did not begin with you,
> I do not end with you, America.
>
> You are the present veneer.
> If my blood has flowed within you,
> Are you not wrought from my people!
>
> (*CEP* 269)

The figure of his ancestral blood flowing within America reverses the statement of John Adams in canto 66, as Pound implicitly claims here, "There is no drop not mine in America." The move to dissociate himself from his country, dismissed as merely "the present veneer," forms part of a larger argument in the poem, the argument that Pound's ancestry reaches back to Europe: "Before they found you with ships / They knew me in Warwick and Cornwall, / They knew me at Crécy and Poictiers" (*CEP* 270). Among other motifs that weave through the poem is that of refusing to flatter his country, a thread that also runs through "Pax Saturni": "I do not join in the facile praises, / In the ever ready cries of enthusiasms." In turn, this refusal to flatter extends to the realm of art and prefigures the many statements in which Pound opposes Melville's position in "Hawthorne and His Mosses": "Have done with the encouragement / of mediocre production" (*CEP* 271).

In addition to his style and techniques, Whitman himself appears by name in the poem: "There is no use your quoting Whitman against me, / His time is not our time, his day and hour / were different." Although these lines renounce his spiritual father, they do not wholly persuade, for unless Pound's poem is parody, and it takes itself too seriously to be a successful one, it renounces Whitman's time without escaping Whitman's voice. Admittedly, Pound's lines are shorter than Whitman's, and the enjambment of "I have seen the dawn mist / Move in the yellow grain" does not reflect Whitman's end-stopped lines. But the only note struck by Pound that does not resonate with Whitman's voice sounds in the first three lines below:

> You may kill me, but I do not accede,
> You may ignore me, you may keep me in exile,
> You may assail me with negations, or you
>   may keep me, a while, well hidden,
> But I am after you and before you,
> And above all, I do not accede.

> (*CEP* 270)

Especially in the context of his relationship to America, Whitman avoids the language of the victim. In prophesying his significance to his country in the 1855 preface, he may imply that his time has not yet come ("The proof of a poet is that his country absorbs him as affectionately as he has absorbed it"), but he shows confidence that it will and does not represent himself, at least in his early career, primarily as the object of violence, neglect, exile, or negation. Such language belongs instead to the Catullan voice. One can imagine the "you" of the first three lines referring to a person, an ambivalently loved and loving one such as Lesbia, as well as to a country.

Of the varying ratios between ambivalence and invective in Pound's early poems, the most interesting belongs to the least overtly satiric one, "From Chebar." With its sudden swerve into talk of being killed, ignored, exiled, or negated by America, this poem reflects many of the same concerns present in the more conciliatory "Epilogue." In the latter poem, the exile returns with products of his labor, a set of experiments in poetic form and technique, which he offers to the fatherland as justification for his wanderings. In the former, however, the speaker anticipates that those products will be ignored or that his exile will be forced rather than voluntary, and so his tone seeks to defy the *Vaterersatz* rather than to placate it. As it turns out, the speaker of "From Chebar" anticipates correctly, at least in relation to the reception of his labors. In a broadcast of July 24, 1943, Pound tells his American audience, "Now as far as I am concerned, you have lost some of my contributions" (*EPS* 374). Having had his productions ignored or undervalued by America, Pound counters by withdrawing from his country and, in effect, withholding those productions.

Along with his incarceration at Pisa or his confinement at St. Elizabeths, Pound's expatriation stands out as a prominent feature of his biography. "Exile" is, at least before his release from St. Elizabeths, a figurative term in Pound's case in a way it most certainly was not for Dante. In his 1908 letter to Williams, he defends what he calls his "unconstrained" or "arrant vagabondism" (*L* 5, 6), perhaps echoing Williams's own terms, but by the time he assembles "Patria Mia," he shows preference for "exile," such as in a passage quoted earlier or in the phrase "voluntary exile" (*SP* 133), used to describe "some reporter" or "some professor" who leaves America for Europe. The themes of wandering and exile run from early poems not included in *Personae*, such as "Purveryor's General" ("We, that through all the world / Have wandered seeking new things . . . / May gather such dreams as please / you, the Home-stayers" [*CEP* 61–62]), to more familiar ones such as "The Seafarer" or "Exile's Letter," and finally to the Odyssean motif that opens the *Cantos*. Parallel to these poems run letters that take up the same theme repeatedly, such as one of May 12, 1923, in which Pound tells Kate Buss, "If any of you people exiled in America wants news from the front you'll have to organize a demand" (*L* 186). This statement deftly reverses figure and ground, as it associates exile with the Home-stayers rather than with the expatriates and revises the stance of the earlier poem "The Rest" (1913): "O helpless few in my country, / O remnant enslaved! . . . / I have beaten out my exile" (*P* 92–93). This reversal is particularly interesting, as it anticipates a reversal in the father-son roles Pound assigns to his country and to himself. Throughout his broadcasts, he asks his audience (both British and American) to investigate certain problems or to ask certain questions and then to come back to him and "tell papa" (*EPS* 90, 128, 200).

But what matters more than the multiplication of examples is the significance of Pound's exile. Although most of his statements leave the impression that he goes to Europe to find what is unavailable to him in America, which is undeniably true, he also goes to solve the problem of ambivalence toward his fatherland. In leaving America he escapes, or attempts to escape, the discrepancy between an idealized America that he loves, the America of the founding fathers, and the actual America that he hates, the America of Theodore Roosevelt, Taft, Wilson, Harding, Coolidge, Hoover, and Franklin Roosevelt. Expatriation enables Pound to erase the actual America from his experience, an erasure that shows clearly in the comparison of two statements. In a letter of September 3, 1928, he brags to Mencken: "I am prob. as well informed as to the events in our vaterland as I wd. be if in residence there" (*L* 219). But obviously his knowledge of the actual America hangs from the slender threads of personal correspondence, journals, and newspapers, for with the snipping of these threads during World War II, a different statement emerges: "I do NOT know what is going on in the U.S., and I am not under any illusion that Roosevelt's press bureau will send out ANY reliable information" (*EPS* 229).

In the absence of firsthand experience of America, Pound can begin to reconstruct his ideal fatherland through the controlled experience of reading. It is no coincidence that his serious study of Jefferson, the Adamses, and Van Buren takes place only in exile. With this reconstruction, he gradually forges a myth of America in both its public and private aspects. In the essay "The Jefferson-Adams Letters as a Shrine and a Monument" (1937–38), for example, Pound sorts "Our national life" into four periods: "American civilisation" (1760–1830); the "period of thinning, of mental impoverishment" (1830–60); "the period of despair, civil war as hiatus" (1870–1930); and the "possibilities of revival, starting perhaps with a valorisation of our cultural heritage" (*SP* 147). As cultural history, this mapping poses several problems. Pound ignores the energies of Puritan culture from the landing at Plymouth Rock through the Great Awakening; he brands as mentally impoverished the period of Emerson, Hawthorne, Poe, Thoreau, Melville, Whitman, and Dickinson, later tagged by Matthiessen with Pound's own cherished phrase, "American Renaissance"; and he lumps under the heading "period of despair" the diverse and exuberant phenomena of American modernism.

But as personal mythmaking, Pound's mapping sketches his ideal America. It reveals, for example, his Neoclassical temperament and his distrust of Romanticism, as it locates the beginning of decline between the deaths of Jefferson and Adams and the early essays of Emerson. In one broadcast from 1943 Pound identifies the specific cause of this decline: "The whole tone of American life went down, slopped, grew foetid, step by step as the Latin classics went into the discard" (*EPS* 408). Dating this decline, he maintains that "up till 1820 people read Latin" (*SP* 153), but afterward the knowledge of the classics began to ebb, to the relief of the usurers, and darkness moved in to take its place. Of course, this arbitrary boundary overlooks, among many others, Thoreau, who graduated in 1837 an accomplished classicist, but Thoreau's case is inconvenient for Pound because it demonstrates that a profound knowledge of the classics does not automatically lead one to share his communal economic vision. In a radio broadcast of November 6, 1941, Pound makes short work of the best classicist of his literary generation: "Thoreau tried to see how little he need bother about other humanity. Amateur move" (*EPS* 19). Against Thoreau, Pound affirms "COHABITATION with other men." Of course, this affirmation assumes the necessity of government ("POLIS, a city, politics, right way for people to live together in a city"), and to Pound government means Jefferson and Adams.

In addition to revealing the contours of his own character, Pound's four-phase division of American history grafts the classical myth of a golden age, which tends toward deterioration, onto the Christian myth of paradise regained, which tends toward amelioration. In the beginning, American civilization shone, but then came the thinning, impoverishment, and despair characteristic of the iron age. Nevertheless, all is not lost, since by returning to the principles of Jefferson and Adams, Americans can reclaim paradise. Such a vision minimizes, among other problems, the differences between an agrarian past and an urban present, between an economy still partially based on slavery and one that is not, and between a population still relatively homogenous and one that has ramified in various racial, ethnic, and religious directions. Still, for Pound "America was a civilised land in those days" (*SP* 152), days when Adams and Jefferson existed "in a full world" (*SP* 156), and he wants the fullness of those days back.

Just as exile offers him an apparent escape from his own ambivalent feelings about his country, so his admiration of Jefferson and Adams helps Pound escape aspects of America he cannot absorb or encompass. As early as "Patria Mia," for example, he indicates that the vastness and variety of America may be beyond him: "You will get no idea of America if you try to consider it as a whole" (*SP* 120). A poet realistic enough to admit this necessarily forfeits the chance to turn the size of America and the diversity of Americans to the same advantage Whitman did. A page later, after several generalizations, the reality principle again causes him to qualify: "It is almost impossible, and it seems quite futile, to make general statements about a country which has no centre, no place by which it can be tested, no place that 'says today what somewhere else will say tomorrow'" (*SP* 121). Pound's need for a center informs the definition of a "nation" with which he opens "Patria Mia": "No nation can be considered historically as such until it has achieved within itself a city to which all roads lead, and from which there goes out an authority" (*SP* 101). According to this definition, America can never be a nation, a conclusion that really means that Pound can never feel at home in such a nation. Hidden in the opening of "Patria Mia" is a prophecy of Pound's eventual move to Italy, a nation with a center, the city to which all roads lead.

A whole, a center, a single place from which authority emanates: the actual America of 1808 could not provide these any more than that of

1908. But in Pound's view, an earlier America, filtered through the writings of intelligent, well-educated men, came much closer than his own to fulfilling his need for wholeness, centeredness, authority, and the stability of what can be tested and relied upon. Of course, these attributes describe not a country but a parent, suggesting once again Pound's deep psychological investment in his own *Vaterersatz*. It is no accident that in the isolation of his radio broadcasts the exile seeking to defend himself against the fragmented, uncentered, unstable aspects of his fatherland lapses into recollection of his American childhood: "Lookin' back and rememberin' my far distant childhood on the corner of 47th and Madison Avenue where there is now such [a?] sumptuous Hotel Accommodation. Thinkin', thinkin of my Great Aunt's family furniture, moved a few blocks up the street. I wonder if the ole grand piano is still workin' for the folks that took over, foreclosed the mortgage, or something, anyhow, sold the old lady up. . . .—now why do I think of that?" (*EPS* 99). Why indeed? One could argue that in a broadcast entitled "To Social Creditors" (April 19, 1942) this personal memory of someone whose mortgage was foreclosed is entirely appropriate. But Pound's reference to "what is occurin' in my psychology" (*EPS* 99) suggests that he realizes the logic of association may be leading him beyond the boundaries of expository discourse into a childhood world free from the complications of wrenching the actual America into coherent wholeness.

In addition to exile and his own national myth, Pound's third defense against America and the feelings it generated in him was his insistent formalism. The earlier formulation that close attention to technique protected him, at least as a younger poet, from Content now combines with the identification of Content as America itself to give Pound's formalism added significance. By emphasizing the surface schemes of verse, he finds the wholeness, centeredness, and stability that the country itself cannot give him. By concentrating on the effectiveness of form to convey his intentions and to cause a reader to feel as he does, he fixes his gaze on what he can control amidst so much that he cannot. In several instances, Pound associates America, Americans, or Americanness directly with poetic form, as in "Patria Mia": "And one wonders what they have to do with lyric measures and the nature of 'quantity'" (*SP* 104). Lurking behind this sentence is the doubt that Americans have anything at all to do with the ordered world of lyric measures or quantity, a doubt Williams made the cornerstone of his aesthetic.

But unlike Williams, or Whitman before him, Pound does not concede to America and Americans the sole authority for generating appropriate forms. In a letter of 1915 to Harriet Monroe, for example, he defines his own role in no uncertain terms: "You constantly think I undervalue élan and enthusiasm. I see a whole country rotted with it, and no one to insist that 'form' and innovation are compatible" (*L* 55–56). Whereas Whitman and Williams insist that the complexity of America demands innovation that departs from traditional form, Pound refuses to yield. The more disorderly America appears to be, the more Pound insists on traditional order: "Of course you need music to understand real versification. But comin' from a duck-board country, I was interested in LATIN order. Order in stone work, in paintin', *Adamo me fecit*" (*EPS* 137). The elided logic of the second sentence suggests a causal relationship: Because I come from a disorderly new country in progress (duckboard is usually laid across wet or muddy ground or flooring), I am necessarily interested in the established order of classical tradition.

For Pound the order of versification finesses the disorder of actual America. Not surprisingly, technical or formal order associates itself in his mind with the presiding genius of his ideal America, Jefferson: "Or say why does it come easier to me, I am hoistin' up over questions of technique, Cummings' neologism, his punctuation. Well I am American. I perceive his technique, which Jefferson, Tom Jefferson, would have justified; which is justified by the measure Jefferson applied to neologism. Namely, new words justified when NECESSARY to express a new meaning" (*EPS* 142). Jefferson not only wrote a treatise on prosody, he also wrote according to a "moderate precept of style," to which Pound again refers in "The Jefferson-Adams Letters" (*SP* 153), that makes him the embodiment of true speech. In the passage above hides another causal relationship: Because I am a citizen of the ideal America associated with Jefferson, I perceive Cummings's technique. Of course, such causality implies that Jefferson, Cummings, Pound, and other masters of technique share one mind, a unified American mind, which, like a central city to which all roads lead, is the core of Pound's national fiction: "If we are a nation, we must have a national mind" (*SP* 148).

Pound's insistence on a unified national mind made him unfit to dwell in a country in which like-mindedness is not a defining feature of its citizenry. The actual America is a nation made up of many kinds of minds, some of which share little with Jefferson or Adams. Exile, his own national myth, and formalism protected Pound from the many-mindedness of actual America until Pisa and this small moment:

> inexorable
>   this is from heaven
>   the warp
>   and the woof
> with a sky wet as ocean
> flowing with liquid slate

> Pétain defended Verdun while Blum
> > was defending a bidet
> the red and white stripes
> > cut clearer against the slate
> than against any other distance
> the blue field melts with the cloud-flow
> To communicate and then stop, that is the
> > law of discourse.

(C 494)

In the Disciplinary Training Center at Pisa, Pound found himself once again face to face with actual America, with Americans and with their flag, here considered not as a symbol or an abstraction, but as a piece of colored cloth against the sky, an aesthetic design in a natural context. This passage associates four of Pound's favorite themes, "the warp and woof" of his thought: the natural world, economic history (Pétain and Blum), America, and the style of true speech. To say that the passage resolves his ambivalence toward America would be to impose too neat an ending on a story that defies it. After all, the quiet description of the Stars and Stripes purposefully avoids any moralizing, closing instead with the blending of sky and flag. But after his release from St. Elizabeths, his return to Italy, and his withdrawal into silence, Pound hints at a final pact. In the foreword to his *Selected Prose*, he modifies, and comes close to retracting, the views that led to his split with America:

> In sentences referring to groups or races "they" should be used with great care.
> re USURY:
> I was out of focus, taking a symptom for a cause.
> The cause is AVARICE.

As the paragraphing of prose dissolves into the lineation of verse, Pound obeys his own law of discourse. Having communicated, he stops, but not before he dates his statement, using the American day to signal his sense of nationality even in exile: "Venice, 4th July, 1972."

FIVE

ELIZABETH BISHOP'S WINDING PATH

IN ELIZABETH Bishop's life and art, Pound's presence cannot compare with Marianne Moore's, which quite appropriately has received considerable critical attention.[1] Nevertheless, his presence remains undeniable. In her adolescence, Bishop began playing a Dolmetsch harpsichord in response to Pound's opinions on music.[2] In her prose piece "A Trip to Vigia," probably written in 1967, she records that she "tried a story about Ezra Pound," adding, "It was very well received but, I felt, not understood."[3] In "Efforts of Affection," her memoir of Marianne Moore written between 1969 and 1979, Pound appears twice, once as the alleged author of a cigar burn on the railing outside Moore's Brooklyn apartment and once as the authority who pronounces all dedications "dowdy" (*Prose* 128, 142). But Bishop's most sustained contemplation of Pound comes in "Visits to St. Elizabeths," first published in *Partisan Review* (Spring 1957) and later collected in *Questions of Travel* (1965), where it appears as the final poem of the volume:

> This is the house of Bedlam.
>
> This is the man
> that lies in the house of Bedlam.
>
> This is the time
> of the tragic man
> that lies in the house of Bedlam.[4]

Here Bishop employs the same rhetorical schemes as her model, the nursery rhyme "This Is the House That Jack Built." Strophes begin with the same phrase (anaphora), end with the same phrase (epistrophe), and succeed one another according to a logic of accumulation. Prosodically, Bishop's poem also mirrors its original, culminating in a twelve-line strophe (eleven in the original) built of seven four-stress lines on top of four two-stress lines, the whole resting on the three-stress foundation "that lies in the house of Bedlam." Against the background of this strong accentualism, individual lines in both Bishop's poem and its model approach an accentual-syllabic regularity, the shortest falling easily into iambic dimeter and the long ones suggesting various configurations of triple meter. As for rhyme, Bishop departs from the exact regularity of "This Is the House That Jack Built," which culminates in the sequence *corn/morn/shorn/torn/forlorn/horn*, although she does allow herself the triplet *war/door/floor* and two couplets. At the close of each strophe, however, she offsets this regularity with a richly suggestive off-rhyming sequence worthy of Dickinson, *time/man/Bedlam*.

Formally, then, "Visits to St. Elizabeths" is no child's play, and other complexities of this poem suggest that it would be naive to think that Bishop alludes to Mother Goose because she wishes to view Pound from a child's perspective.[5] Instead, the effect of her allusion recalls that of Thoreau's use of the same model in *Walden*:

> Finally, there were the self-styled reformers, the greatest bores of all, who thought that I was forever singing,—
>
> This is the house that I built;
>
> This is the man that lives in the house that I built; but they did not know that the third line was,—
>
> These are the folks that worry the man
>
> That lives in the house that I built.
>
> I do not fear the hen-harriers, for I kept no chickens; but I feared the men-harriers rather.[6]

This passage comes, fittingly enough, at the close of the chapter "Visitors." Whether or not Bishop had this passage in mind when she began to meditate on her own status as a visitor, its treatment of "self-styled reformers, the greatest bores of all" anticipates at least one of Bishop's negative feelings toward Pound, that behind her epithet "the tedious man." Thoreau's allusion to the nursery rhyme exposes not his own childish simplicity but that of the self-styled reformers who think that he thinks his experiment in house building is as innocent as Jack's. Likewise, Bishop's allusion points not to her perspective but to Pound's. Whereas Thoreau, the occupant, pictures himself chanting the nursery rhyme to implicate his visitors, Bishop, the visitor, chants the rhyme to implicate the occupant.

Although Bishop borrows the insistent formal patterns of a poem children read or have read to them, she does so to illuminate adult fixations. It would be a mistake to consider this borrowing "ironic," for genuine irony arises only where difference or incongruity exists, as it would if Pound were not at all childish. But what makes Bishop's poem powerful is that Pound exhibited so many regressive impulses, impulses that link him to childhood in an all-too-literal way, as two of Bishop's epithets, "cranky" and "cruel," suggest. "Visits to St. Elizabeths" uses the complementary figures anaphora and epistrophe mimetically rather than parodically, confirming Longinus's reading of the first of these figures as imitations of the thoughts or actions they express.[7] Although

"This Is the House That Jack Built" has been both the object and the instrument of parody for more than 150 years,[8] simple parody would render the poem a piece of light verse; mimesis makes it a much grimmer exploration of, and commentary on, the nature of some of Pound's thinking and writing, characterized as these often are by predictable beginnings (anaphora) and even more predictable endings (epistrophe). With the campaign for Pound's release in the background when the poem appeared in 1957, and with Bishop's own ambivalent feelings toward him complicating her presentation, "Visits to St. Elizabeths" acquires a seriousness for which simple parody cannot account.

The mimetic nature of the poem becomes apparent when its final strophe sits beside that of "This Is the House That Jack Built":

> This is the soldier home from the war.
> These are the years and the walls and the door
> that shut on a boy that pats the floor
> to see if the world is round or flat.
> This is a Jew in a newspaper hat
> that dances carefully down the ward,
> walking the plank of a coffin board
> with the crazy sailor
> that shows his watch
> that tells the time
> of the wretched man
> that lies in the house of Bedlam.
>
> (*Poems* 135)

> This is the farmer sowing his corn,
> That kept the cock that crowed in the morn,
> That waked the priest all shaven and shorn,
> That married the man all tattered and torn,
> That kissed the maiden all forlorn,
> That milked the cow with the crumpled horn,
> That tossed the dog,
> That worried the cat,
> That killed the rat,
> That ate the malt
> That lay in the house that Jack built.
>
> (Opie 231)

In the world of Mother Goose, metonymy rules. Every person, animal, and action is associated with, and leads directly to, another, so that a continuous chain of relations and events unfolds. This world is a stable one in which the animate and inanimate function in determined ways, making the house that Jack built the center of a tightly structured universe. Admittedly, this world is neither perfect nor wholly unambiguous. Rats infest houses and eat malt; cats kill rats; dogs worry cats; cows toss dogs with crumpled horns; and maidens are forlorn, calling into question their relationships with men all tattered and torn. Nevertheless, an ordered chain of being prevails.

The syntactic sign of this stable order is the continuous subordination enforced by the relative pronoun "that." Since everything has a place and a function, everything can be subordinated relative to something else, both in the chain of being and in the syntagmatic chain that represents it. But in Bishop's poem this subordination falters and with it the stability of the world inside the house of Bedlam. Traces of that subordination still linger (for example, "with the crazy sailor / that shows his watch / that tells the time / of the wretched man"), but it does not encompass "the soldier home from the war," who has no grammatical, and presumably little existential, relation to the other members of the ward. In the world of "Visits to St. Elizabeths," a man can exist apart from all that goes on around him, preserving an isolation Pound himself embodied. Furthermore, the faltering structures of subordination come to represent Pound's own thinking about the world, a world he insisted was economically ordered in as clear and determined a way as everything in Jack's world.

The presence or absence of subordination determines the structure of many of Bishop's poems, and I will discuss this feature of her work later, but for the moment I want to concentrate on what Pound meant to Bishop. Although first published in 1957, "Visits to St. Elizabeths" carries the parenthetical date "1950" after its title. In 1950, Bishop was serving as consultant in poetry at the Library of Congress, her term having begun in 1949. In a letter of June 28, 1953, written to Lowell, she refers to this period as "that dismal year in Washington."[9] Dismal or not, the year in Washington represented a public recognition of her achievement as a poet, a recognition that contrasted starkly with Pound's situation at the same time in the same city. At least in part, the underlying ambivalence of "Visits to St. Elizabeths" originates in this contrast. Bishop, who has little to say about her identity as an American poet but who has garnered one of America's highest honors, is visiting Pound, who has much to say about his identity as an American but who has narrowly escaped his country's greatest dishonor, a conviction for treason.

But the timing of the poem also has other significance. One could argue that it simply took the deliberate Bishop seven years to complete "Visits to St. Elizabeths," as it took her many years to complete "The Moose." Or one could argue that the idea for a poem about Pound lay dormant in her mind until the campaign for his release began to gather considerable support, at which time the composition of such a poem became more urgent. Both arguments have merit, but neither considers the major change in Bishop's life during the seven-year hiatus. In 1950, Bishop had never seen Brazil; by 1957, she had been living there for six years. When she visited Pound, he alone had been an expatriate, but by the time she published the poem about those visits, she herself had become one, too.[10]

The placement of "Visits to St. Elizabeths" in *Questions of Travel* suggests that this biographical development is not at all beside the point. Closing the volume, which consisted originally of the "Brazil" section of eleven poems, the prose piece "In the Village," and the "Elsewhere" section of eight poems, the poem about Pound provides the last word on many of the issues the volume considers, among them expatriation and insanity. Returned to this context, "Visits to St. Elizabeths" reveals another dimension, that of Bishop's divided feelings not just toward Pound but also toward America.

The penultimate poem of the volume, "From Trollope's Journal," confirms that America hovers over the close of *Questions of Travel* and prepares for the meditation on Pound. Originally published in *Partisan Review* in November of 1961, this dramatic monologue, a double sonnet, has received almost no critical attention. The poem is unique in Bishop's canon, not because of its conventional prosody (consider "Sestina" or the villanelle "One Art") and not because of its status as a dramatic monologue (consider "Jerónimo's House," "Songs for a Colored Singer," or "Crusoe in England"), but because of its sustained, direct treatment of American history, a treatment typical of Lowell at many points in his career but not of Bishop. An exception to this statement might be the single sentence "The War was on" in "In the Waiting Room," but this moment is slight by comparison with "From Trollope's Journal."

Like "Visits to St. Elizabeths," "From Trollope's Journal" carries a parenthetical date, "Winter, 1861," exactly one hundred years before the publication of Bishop's poem. As the poem makes abundantly clear, Washington in the winter of 1861 was not a pleasant place to visit. After the humiliation of Irvin McDowell's army at the battle of First Bull Run in July, Lincoln had appointed George B. McClellan commander of all troops in the Washington area, charging him with the creation of a new army. Through the fall and winter, the cautious McClellan prepared for what would turn out to be the fiasco of the Peninsular Campaign (March-July 1862). As for Washington itself during this period, the Civil War historian Bruce Catton describes it this way: "Almost daily new Northern regiments were reaching Washington.

Soon herds of cattle en route to commissary butchers were familiar sights in the city streets, and mountains of provisions rose in warehouses. Within two months McClellan's Army of the Potomac had swelled to a staggering force of 168,000, four times the size of the enemy beyond Manassas."[11]

Enter Anthony Trollope, who had secured a nine-month leave from the secretary of the post office to fulfill his long-standing ambition to travel to America and write a book about it, as his mother, Frances Milton Trollope, had done in *Domestic Manners of the Americans* (1832).[12] Trollope's status as an English observer in Washington became complicated by the affair of the *Trent*, a British ship from which a U.S. naval officer, Captain Charles Wilkes, removed two representatives of the Confederacy to Europe, James M. Mason and John Slidell, after firing twice across its bows from his own ship, the U.S.S. *San Jacinto*, on November 8, 1861, in the Bahama Channel.[13] The subsequent outrage in England nearly precipitated war with the United States, and British intervention on behalf of the Confederacy, which the Lincoln administration feared, almost became reality.

Against this tense background, Trollope's situation could not have been enviable. In a letter of December 17, 1861, written to Kate Field, he describes the chopping of the anthrax on his forehead, a detail that Bishop includes in her poem, and admits that he is "anxious to get out and see the people before war is declared" between Britain and the United States, a development that suddenly would render him not only a foreigner but also an enemy.[14] Trollope concludes the "Washington" chapter of his *North America* (1862) with the observation that because society in Washington was "considerably cut up" by the war, the place itself was "somewhat melancholy."[15] With this judgment Bishop could not help but concur, recognizing in the Englishman a figure for her own estrangement during the dismal year in Washington. His "journal" appears to be her own imaginative creation, since Trollope's journals have not been published, and her fictional version of the doctor's comments to his patient resonate with her own sense of malaise: "We talked about the War, and as he cut / away, he croaked out, 'Sir, I do declare / everyone's sick! The soldiers poison the air'" (*Poems* 132).

"From Trollope's Journal" prepares for "Visits to St. Elizabeths" by focusing on Washington, the heart of political America, on its unhealthy atmosphere, and on the response to that atmosphere of a visitor, in this case one coming from abroad. Another link between the two poems is that for Pound the American Civil War clearly marks the fall into usury and "eighty years of decadence" (*SP* 310). In "What Is Money For?" (1939), he argues, "Bankhead proposed Stamp Scrip in the U.S. Senate, possibly only 100 per cent honest monetary proposal made in U.S. legislature since American civilisation was destroyed by and after the Civil War (1861–65)" (*SP* 300–301), and in "A Visiting Card" (published in Italian 1942; translated 1952), he adds, "Right in the middle of this war the Government was betrayed and the people were sold into the hands of the Rothschilds, through the intermediaries John Sherman, Ikleheimer, and Van der Gould" (*SP* 309–10). These comments reflect Pound's assurance that a particular historical event has specific cultural and economic relationships to other events that he can identify and trace, an assurance that belongs to the world of "This Is the House That Jack Built."

For Bishop, then, "Visits to St. Elizabeths" involves a vexing mixture of identification, rejection, and guilt. Like Pound, she is a poet who has found America uninhabitable, and so, at least temporarily, has rejected it. But in turn she must also reject Pound whom she finds, in some respects, cranky, cruel, and tedious. Furthermore, she cannot escape all feelings of guilt at being implicated in Pound's situation, as in 1950 she functions in part as the symbol of officially sanctioned American poetry, the consultant in poetry at the Library of Congress. As such, she benefits at the hands of the same government that punishes Pound. The title of Bishop's poem intimates the self-reflexive nature of her visits to him and anticipates the discovery of her own identity in "In the Waiting Room": "you are an *I*, / you are an *Elizabeth*."[16] Who is the object of these visits? Is it only Pound or is it perhaps Bishop's mother, whom she never visited in the sanitorium and whose insanity returns for the adult to confront, despite the efforts of the child-narrator to repress it in "In the Village"? Or is it also the part of Bishop reflected in Pound's situation, the poet singled out for special treatment, good or bad, by a country often indifferent to poets? The inclusion of her own name in the title suggests all of these, but the title resonates beyond Bishop's name, for it also points to Saint Elizabeth herself, wife of Zacharias, who "was barren" and "well stricken in years" (Luke 1:7) before she became the mother of John the Baptist. Although a Baptist in childhood and an unbeliever afterward, Bishop, now living in Catholic Brazil and immersed in the translation of *The Diary of "Helena Morley,"* which she published the same year as "Visits to St. Elizabeths," could not fail to appreciate the typological possibilities of a woman's life suddenly changed from barrenness to fertility. After the dismal year in Washington (she published no original poetry or fiction in 1950), she left America in 1951 and began a new life in a new world at the age of forty.

The many currents running through "Visits to St. Elizabeths," formal, allusive, contextual, historical, political, autobiographical, typological, make it a rich poem for Bishop. Despite, or because of, its importance, she felt some uncertainty about the poem, remarking in a letter of May 1, 1957, to Isabella Gardner: "I am glad you liked the Pound poem—I really couldn't tell myself whether it had conveyed my rather mixed emotions."[17] The adjective *wretched*, aptly chosen to describe Pound in the final strophe, encapsulates these divided feelings, for it can mean both "miserable," in which case Bishop would be expressing sympathy for someone else in a dismal situation, and "contemptible" or "despicable," in which case she would be passing judgment on him. Since the succession of epithets substituted for Pound's name throughout the poem makes obvious Bishop's mixed emotions toward him, she is either being disingenuous in the letter to Gardner or, more likely, hinting that her mixed emotions extend beyond Pound himself to all he stands for in her mind: reward, punishment, poetry, expatriation, America. In this way, Pound functions for Bishop as Whitman functions for Pound; he becomes the immediately available human object of ambivalent feelings toward America itself.

First published in the *New Yorker* in July of 1951, the year after her visits to Pound and a few months before her departure for Brazil, "View of the Capitol from the Library of Congress" reveals these ambivalent feelings:[18]

> Moving from left to left, the light
> is heavy on the Dome, and coarse.
> One small lunette turns it aside
> and blankly stares off to the side
> like a big white old wall-eyed horse.

> (*Poems* 69)

In briskly rhymed iambic tetrameter, Bishop devotes this first stanza exclusively to sight. Since the Library of Congress lies southeast of the Capitol dome, she would watch sunlight travel across its southern face during the day, the face on the left for anyone looking from the library. But already something is amiss, for one usually speaks of movement from right to left or left to right, not "left to left," which suggests a deliberate thwarting of the conventions of perspective. The phrase insists that the movement of light be observed according to the perspective of a fixed speaker watching the light move from her left further to her left. To deny that the first left lies to the right of the second one, and so not to say from "right to left," suggests a perversity or idiosyncrasy, one appropriate to the "big white old wall-eyed horse" to which the dome is compared. The choice of the adjectives "heavy" and "coarse" to describe the light contributes further to this general sense of imbalance and clumsiness.

The second, third, and fourth stanzas develop the skewed, thwarted aspects of the scene, but now with respect to the sense of hearing:

> On the east steps the Air Force Band
> in uniforms of Air Force blue
> is playing hard and loud, but—queer—
> the music doesn't quite come through.
>
> It comes in snatches, dim then keen,
> then mute, and yet there is no breeze.
> The giant trees stand in between.
> I think the trees must intervene,
>
> catching the music in their leaves
> like gold-dust, till each big leaf sags.
> Unceasingly the little flags
> feed their limp stripes into the air,
> and the band's efforts vanish there.

The adjective "queer" describes the whole scene, its disconnections of sight from sound and of effort from accomplishment. In contrast to Whitman's celebration "I Hear America Singing," this poem admits that the speaker fails to hear America singing, not because she is deaf, but because what there is to be heard is somehow weak, inadequate, and ineffectual. The general lassitude or insufficiency finds its visual emblem in the "little flags" that "feed their limp stripes into the air."

This moment of looking at national emblems, while patriotic music plays, recalls the moment in canto 80 when Pound at Pisa watches while "the red and white stripes / cut clearer against the slate / than against any other distance / the blue field melts with the cloud-flow" (C 494), as the "Battle Hymn of the Republic," or something comparable, blares over the loudspeakers. Although Bishop at the Library of Congress finds herself in a much different situation from that of Pound at Pisa, the two moments share a sense of dissociation or detachment from national symbols, symbols that have been rendered unfamiliar and uncanny by the contexts of their observers. Oddly, Bishop's estrangement carries a more negative charge than does Pound's, which blends the abstract design of the flag into its natural background. In contrast, Bishop's poem sets nature, in the form of giant leafy trees, in opposition to the efforts of the Air Force Band.

But Bishop's estrangement may not be so odd after all. Her various comments about the band's music invite readings that point in different directions. Although the band plays "hard and loud," "the music doesn't quite come through"; instead, "it comes in snatches, dim then keen, / then mute." As implicit comments about an American ethos, these statements constitute a broad indictment. As veiled judgments of certain kinds of American "music," or poetry, they reveal a sly criticism. But as oblique confessions about her own art, they suggest a larger complaint:

> Great shades, edge over,
> give the music room.
> The gathered brasses want to go
> *boom—boom.*

After four stanzas of full tetrameter lines, the switch to a stanza in which the penultimate line is the only one to fulfill the metrical norm constitutes not just a variation for the sake of closure but also a radical diminishment. This formal diminishment mirrors and mocks the attenuated performance of the Air Force Band, the "*boom—boom*" of its brasses reduced by distance and the trees to a pathetic puniness like that of the final line.[19]

But the implied criticism of this stanza, along with its petition to the "great shades" to make room for the music, also entangles the poet herself. When she became poetry consultant, Bishop had published only one volume of poems, *North and South* (1946). Her second volume, *A Cold Spring* (1955), still lay six years in the future. Various comments made throughout her career exhibit her self-consciousness about the relatively small amount of her own poetic production.[20] In "Efforts of Affection," for example, she savors the salutary effects of her visits to Moore: "Yet I never left Cumberland Street without feeling happier: uplifted, even inspired, determined to be good, to work harder, not to worry about what other people thought, never to try to publish anything until I thought I'd done my best with it, no matter how many years it took—or never to publish at all" (*Prose* 137). Behind such an affirmative statement simmers anxiety about what other people think, about the time that production takes, and about the pressures to publish. Bishop's canon advertises the virtues of resisting these anxieties, but still they surface throughout her work, as they do in "View of the Capitol."

In particular, this anxiousness about production attaches itself to the giant trees that "intervene, / catching the music in their leaves / like gold-dust, till each big leaf sags." The enjambment here, the only one between stanzas, cuts an especially effective formal figure of intervention, the silent gap between stanzas interrupting and momentarily muting what should be the continuous syntax of a single sentence. The giant trees keep the external music from reaching Bishop; they thwart, block, and interfere. But they also aggravate a fear that her own internal music may be thwarted or blocked. Most disturbing is the ambiguous quality of the trees, which loom with a menacing phallic stature but also replicate the swelling of the womb in gestation, their leaves growing full and ripe with music.

The composite nature of the trees informs the epithet "great shades" with added significance. Inevitably, the phrase suggests the ghosts that make poetic production difficult and doubtful, those of earlier poets from George Herbert to Marianne Moore, poets of both sexes whose works overshadow the view of a poet with one book to her name, especially when she now finds herself, in turn, so obviously in the public view. But "great shades" also reaches beyond poetry itself to the civil and political life of a nation, for which the Capitol stands as a synecdoche, its own great shade moving from right to right (as the light moves left to left) all the while Bishop looks on. In a complex moment, then, Bishop realizes that the Air Force Band suffers from the same overshadowed condition she does at the same time that it represents the overshadowing presence of a national consciousness, a consciousness Bishop herself does not find either fertile or invigorating. As in "Visits to St. Elizabeths," her own survival depends on her rejection of something or someone with which she cannot help but identify.

For Bishop, at least in 1950, the connection with America proves fruitless.[21] It does not stimulate her to celebration, as it did Whitman; it does not provoke her into criticism and reform, as it did Pound; it does not even lead her into an internalized, personalized version of itself, as it did Dickinson. Some might argue that the poems originating in her experience of Key West, such as "Florida," first published in 1939, represent possible exceptions, but if so, they also represent a relatively slim vein that Bishop had ceased to mine by 1950. In this context of her detachment from America, certain remarks become particularly challenging. In an interview conducted in 1966, she recalls the genesis of her career: "I wrote a good deal, starting at the age of eight. When I was twelve I won an American Legion prize (a five dollar gold piece) for an essay on 'Americanism.' This was the beginning of my career. I can't imagine what I said on *this* subject!"[22] In a revealing moment, Bishop identifies the beginning of her career with Americanism, an origin that she then buries by suggesting that she cannot remember her thoughts on the subject. Whether or not her memory falters because she now has no thoughts on the subject or because her present thoughts revise her earlier ones in ways that might make the latter too embarrassing remains unclear. At any rate, this recollection makes troublesome a statement earlier in the same interview: "To summarize: I just happened to come here [Brazil], and I am influenced by Brazil certainly, but I am a completely American poet, nevertheless" (*Art* 290).

What could the phrase "a completely American poet" mean to Bishop?[23] The example of Pound demonstrates clearly that a poet can spend most of his or her life abroad and still identify strongly with aspects of America, especially with moments in its literary and political history. But in the case of Bishop, such an identification becomes questionable, particularly when one turns from her poems to her prose pieces. Although her editor, Robert Giroux, ordered the pieces after her death, the opening sequence of Bishop's *Collected Prose* effectively dramatizes an autobiographical structure she must have carried in her own mind, that of the fall into Americanism:

> The War was on. In school at recess we were marched into the central hall, class by class, to the music of an upright piano, a clumping march that has haunted me all my life and I have never yet placed. There we pledged allegiance to the flag and sang war songs: "Joan of Arc, they are ca-alllll-ing you." I hated the songs, and most of all I hated saluting the flag. I would have refused if I had dared. In my Canadian schooling the year before, we had started every day with "God Save the King" and "The Maple Leaf Forever." Now I felt like a traitor. I wanted us to win the War, of course, but I didn't want to be an American. When I went home to lunch, I said so. Grandma was horrified; she almost wept. Shortly after, I was presented with a white card with an American flag in color at the top. All the stanzas of "Oh, say, can you see" were printed on it in dark blue letters. Every day I sat at Grandma's feet and attempted to recite this endless poem. We didn't sing because she couldn't stay in tune, she said. Most of the words made no sense at all. "*Between his loved home and the war's desolation*" made me think of my dead father, and conjured up strange pictures in my mind. (*Prose* 26–27)

Giroux notes that "The Country Mouse," from which this paragraph comes, was "probably written in 1961" (*Prose* 277), the year Bishop published "From Trollope's Journal" and five years before the interview in which she claims she cannot remember her twelve-year-old thoughts on Americanism. In this passage, however, she has no difficulty remembering her six-year-old thoughts on the subject: "I didn't want to be an American." Once again, this resistance to America and Americanism surfaces in the presence of national emblems, the flag in school or on the white card and the music of war songs or that "endless poem," "The Star-Spangled Banner." In contrast, Bishop's recollection of her Canadian school, the subject of the piece "Primer Class" (probably written in 1960), which Giroux places immediately before "The Country Mouse," shows her taking pleasure in national emblems, both auditory ("God Save the King" and "The Maple Leaf Forever") and, in "Primer Class," visual: "By the time school started, I could read almost all my primer, printed in both handwriting and type, and I loved every word. First, as a frontispiece, it had the flag in full color, with 'One Flag, One King,

One Crown' under it" (*Prose* 5). As Bishop links the beginning of her writing career to Americanism, here she links the beginning of her reading career to Canadianism, the latter suggesting none of the ambivalences and ambiguities of the former: "I loved every word."

But with the move in 1917 to Worcester, Massachusetts, which makes her feel as if she "were being kidnapped" (*Prose* 14), comes the fall into Americanism and, with it, many difficult identifications and rejections. "The Country Mouse" opens with descriptions of Bishop's paternal grandparents, noting among other details that her father's father is walleyed: "At least, one eye turned the wrong way, which made him endlessly interesting to me" (*Prose* 13). This detail associates Bishop's "too tall" (*Prose* 13) American grandfather with the Capitol dome, the "big white old wall-eyed horse," and identifies him with the "great shades" who overshadow her. But even more unnerving is the identification of America with Bishop's own dead father, an identification suggested by both a line from the rarely heard fourth verse of "The Star-Spangled Banner" ("*Between his loved home and the war's desolation*") and, earlier, one from "My Country, 'Tis of Thee": "*Land where my father died / Land of the pilgrims' pride*—for a long time I took the first line personally" (*Prose* 24).

For Bishop, then, America is quite literally the fatherland, the *patria* of great shades toward which Pound also expresses so much snarled feeling. Not surprisingly, the swirl of complex associations in "The Country Mouse" includes one that points indirectly to Pound: "Now I felt like a traitor." Of course, Pound himself maintained that he never felt like a traitor, while Bishop feels she has betrayed not America but Canada, her motherland. Still, Bishop's admission of treasonous feeling, private and personal as its context may be, complicates the statement "I am a completely American poet." Her affections and loyalties are at best divided between two countries, as well as between the maternal and paternal sides of her family, a division that illuminates further the composite gender of the giant trees in "View of the Capitol." The assertion of her complete Americanism either denies these ambivalent feelings or suggests that such feelings are part of what it means to Bishop to be completely American. In the unrehearsed, often unrevised text of an interview, both these statements may be true, but the latter certainly ties Bishop to both Dickinson and Pound, whose feelings for America reflect the divided aspects of their respective family romances.

The mixture of personal psychology into national consciousness makes "In the Waiting Room," first published in the *New Yorker* in 1971, especially significant. This poem has been the object of much critical discussion, most of which focuses on the extraordinary moment when the speaker realizes her own phenomenological status as both subject and object, both a first-person *I* and a third-person *Elizabeth*.[24] But this personal moment, a prose version of which closes "The Country Mouse" (*Prose* 32–33), also locates its self-discovery within the larger context established by the earlier prose memoir. The simple sentence "The War was on," which both opens the long paragraph quoted above and appears in the final strophe of the poem, links the latter to the exploration of America and Americanism. The speaker's discovery that she is "one of *them*" (*Poems* 160; "*one* of them" in *Prose* 33) means not only that she realizes she is a person with a name and a body but also that she is an inhabitant of Worcester, Massachusetts, an American, during the Great War. The child's fall into self-consciousness includes a fall into historical and national consciousness, a consciousness suggested by the title of the magazine she reads, *National Geographic*, which purports to explore different areas of the world but which does so from an expressly American point of view. This discovery of nationality, which begins with hearing the voice of Aunt Consuelo (Aunt Jenny in *Prose*) and identifying that voice with her own, recalls the reference in "The Country Mouse" to Joan of Arc, whose own awakening to a national consciousness also began with hearing voices: "'Joan of Arc, they are ca-alllll-ing you.'" In the case of Saint Joan, "they" are Saint Michael, Saint Catherine, and Saint Margaret, whose voices led eventually to trial, imprisonment, and execution. In the case of the young American girl newly arrived from Canada, they are the different aspects of "the family voice / I felt in my throat" (*Poems* 161), a composite voice that mixes the personal with the national and makes her feel, as in her own way the fifteenth-century French farm girl must have felt, "'you're in for it now'" (*Prose* 33). Like the clumping march played at school on the upright piano, the fall into Americanism establishes a basic structure of Bishop's thinking and writing; and yet, as the march haunts her because she cannot place it, that structure remains an elusive one defying simple placement.

2

Bishop's career does not step to the march of any one structure. Uninterested in "big-scale" myths (*Art* 295), she did not don and shed the many mythological coats Yeats did. As an unbeliever, she did not undergo the transformation of conversion along with Eliot. Always "opposed to political thinking as such for writers" (*Art* 293), she did not generate Auden's history of political commitments. Unlike Lowell, she did not transform her attitudes toward poetic style and form midcareer. Instead, Bishop's Americanism is one of many structures that surface discontinuously in her writing, as it does in "Visits to St. Elizabeths,"

"From Trollope's Journal," "View of the Capitol from the Library of Congress," and "The Country Mouse," only to submerge again and defy exact placement in a hierarchy of values and beliefs. Americanism in itself does not provide the key to Bishop's work; no one idea does. Nevertheless, her Americanism, with its many complicated links, both explicit and implicit, reflects Bishop's habit of joining without necessarily unifying; yet, as with instances of that Americanism, what appears to be set down discontinuously, discretely, and without plan often reveals a larger pattern.

One way of describing this larger pattern recalls Nathan Scott's objection to the apparent structurelessness of Bishop's canon: "The poems altogether seem to be an affair of 'Everything only connected by "and" and "and." ' "[25] In the poem "Over 2,000 Illustrations and a Complete Concordance," first published in 1948, this line describes both the syntax of biblical narrative and the experience of traveling. Bishop uses biblical syntax, a formal structure of written language, as an image for the phenomenology of time and the relentlessly sequential nature of its forwardness. For the traveler, one event or perception appears to follow another with little or no necessary relation between them, other than that established by temporal sequence:

> And at St. Peter's the wind blew and the sun shone madly.
>
> . . . .
>
> And at Volubilis there were beautiful poppies
> splitting the mosaics; the fat old guide made eyes.
>
> . . . .
>
> And in the brothels of Marrakesh
> the little pockmarked prostitutes
> balanced their tea-trays on their heads
> and did their belly-dances.
>
> (*Poems* 58)

"Everything only connected by 'and' and 'and' " describes not only the syntax of the Bible, that "heavy book," and the phenomenology of travel; it also describes Bishop's own syntax and, by extension, her sense of poetic form and structure. Clearly, this poem constitutes a piece of self-referential commentary and demonstration in the tradition of the *ars poetica*. But Scott's criticism turns Bishop's line against her, implying that a connection by "and" and "and" is somehow insufficient, even though it is not at all clear that Bishop agrees. How should one read the "only" in "only connected"? Does it mean "merely," indicating that the speaker wishes for more definite connections, perhaps in the form of subordinating conjunctions? Or does it mean "solely," indicating that "and" only connects, but never arranges, allowing meaning and pattern to emerge from the connection instead of imposing them on it?

The sly twinkle of Bishop's own self-referential joke (connecting two "ands" with a third) points not so much to an existential disappointment as to an irony present from the first lines: "Thus should have been our travels: / serious, engravable" (*Poems* 57). Although disconnected images from the speaker's travels may not appear to carry the iconic weightiness of "serious" engravings in an illustrated Bible, they manage to convey a sense of urgency that the engravings do not: "It was somewhere near there / I saw what frightened me most of all" (*Poems* 58). The psychological texture of this statement, or of the later desire to see "this old Nativity while we were at it," depends for its power on the pressing, crowding immediacy of the speaker's perceptions. Behind "Over 2,000 Illustrations" hovers an argument that this immediacy, or the poetic illusion of it, cannot survive in the carefully wrought, overly solemn representations of an illustrated Bible or in the kind of iconic art for which it stands.

Beyond its immediate context, Bishop's image of biblical narrative syntax has deeper resonance. "Everything only connected by 'and' and 'and'" points to parataxis, which Robert Alter describes this way:

> Parataxis, we should recall, means placing the main elements of a statement in a sequence of simple parallels, connected by "and," while hypotaxis arranges statements in subordinate and main clauses, specifying the relations between them with subordinate conjunctions like "when," "because," "although." Thus, the sentence "Joseph was brought down to Egypt and Potiphar bought him" is paratactic. The same facts would be conveyed hypotactically as follows: "When Joseph was brought down to Egypt, Potiphar bought him."[26]

Alter goes on to read parataxis as a formal emblem of "the vigorous movement of biblical writing away from the stable closure of the mythological world and toward the indeterminacy, the shifting causal concatenations, the ambiguities of a fiction made to resemble the uncertainties of life in history."[27]

A figure of indeterminacy, shifting causal concatenations, and the uncertainties of life in history, parataxis is not only an appropriate structure for biblical narrative but also for Bishop's poetry, as it suppresses continuity and connections in favor of discontinuity and gaps.[28] In many respects, the house of Bedlam in "Visits to St. Elizabeths," where connections dissolve and subordination falters, represents parataxis writ large, as does the discontinuous, interrupted music of the Air Force Band in "View of the Capitol." But an even more explicit image of discontinuities and gaps comes in the early story "The Sea and Its Shore" (1937), in which Edwin Boomer studies the various scraps and sheets of writing he collects on the beach, attempting to read them as continuous narratives, only to have the narrator comment: "It might be two nights more, or two weeks, however, before he would find the next step in this particular sequence" (*Prose* 176). As a description of the process of poetic composition, the narrator's remark aptly describes Bishop's own practice. But as an image of how one interprets the separate pieces of experience, it does not. The fictional Boomer believes that all his intermittent, sporadic "studies" will amount to a continuous, structured narrative. He forges explicit connections between discrete elements, whereas Bishop often chooses to subvert such connections.

In Bishop's life and work, gaps come in all shapes and sizes. In the fourth of his sonnets to Bishop in *History* (1973), Lowell closes with his image of these gaps:

> Do
> you still hang your words in air, ten years
> unfinished, glued to your notice board, with gaps
> or empties for the unimaginable phrase—
> unerring Muse who makes the casual perfect?[29]

On one level, Lowell refers here to Bishop's habit of starting poems, putting them aside, and finishing them much later, poems such as "The Moose," finally published in 1972 yet begun many years earlier. But with his image of the inchworm, which immediately precedes these lines ("Have you seen an inchworm crawl on a leaf, / cling to the very end, revolve in air, / feeling for something to reach to something?"), Lowell makes it clear that Bishop's method of poetic composition stands in his mind as a synecdoche for her way of living and looking from "the very end" of what is solid and known toward some invisible and perhaps unreachable link or connection, at once an image of transcendence and uncertainty. Most moving is the final line, which leaves unsettled whether "unerring Muse" refers to Bishop's muse or to Bishop herself, now mythologized as Lowell's muse.

Even if the indeterminacies, shifting causal concatenations, and uncertainties of Bishop's life in history, as represented by her methods of composition, leave her readers, like the inchworm, "feeling for something to reach to something," instances of discontinuity and parataxis in her work suggest that she inclines toward deliberate omissions. In her early undergraduate piece "Time's Andromedas" (1933), she describes watching birds migrate south and noticing "the spaces between the birds" (*Art* 271). As this perception expands into a figure of rhythmic norm and variation, she comments: "The interspaces moved in pulsation too, catching up and continuing the motion of the wings in wakes, carrying it on, as the rest in music does—not a blankness but a space as musical as all the sound" (*Art* 271–272). "Not a blankness": the comment describes not only the spaces between groups of birds or between sounds in music but also those between elements in the paratactic structures of discourse. Unlike simple juxtaposition, which pairs one thing with another in the hope of inventing or discovering a connection between them, parataxis deliberately buries or undoes the obvious and even causal connections of hypotaxis. Juxtaposition aims to generate or arrive at design, whereas parataxis works to deflect or disguise design. Juxtaposition seeks to bridge the gap between elements, where parataxis works to enforce that gap. As a result, the syntactic space between paratactically joined elements is not the blankness of nothing that is not there, but, if a blankness at all, of the nothing that is.

Parataxis structures the first line of the first poem of Bishop's first book, a line that anticipates much to come: "Land lies in water; it is shadowed green" (*Poems* 3). First published in 1935, "The Map" opens *North and South* (1946), and Bishop's canon, with many of the themes and tones several of her critics have discussed. To these discussions, I would add that "The Map," while not without hypotaxis ("where," "as if," and "as when" do the occasional work of subordination), demonstrates Bishop's habit of placing the main elements of a statement in a sequence of simple parallels with minimal, if any, connection:

> The names of seashore towns run out to sea,
> the names of cities cross the neighboring mountains
> —the printer here experiencing the same excitement
> as when emotion too far exceeds its cause.
>
> .   .   .   .
>
> Are they assigned, or can the countries pick their colors?
> —What suits the character or the native waters best.
> Topography displays no favorites; North's as near as West.
> More delicate than the historians' are the map-makers' colors.

The first excerpt contains a good example of formal mimesis, as after two paratactically linked lines Bishop moves to hypotaxis ("as when"). The shift to subordination suggests a release into discursiveness, as the speaker, in reaching for a connection between printed words (names on a map) and some corresponding emotion, experiences the same excitement as the printer, an excitement that causes her to relax the restrained pattern, in which discursive connection is withheld, established by the paratactic first line of the poem.

The second excerpt justifies the many readings of "The Map" as an *ars poetica*, one that anticipates, among other poems partly about poetry, "Over 2,000 Illustrations and a Complete Concordance." But whereas the later poem considers everything only connected by "and" and "and," "The Map" considers everything only connected by "or" and "or." Five times in this poem Bishop uses "or" to introduce an alternative that qualifies a statement or question. Like topography, "or" displays no favorites, as qualifications lead away from the stability of direct statement toward choice and indeterminacy. This conjunction may coordinate the elements of discourse, and so edge away from parataxis, but it also denies the conveniently hierarchical arrangements of hypotaxis. Those who read in the final comparison of the historian and the map-maker a fable of reality and the imagination are undoubtedly correct; the map-maker inhabits a middle ground between strict empiricism and pure invention, a ground where Bishop the poet dwells. But in light of Bishop's career the final lines tempt one to read them as a warning to her readers and critics: In the poems and years that follow, you will expect me to favor one direction in the topographic mapping of my inner world to justify the clumsiness of the literary historical chronicle; I can't and I won't.

In making significant use of the play between parataxis and hypotaxis, "The Map" is not unique in Bishop's canon. Particularly striking are the poems that use parataxis as a closural device. Consider the endings of "Arrival at Santos" ("We leave Santos at once; / we are driving to the interior" [*Poems* 90]); "The Riverman" ("The Dolphin singled me out; / Luandinha seconded it" [*Poems* 109]); or, most powerfully, "Cape Breton":

> The birds keep on singing, a calf bawls, the bus starts.
> The thin mist follows
> the white mutations of its dream;
> an ancient chill is rippling the dark brooks.

(*Poems* 68)

In the first two examples, parataxis suppresses the obvious links of temporal sequence: before one drives to the interior, one must leave, just as one must be singled out before one can be seconded. But in the excerpt from "Cape Breton," the suppressed links are not so obvious, or at least not so obviously the links of narrative temporality. Instead, the paratactic joining of thin mist and ancient chill reflects a simultaneity of perceptions, not a sequence of events, in the speaker's mind. This last example, with its menacing final line, associates parataxis with death and the dissolution of human consciousness in a nonhuman world.

But Bishop's use of parataxis does not produce a consistent effect. In "Cirque d'Hiver," for example, the sequence of simple parallels accumulates without subordination until the end of the third stanza, when both syntax and suggestion expand: "He feels her pink toes dangle to-ward his back / along the little pole / that pierces both her body and her soul / and goes through his, and reappears below" (*Poems* 31). Here the subordination of hypotaxis ("that pierces both her body and her soul") releases Bishop's verse from the limits of the restrained paratactic open-ing. If anything, parataxis in this poem associates itself with the culling of erotic stimuli from minute description more than with the cessation of these in the drive toward death, whereas hypotaxis signals the mo-ment of penetration and the drive toward cessation when the toy horse "canters, then clicks and stops, and looks at me."

Likewise, the familiar poem "The Fish" can be reread profitably as a configuration of simple parallels and more complex subordinations, culminating in the paratactic connection reminiscent of biblical syntax: "And I let the fish go" (*Poems* 44). The careful avoidance of subordina-tion, as in "so I let the fish go," reveals the speaker's reluctance, even refusal, to impose a more obvious moral closure on her narrative. In-stead, Bishop reserves subordination for the shift from the speaker's simple narration of her fish story to an imaginative identification with the fish she catches. Through the first twenty-one lines, the only con-junction is "and," and several statements are linked without conjunc-tions at all. Then, as the first-person speaker shifts from "I caught" to "I thought," comes hypotaxis:

> While his gills were breathing in
> the terrible oxygen
> —the frightening gills,
> fresh and crisp with blood,
> that can cut so badly—
> I thought of the coarse white flesh
> packed in like feathers.
>
> (*Poems* 42)

In this poem, with its paratactic skeleton of "I caught," "I thought," "I looked," "I admired," "I stared and stared," "And I let the fish go," hypotaxis signals the journey to the interior, as the mere recounting of events yields to personal reflection on, and appreciation of, those events. As in "The Map," in which hypotaxis accompanies the printer's excitement "as when emotion too far exceeds its cause," parataxis in "The Fish" governs emotion, whereas hypotaxis releases it, even in the vision of a "pool of bilge / where oil had spread a rainbow" (*Poems* 43).

But before turning finally to examples from a later poem, "North Haven," an elegy for Lowell published in December 1978, less than a year before her own death, I want to consider briefly Bishop's use of parataxis in the larger contexts of primitivism and literary history.

Primitivism in art fascinated Bishop. In addition to the two often-discussed poems "Large Bad Picture" (1946) and "Poem" (1972), which stand near either end of her publication chronology, recalling the palindrome that reads the same forward and backward, Bishop's *Collected Prose* contains several examples of this fascination. In "The Country Mouse," the young Bishop discovers "some paintings I now realize were primitives" (*Prose* 25). In "The U.S.A. School of Writing," published in 1983 but probably written in 1966, Bishop contrasts two types of primitivism: "There seemed to be one thing common to all their 'primitive' writing, as I suppose it might be called, in contrast to primitive painting: its slipshodiness and haste. Where primitive painters will spend months or years, if necessary, putting in every blade of grass and building up brick walls in low relief, the primitive writer seems in a hurry to get it over with" (*Prose* 46). Along with this passage, the two original watercolors by Bishop on the covers of her *Complete Poems, 1927–1979* and her *Collected Prose* suggest that her sympathies lay with primitive painters. These sympathies certainly inform her assessment of Gregorio Valdes in the piece named for him, published in 1939. Having admitted that "Gregorio was not a great painter at all, and although he certainly belongs to the class of painters we call 'primitive,' sometimes he was not even a good 'primitive' " (*Prose* 58), Bishop closes her appreciation by pondering the "partial mystery" of Gregorio's painting: "But surely anything that is impossible for others to achieve by effort, that is dangerous to imitate, and yet, like natural virtue, must be both admired and imitated, always remains mysterious" (*Prose* 59).

In probing the mysterious virtue of primitive painting, Bishop's consideration of Gregorio Valdes returns us to another example of primitivism, not only stylistic but also historical, the set of ancient written texts we call the Bible. Alter warns that the characteristic narrative procedures of the ancient text "should not lead us to any condescending preconception that the text is therefore bound to be crude or simple." In fact, "the whole notion of 'primitive narrative' is a kind of mental mirage engendered by modern parochialism," which subjects the supposedly primitive narrative "to tacit laws like the law of stylistic unity, of noncontradiction, of nondigression, of nonrepetition, and by these dim but purportedly universal lights" finds it "to be composite, deficient, or incoherent."[30] This critique of "modern parochialism" applies not only to those who dismiss ancient narrative procedures, such as parataxis, as deficient (those who take the "only" in "everything only connected by 'and' and 'and' " to mean "merely"), but also to others who subject a poet's canon and career to tacit laws of unity, noncontradiction, nondigression, and nonrepetition, insisting instead on progress, growth, and development. The analogy between her paratactic style and the discontinuous aspects of her Americanism reveals how Bishop defies such laws. Deliberately avoiding unity, as she does in her prosodic practices generally,[31] she employs formal and stylistic strategies, such as parataxis, that may be associated with the mysterious natural virtue of the primitive in all its deceptive simplicity and apparent artlessness.

One irony of Bishop's life and work is that, in opting for the supposedly crude, simple, composite, deficient, or incoherent strategies of primitivism, she reveals herself to be more radically modernist than Yeats, Eliot, Auden, or Lowell, with whose self-consciously structured careers hers has been compared unfavorably.[32] Easthope formulates this linguistic description of the modernist mode: "The coherence of the syntagmatic chain is disrupted by various fissures, dislocations and *lacunae*, and opened up to forms of parataxis."[33] As his fourth sonnet to Bishop demonstrates, Lowell recognizes precisely this aspect of her compositional method and, by implication, both the life behind it and the work it engenders. As Bishop's elegy "North Haven" makes clear, she, too, understands a crucial difference between Lowell and herself:

> *I can make out the rigging of a schooner*
> *a mile off; I can count*
> *the new cones on the spruce. It is so still*
> *the pale bay wears a milky skin, the sky*
> *no clouds, except for one long, carded horse's-tail.*
>
> (*Poems* 188)

Bishop's poem answers Lowell in at least two ways.[34] First, it opens with this italicized stanza in which she conjures up Lowell's voice, although the paratactic structure of the opening lines reveals her signature. With its family resemblance to the Spenserian stanza or the stanza of Milton's "On the Morning of Christ's Nativity," Bishop's stanza originates in, and identifies itself with, Lowell's voice, pretending to be the vehicle of his thought and conversation, as well as of poetic tradition. When she enters and continues that conversation, she answers Lowell, using the terms, or the form, he appears to have established. The formal scheme of the poem, a five-line stanza made of four pentameters and a final alexandrine, dramatizes the thematic play between repetition and revision, as every fifth line changes the pattern, a change Bishop's rhyming associates with deranging (sadly appropriate for Lowell) or rearranging.

Second, she answers Lowell's sonnet to her by adopting his figuration of human life and consciousness as *poiesis*, once again represented by a poet's compositional method. An obsessive reviser of his own work, both published and unpublished, Lowell exercised fully his power to change his creations, to create the fiction of a coherent career through revision. Bishop turns this revisionary power to change a poem, a transitive kind of change, into the existential power to change at all, an intransitive kind of change, which ends with death. As long as Lowell lived, he could revise his canon and, with it, its poem of his life, shaping his own progress, growth, and development. Now that he is dead, both the poems and the progress remain fixed: "The words won't change again. Sad friend, you cannot change." For a poet as obsessed with perfection as Lowell, death is therefore a loss, since it precludes further self-fashioning; for a poet like Bishop, it is a mere end, as well as part of a process of contingency long since accepted.

Unlike Lowell, Bishop was not a reviser: "Some poets like to rewrite, but I don't" (*Art* 299). Unlike him, as "North Haven" suggests, she exercises the power to change in a qualified and tentative way: "The islands haven't shifted since last summer, / even if I like to pretend they have." Following the metaphor attributed to Lowell ("*no clouds, except for one long, carded horse's-tail*"), Bishop's reluctance to let her imagination tamper with nature stands out sharply. Instead, she prefers the simple registration of the wildflower catalogue, departing only modestly into metaphor with the line "the Fragrant Bedstraw's incandescent stars." This deference to nature, albeit a nature mediated through the elegiac motif of the flower catalogue, culminates in the statement near the center of the poem: "Nature repeats herself, or almost does: / *repeat, repeat, repeat; revise, revise, revise*." As in "The Map," the "or" undoes simple predication. Nature repeats herself annually, but with revisions, such as the new absence of an old friend. Behind Bishop's careful attention to the natural world hovers the suggestion that, in contrast, Lowell's restless revisions of the poem of his life aim at a continuity and a completeness that are not natural, even if we like to pretend they are. More natural, at least to Bishop, are the unrevised discontinuities she formalizes in her paratactic schemes.

3

Parataxis is an appropriate image for Bishop's complicated Americanness, which resists the convenient connections and subordinations of Whitman's or Williams's or even Pound's. It is also an appropriate image of Bishop's treatment of what, in a description of Lowell's *Life Studies* (1959), she refers to as "those 'ironies of American History'" (*Art* 285), a phrase she holds at arm's length by encasing it in quotation marks. Unlike Whitman or Williams or Pound, Bishop does not attempt to piece together a continuous vision of America, celebratory or critical; yet more obviously than Dickinson, she does introduce the ironies of

Americanism and American history into her poems, albeit occasionally and indirectly. In addition to "Visits to St. Elizabeths," "From Trollope's Journal," and "View of the Capitol from the Library of Congress," she published the sestina "A Miracle for Breakfast" (1937), which she calls "my Depression poem" and "my 'social conscious' poem" (*Art* 297); the allegorical "Roosters" (1941), which she describes as being "more or less" about the Second World War (*Art* 320);[35] and "Songs for a Colored Singer" (1944), which uses the dramatic monologue to cross racial boundaries. Furthermore, at least two of the Brazil poems carry distinct resonances for American readers, "Brazil, January 1, 1502" (1960), which considers the intrusion of Europeans upon the Western Hemisphere, and "The Burglar of Babylon" (1964), which opposes the poor of "Babylon slum" to the "rich with their binoculars" (*Poems* 116–17).

Parataxis shapes Bishop's fiction of form, then, as Emersonian organicism shapes Whitman's, the resistance to that organicism shapes Dickinson's, the principle of effective form shapes Pound's, or the notion of measure shapes Williams's. This statement does not mean that neither Whitman nor Dickinson nor Pound nor Williams ever arranges poetic materials side by side in paratactic fashion; each often does just that, as the example of Pound's *Cantos* makes clear. But in the case of Pound, for instance, parataxis serves an explicit aesthetic ideology, and the link between parataxis and that ideology is obvious. Pound's notion of an Ideogrammic Method and the paratactic structures of his *Cantos* suit one another. In other words, there is nothing paratactic about the link between parataxis and ideology; Pound subordinates the former to the latter. In Bishop's case, however, the link between parataxis and an explicit aesthetic ideology is missing, since she offers no such ideology. Implicit fragments of that ideology lie scattered throughout her writing, waiting to be pieced together. But the relationship of fragment to fragment is itself paratactic, as would be that between any ideology her readers construct and her use of parataxis. One does not subordinate the other; they simply exist side by side.

This absence of an obvious connection between poetic theory and practice associates Bishop with Dickinson, and it comes as no surprise that Bishop admired Dickinson partly for her reticence: "It is nice for a change to know a poet who never felt the need for apologies and essays, long paragraphs, or even for long sentences."[36] But although both poets usually avoid "apologies and essays," and so suppress the connection between theory and practice, Bishop differs from Dickinson in at least one crucial way. Between Bishop and Dickinson falls the first generation of modern poets, a generation that elevated prose apologies for poetic practices to the status of an independent genre. With the polemical self-

defenses of, among others, Pound and Williams before her, Bishop necessarily admires Dickinson's refusal to explain herself with a certain
touch of nostalgia, a longing for an earlier phase of American poetic
history when poets were not automatically expected to fire off manifestoes or consent to interviews. Of course, such prose apologies for poetic
practices existed long before the coming of modernism, as Poe's decep-
tively explicit essay "The Philosophy of Composition" (1846) demonstrates, and it may be somewhat naive of Bishop to infer that Dickinson
"never felt the need" to explain herself. But Bishop's comment, published the year after she completed her term as poetry consultant, carries
the unmistakable tone of someone who wishes to avoid the kinds of
explicit self-description her public status forces upon her.

Nevertheless, either because she cannot or because she chooses not
to, Bishop does not avoid all self-description. Certain remarks in her
prose pieces and in interviews describe aspects of her craft. In a 1966
interview, for example, she claims to wish she had "studied nothing but
Latin and Greek in college," identifying herself with the kind of classical
training Pound so adamantly preached, and adds: "Writing Latin prose
and verse is still probably the best possible exercise for a poet" (*Art*
292). In "Efforts of Affection," she devotes three or four pages to
Moore's prosody, making observations that reveal her own awareness
of ways in which rhyme, meter, and free verse can accommodate one
another (*Prose* 138–41). In a talk she gave in 1977, she admits that she
is "saturated" with the meters, rhymes, and phrasings of hymns, further
associating her with Dickinson, although she also claims that she
learned more about meter from nursery rhymes than from hymns.[37]

Classicism, traditional prosody, free verse, hymns, and nursery
rhymes all contribute to Bishop's sense of poetic craft, combining the
ancient with the contemporary, the sacred with the secular, and high
culture with popular art to form her own eclectic technique. But while
this formal inclusiveness enriches Bishop's poetic practice, it does not
lend itself easily to the production of manifestoes, apologies, and polemical assertions, all of which tend toward self-revelation, reductive-
ness, and exclusion, principles inimical to Bishop's aesthetic sensibility.
For this reason, much of her commentary on her own art, or on poetry
in general, embeds itself in her poems. For Bishop, the *ars poetica*
acquires a significance it cannot have for Pound or for Williams or for
any poet who supplements his or her poems with abundant prose
explication.

In Bishop's case, as in Dickinson's, the *ars poetica* internalizes the
binary relation between commentary and illustration, relinquishing the
support of prose explication and rendering its arguments in the figura-

tive mode of poetry. Bishop's poetry includes three strains of *ars poet-ica*. First, like Dickinson, she has poems that generate useful metaphors for discussing her art and so become self-descriptive in an oblique, non-literal way, poems such as "The Map." Second, unlike Dickinson, whose self-descriptive poems (for example, "Four Trees—upon a soli-tary Acre—") remain uncompromisingly covert and elliptical, Bishop also writes poems that are explicitly about writing, poems such as "Over 2,000 Illustrations and a Complete Concordance," which con-fronts the nature of biblical parataxis, or "One Art," which considers the transformation of loss into writing: "The art of losing's not too hard to master / though it may look like (*Write* it!) like disaster" (*Poems* 178). I shall return to this category shortly.

A third, once-removed category of *ars poetica* consists of poems about visual art that are also implicitly about poetic art. Into it fall three poems that have received considerable critical attention, "The Monu-ment" (1939), "Large Bad Picture" (1946), and "Poem" (1972). In the case of the last, Bishop makes explicit the self-descriptive aspects of her *ekphrasis*, for the title "Poem" functions not as a place-holding ci-pher on the order of "Untitled" but as an indication of the true subject of her meditation: "Art 'copying from life' and life itself, / life and the memory of it so compressed / they've turned into each other. Which is which?" (*Poems* 177).[38] Here Bishop enters the long-standing debate on the nature and value of mimesis not only to comment on her own art but also that of Lowell, whose "Epilogue" in *Day by Day* (1977) takes up with more self-doubt Bishop's ekphrastic questioning of the limita-tions memory imposes:

> Those blessèd structures, plot and rhyme—
> why are they no help to me now
> I want to make
> something imagined, not recalled?
> I hear the noise of my own voice:
> *The painter's vision is not a lens,*
> *it trembles to caress the light.*[39]

Lowell prays that "the grace of accuracy / Vermeer gave to the sun's illumination" will rescue his poems from the status of mere snapshots, "lurid, rapid, garish, grouped, / heightened from life," whereas Bishop finds in the amateur painting of her great-uncle an analogy for her own "look": "Our visions coincided—'visions' is / too serious a word—our looks, two looks." In her hands, the ekphrastic *ars poetica* shies away from reading the great works of art history, preferring instead the con-temporary work of Joseph Cornell or the primitive paintings of her great-uncle. An interesting case here is "Over 2,000 Illustrations," which could also belong to this category, as it begins with a look at anonymous engravings of biblical scenes.

Returning to the second category, that of poems explicitly about writing, one can follow some of Bishop's one-word titles to further examples. Originally published in 1945, "Anaphora" closes *North and South* and the journey that "The Map" opens. Since "anaphora" is the name classical rhetoricians give to the repetition of beginnings, the placement of Bishop's poem in a terminal position constitutes a wry joke, one that reveals deeper meaning in the context of its dedication, added in *Complete Poems* (1969), "In memory of Marjorie Carr Stevens." By calling attention to the act of beginning as one has begun before, Bishop's title attempts to soften both the closure of her own volume and the closure of human life.

The poem focuses on the astronomical prototype of repeated beginnings, daybreak: "Each day with so much ceremony / begins, with birds, with bells, / with whistles from a factory" (*Poems* 52). Bishop's suspended syntax defers the verb "begins" to the beginning of the second line, a self-descriptive moment enhanced by the alliteration of "begins," "birds," and "bells," a sequence that forces its reader to experience alliteration as a kind of phonemic anaphora: as each day begins the same, so each word begins the same. After the opening lines of anticipation, the sun finally appears in the ninth line as "he":

> Oh promptly he
> appears and takes his earthly nature
> instantly, instantly falls
> victim of long intrigue,
> assuming memory and mortal
> mortal fatigue.

Here the final quatrain of shorter lines recalls the wheel of medieval romances, originally a device for stanzaic closure, but in Bishop's poem also a figure for the fall into a smaller, more limited "earthly nature" marked by memory and mortality.

"Anaphora" allegorizes the downwardness of reading verse on the printed page, interpreting it as an emblem of the figurative fall into memory and mortality, as well as of the literal fall, from the perspective of an earthly observer, of the sun from its apex. In the second stanza, identical to the first in format, this general falling enlarges to include the social and economic sinking "through the drift of classes / to evening to the beggar in the park," who, in his or her preparation for "stupendous studies," suggests a cousin of Stevens's man "in that old coat, those sagging pantaloons," transformed by imagination into major man in

"Notes toward a Supreme Fiction" (1942) three years before Bishop's poem.[40] The object of the beggar's studies, like that of Stevens's ephebe, is nothing less than the sun itself, which initiates "the fiery event / of every day in endless / endless assent." With this close "Anaphora" replicates in miniature the progress of *North and South*, ending with an image of beginning, clinched here by the unavoidable pun ("assent"-"ascent") inscribed at the point of furthest typographical descent.

Behind "Anaphora" hovers Whitman, whom Bishop admired early in her life.[41] Not only is he the American poet of anaphora, but he is also the American poet who defies most vehemently the darker side of daybreak: "Dazzling and tremendous how quick the sunrise would kill me, / If I could not now and always send sunrise out of me" (*CP* 52). Sunrise challenges Whitman by putting "upward libidinous prongs" that threaten to overshadow his own erotic power, mocking him with "the mocking taunt, See then whether you shall be master!" Sunrise challenges Bishop by immediately suggesting sunset, the fall necessitated by every rise and so an image of the closure that begins with beginning, especially the closure death brings. For both poets, sunrise occasions thoughts on human limitation, but for Whitman it is the magnitude of a single sunrise that most daunts him, while for Bishop it is the repetition of successive sunrises.

In the rhetorical scheme anaphora, Bishop recognizes a metaphor for repeated beginnings. Remarkably, the poem titled "Anaphora" makes no significant use of this scheme, although two successive lines begin with "sinks through the drift of" and the two sonnet-like stanzas imply repetition. If the poem did make significant use of anaphora, as "Visits to St. Elizabeths" does, it would be self-descriptive in the same obvious way as a sonnet about a sonnet. But since it does not, the title has no immediate literal significance and asks to be construed as wholly figurative. Anaphora serves Bishop as a figure for the repeated beginnings of days, which in turn suggest the repeated beginnings of human lives. But, by its positioning in *North and South*, it also serves her as a figure for the repeated beginnings of various written structures, not just lines or stanzas but also poems, volumes, and entire canons. After all, *North and South* represents the opening of Bishop's own canon. As such, it both repeats the opening of other poets' canons and, as Bishop reads it, anticipates the closure of her career as well. Anaphora, a particular kind of repetition, functions as a synecdoche for all repetition and ultimately for the destination toward which all human repetitions tend. The inverse of refrain, anaphora views termination from the other end of the telescope.[42] "In my beginning is my end" begins Eliot's "East Coker" (1940), and Bishop's "Anaphora" testifies to her acknowledgment of the same truth.

At the close of Bishop's career lies a second poem with a one-word title, "Sonnet," which appeared in October of 1979, the month she died. If "Anaphora" meditates on repetition, both in writing and in living, by concentrating on acts of beginning, "Sonnet" meditates on freedom by concentrating on enclosure:

> Caught—the bubble
> in the spirit-level,
> a creature divided;
> and the compass needle
> wobbling and wavering,
> undecided.
> Freed—the broken
> thermometer's mercury
> running away;
> and the rainbow-bird
> from the narrow bevel
> of the empty mirror,
> flying wherever
> it feels like, gay!

(Poems 192)

Fifty-one years earlier Bishop published another poem titled "Sonnet" ("I am in need of music that would flow") in the *Blue Pencil* (June 1928), the literary magazine of Walnut Hill School. With its references to "music," "melody," and "rhythm," the earlier poem also amounts to an *ars poetica*, but its awareness of its own patterning, a modified Petrarchan scheme, does not suggest a larger fiction of form.

By contrast, the later sonnet allegorizes its own scheme in original ways. Its basic motif of bondage versus freedom associates the 1979 "Sonnet" with other sonnets about the sonnet, among them Wordsworth's "Nuns Fret Not at Their Convent's Narrow Room" and Keats's "On the Sonnet."[43] This motif also surfaces elsewhere in Bishop's work, particularly in the story "In Prison" (1938), which includes the Emersonian credo " 'Freedom is knowledge of necessity' " (*Prose* 191), and in the memoir "Efforts of Affection," in which Bishop comments tellingly on the mixture of freedom and limitation in Moore's formal practices: "Now that everything can be said, and done, have we anyone who can compare with Marianne Moore, who was at her best when she made up her own rules and when they were strictest—the reverse of 'freedom'?" (*Prose* 145).[44] Bishop's placement of the word "freedom" in quotation marks signals a skepticism about freedom in art that also characterizes Williams's pronouncements that no verse can be free and still be verse. But long before arguments about free verse furnished the twentieth century with material for polemical debate, lyric poems began meditating on the emancipating power of their own self-enclosure.

In itself, then, the freedom-in-bondage motif does not make Bishop's *ars poetica* original. Rather, its originality lies in the changes it rings upon that motif by manipulating its own form. Instead of iambic pentameter, Bishop opts for two-stress accentualism. Instead of a Petrarchan or Shakespearean or other rhyme scheme, she rhymes irregularly, if at all, often with the kind of unaccented rhyme perfected by Moore (for example, *bubble-needle* or *mirror-wherever*). In fact, the poem generates Dickinsonian acoustics that cause the ear to string words together on the thinnest phonemic filaments. Does "wavering" rhyme with "broken," or does each stand unmated? The wavering, broken quality of this rhyme suggests that this question is precisely the point. Likewise, does "mercury" rhyme with "-bird," as well as with both "mirror" and "wherever"? How about "-level," which could complete an unaccented rhyme with "bubble" and "needle" early in the poem, but will discover its own exact rhyme with "bevel" near the end? On its auditory plane, Bishop's poem alters the rhyming conventions of the sonnet to permit multiple pairings and connections, pairings and connections that tone down the overt rhymes of her 1928 "Sonnet" as they heighten a reader's sensitivity to sound.

Nevertheless, Bishop's title insists aggressively that even though her poem abandons metrical and rhyming conventions that define a sonnet, her poem must still be read as a sonnet. The effect would be much different if the poem were titled, say, "Caught and Freed," with a wink at Frost's "Bond and Free." In that case, a reader might recognize that the poem has fourteen lines, interpret this number as a signal from Bishop that she wants her poem loosely compared with sonnet tradition, and decide that she wishes to demonstrate her own independence from it. But to insist that, no, this is a sonnet, and not the distant cousin of one, is to insist on orthodoxy, or rather on a competing, antithetical vision of orthodoxy. Instead of merely loosening established conventions, as Lowell does in the unrhyming sonnets of *History*, and remaining under the general rubric of tradition, Bishop substitutes her own conventions, announces with her title that these conventions are just as legitimate as already existing ones, and attempts to challenge her readers' notions of what constitutes tradition.

"Sonnet" divides its fourteen lines into two sentences, one of six lines and one of eight. In turn, each sentence falls into two parts connected by a paratactic "and," the first into two three-line halves, the second into one part of three lines and one of five. The entire poem contains no finite verb, instead relying wholly on past and present participles. While all these divisions would amount to careful, deliberate patterning in any poem, they gather added significance in one that claims to be a sonnet. Specifically, Bishop preserves the Petrarchan division between octave and sestet, except that she reverses them.[45] The conventional turn between the two occurs after a complete line, not in the middle of one, as in a Miltonic or Wordsworthian sonnet. Furthermore, she maps the two-part Petrarchan structure onto the four-part Shakespearean one, replacing the conventional sequence of three quatrains and a couplet with three tercets and a longer section of five lines.

As she reverses the Petrarchan pattern of octave and sestet, so she reverses the Shakespearean progress toward condensation and compression, allowing her final sentence to lengthen beyond the limits of either couplet or quatrain. Bishop pins this elaborate structure of overlapping, inverted patterns together with the only three exact rhymes in her poem. The rhyming of "divided" and "undecided" enforces the separateness of the sestet by linking the final lines of its two halves. Likewise, the rhyming of "away" with "gay" ties up the two parts of the octave and ties the octave off from the sestet. Finally, the rhyme of "level" with "bevel," each word coming in the second line of its respective section, clasps sestet to octave.

If "Sonnet" were not a sonnet, the obvious association of the six-line part with being caught and the eight-line one with being freed would be mimetically appropriate, as would the lengthening of the final syntactic section to fly, like the rainbow-bird, "wherever / it feels like." These correspondences are the stuff of mimesis but not necessarily of an *ars poetica*; yet because the poem calls itself "Sonnet," it comments on enclosure and freedom in human life by commenting on enclosure and freedom in a fixed verse form. When a reader grants "Sonnet" its sonnetness, the poem generates meaning it would not otherwise have, meaning that involves a recognition of the inversion, which depends entirely on a knowledge of Petrarchan convention.

As Bishop inverts octave and sestet, so she inverts freedom and enclosure. The poem links four objects, three of them instruments of measurement, appropriately enough for a carefully designed poem that contemplates its own scheme, and the fourth a figure of representation, a carved bird. Bishop appears to contrast the enclosure of the bubble within the level's alcoholic solution (the literal meaning here of "spirit") and of the compass needle with the free movements of the mercury and of the bird. The problem, of course, is that the boundary between enclosure and freedom is not at all clear. The compass needle remains free to wobble and waver, for example, but the carved bird, even though it represents flying, cannot actually leave the mirror. Likewise, the bubble in the level moves to measure a vertical or horizontal surface, but the mercury of a broken thermometer, for all its "running away," can no longer move to measure temperature.

Like the compass needle, the poem itself remains undecided on which direction to point. Its superficial identification of the mercury and the bird with freedom radically qualifies the nature of that freedom. Meanwhile, it cannot side whole-heartedly with "Nuns Fret Not at Their Convent's Narrow Room" by maintaining the paradox that enclosure means freedom. At this point the sonnetness of "Sonnet" unfolds further meaning. Readers of sonnets know that, more often than not, they should expect the sestet to resolve matters complicated in the octave. In turn, this important function assigned by convention to the sestet partly redresses the imbalance created by the sonnet's characteristic asymmetry. The sestet may be shorter, but its argumentative significance is as great as, if not greater than, the octave's.

In Bishop's poem, however, neither the sestet nor the octave resolves anything. Neither has the subordinate job of clearing up what the other has complicated. If the sestet and octave were reversed, so that the poem began "freed" and ended "undecided," neither freedom nor enclosure would look significantly less ambiguous. The relationship between sestet and octave, then, is an example of parataxis. The two lie side by side, defying the expectation that their pairing should amount to a completed argument. This defiance forms the heart of Bishop's revisionary challenge to sonnet tradition, as her poem calls attention to its own patterns to deny the very assumptions sonnets make about themselves and the world they inhabit.

Like "Sonnet," "Sestina" (1956) brandishes a title that announces its self-consciousness, promising to examine its own form and, in the process, poetic form in general. As "Some Dreams They Forgot" (1933) demonstrates plainly that Bishop can give a sonnet another kind of title, so the earlier sestina "Miracle for Breakfast" (1937) shows that her self-descriptive, generic labeling of the later poem represents a deliberate choice, not a faltering of imagination. In correspondence with Moore about "Miracle for Breakfast," Bishop comments on the elaborate form attributed to Arnaut Daniel and subsequently employed by the troubadours of Provence and by Dante and Petrarch in Italy.[46] In a letter of September 15, 1936, she admits certain flaws and then dismisses the form: "I realize there are awful faults—one being vague, another extremely impolite, if true, display of your 'influence'; the sestina is just a sort of stunt."[47] These are the confessions and disclaimers of a twenty-five-year-old apprentice writing to her mentor. The statement about the faults of "A Miracle for Breakfast" are mostly accurate. But the dismissal of the sestina as a stunt reveals more about the young poet's defensive techniques than it does about the form itself.

More useful comments come in a letter of January 5, 1937: "It seems to me that there are two ways possible for a sestina—one is to use unusual words as terminations, in which case they would have to be used differently as often as possible—as you say, 'change of scale.' That would make a very highly seasoned kind of poem. And the other way is to use as colorless words as possible—like Sydney, so that it becomes less of a trick and more of a natural theme and variations. I guess I have tried to do both at once."[48] The six terminal words of any sestina will locate it on a spectrum running from "a natural theme and variations," in which neither the words chosen nor their uses are particularly striking, to a "change of scale," in which both the words and their uses suggest novelty and variation. In "A Miracle for Breakfast," in which she claims she has blended the two extremes, Bishop uses "coffee," "crumb," "balcony," "miracle," "sun," and "river." All six are nouns in the first stanza, and all six appear as nouns throughout the poem, with the lone exception of "to crumb" in the third stanza.

Bishop maintains quite rightly that she has included both "unusual" and "colorless" words, with "coffee," "crumb," and perhaps "balcony" representing the former, "sun," "river," and perhaps "miracle" the latter. All are singular, two of them monosyllables, two disyllables, and two trisyllables. By contrast, "Ye Goatherd Gods," the double sestina from Sidney's *Arcadia*, uses entirely what Bishop would call "colorless" words, six general nouns: "mountains," "valleys," "forests," "music," "morning," and "evening." Three are plural and three singular, but all are disyllabic, guaranteeing that each of Sidney's seventy-five pentameter lines will close with a feminine ending. Since most of his lines also correspond to discrete syntactical units, a certain rhythmic predictability becomes inevitable. Some readers might consider this predictability "natural," as Bishop seems to, whereas others may find it monotonously numbing.

At this point, it would be convenient to argue that "Sestina" succeeds where "A Miracle for Breakfast" does not because it uses six terminal words closer to the "unusual" end of the spectrum: "house," "grandmother," "child," "stove," "almanac," and "tears." But once again all six are nouns and function as nouns throughout the poem. Five are singular and four monosyllablic. The most unusual word is "almanac," with "stove" not far behind, but "house," "child," and "tears" are as colorless as any in Sidney's poem. Clearly, neither the power nor the success of "Sestina" depends on Bishop's choosing unusual terminal words. On this spectrum, both her sestinas fall into approximately the same place.

What, then, accounts for the palpable difference between the poems, as well as for Bishop's self-conscious labeling of the later one? Certainly, one significant feature of "Sestina" is its transformation of the grandmother's tears into opportunities for figuration, associating them in turn with teakettle, tea, buttons, moons on the pages of an almanac, and seeds to be planted.[49] "A Miracle for Breakfast" attempts to discover similar opportunities in the word "crumb," yet fails to endow each appearance of the word with a unique specificity. But the question then becomes: What is there about the transformation of the tears that can be described, however obliquely, by the title "Sestina"? One answer might be that etymologically *sestina* points to the number six and suggests a sixfold structure, one that ensures a reader will have at least six (or seven, including the *envoi*) meetings with a particular word and whatever it signifies. If Bishop wished to call attention to the ways in which the formal permutations of a given signifier represent the figurative permutations of a given signified, her title would make sense. By analogy with Stevens's title "Thirteen Ways of Looking at a Blackbird," Bishop's title could be paraphrased "Six (or Seven) Ways of Looking at a Grandmother's Tears." The sestina, with its chemistry of repetition and variation, becomes a metaphor for figuration and uncanniness, as both depend on a mixture of sameness and change.

But the differences between "Sestina" and "A Miracle for Breakfast" also show clearly that in the twenty years between the two Bishop learned a lesson about the sestina in particular and about poetic form in general. Specifically, she learned how to make "a sort of stunt" appear to be "less of a trick," a crucial lesson not just for writers of sestinas but for any poet attempting to write verse in the shadow of the Romantic myth of organicism. Here the literary historical consciousness implicit in her second letter to Moore manifests itself, albeit in a somewhat confused way. As a post-Romantic poet, Bishop knows enough to value the apparent naturalness of "a natural theme and variations." But to associate such naturalness with Sidney makes no sense, as his double sestina is a much greater trick than either of her single ones, and, what is more, just as self-conscious, if not more so. In the Second Eclogues of book 2 of the revised *Arcadia*, Sidney introduces his poem as "this double Sestine," both identifying its prosodic form and calling attention to his own technical skill. But even without this self-conscious labeling, Bishop could not possibly hear in Sidney's uniform, end-stopped lines the same kind of naturalness she heard, for example, in a poem by Moore.

Bishop's twentieth-century awareness of literary history makes her defensive about the tricky, artificial aspects of poetic form, a defensiveness neither Sidney nor other pre-Romantic writers of sestinas would have shared to the same extent. Or, to put the matter differently, because all poetic forms are tricky and artificial to one degree or another, her modern perspective makes her wish to disown or disguise her own poetic stunts, especially when such stunts risk appearing merely mechanical and exhibitionist. Accordingly, Bishop's task becomes that of naturalizing the artificial, a task epitomized by the writing of a sestina in an age when many believe that poetry is supposed to represent the language of people speaking to one another. The solution to her task lies in neither of the "two ways possible for the sestina," which she outlines to Moore, but in a third alternative.

Bishop's formal sophistication in the later sestina becomes especially evident in its third stanza:

> She cuts some bread and says to the child,
>
> *It's time for tea now*; but the child
> is watching the teakettle's small hard tears
> dance like mad on the hot black stove,
> the way the rain must dance on the house.
> Tidying up, the old grandmother
> hangs up the clever almanac
>
> on its string. Birdlike the almanac
> hovers half open above the child.
>
> (*Poems* 123)

What makes this stanza an example of apparent naturalness is not the relative colorlessness of its terminal words but the loose fit of syntax to stanza. In any sestina, the most glaringly artificial moments will come at the beginnings of stanzas, when the sixth terminal word of the previous stanza must also end the first line of the new one, producing an identically rhyming couplet that may have gratified the Provençal ear but that inevitably cloys the modern.

In the example above, Bishop hides these identical rhymes, one at the opening of the stanza and one at its close, with four concealing enjambments, two across stanza boundaries, diluting the rhymes on "child" and "almanac." By contrast, "Ye Goatherd Gods," with its twelve self-enclosed stanzas, has no such moments, nor, for that matter, does "A Miracle for Breakfast," although the transition between its fifth and sixth stanzas shows Bishop experimenting with a more modest, and less successful, concealment: "—I saw it with one eye close to the crumb— / and galleries and marble chambers. My crumb / my mansion, made for me by a miracle" (*Poems* 18–19). The syntactic stop before the stanza division assures that the rhyme will not evade the ear entirely, even though the new stanza enjambs its first line.

Another development in Bishop's technique involves the distribution of syntax within a single stanza rather than between or among two or three stanzas:

> But secretly, while the grandmother
> busies herself about the stove,

the little moons fall down like tears
from between the pages of the almanac
into the flower bed the child
has carefully placed in the front of the house.

In this, the sixth, stanza, stanza and sentence coincide exactly, although individual lines do not always coincide with phrases. The resulting single-sentence unit reads like many a short imagist poem, this one wavering between the four-stress accentual norm operating throughout "Sestina" and free verse. Conversely, "A Miracle for Breakfast" contains no stanzas unpunctuated by sentence divisions, so that its overall movement is more halting and labored. In the example above, Bishop manages to sustain the illusion that her stanza houses her sentence in an organic, inevitable way; it has six lines not because it must conform to a fixed prosodic scheme invented by Arnaut Daniel but because its small narrative takes six lines to complete, falling from line to line like the little moons falling into the flower bed. If Bishop did no more than write a sestina that does not read like other sestinas, her accomplishment would be great enough. But her *ars poetica* includes an image of its own scheme, one that points beyond itself to Bishop's vision of how she arranges language into lines and, eventually, into poems:

It was to be, says the Marvel Stove.
I know what I know, says the almanac.
With crayons the child draws a rigid house
and a winding pathway. Then the child
puts in a man with buttons like tears
and shows it proudly to the grandmother.

After two single-sentence endstopped lines, the enjambment "a rigid house / and a winding pathway" functions mimetically, the syntax winding around a line ending as the pathway winds. But if the enjambment reflects the sense of these lines, the reverse is also true, for these lines contain Bishop's emblem for the sestina itself: a rigid stanzaic house around which the pathway of syntax winds.

The title, then, plays many roles. First, it announces that its subject will be the sestina itself, including nothing less than how to write a fresh one nearly eight hundred years after the invention of the form. Second, it elbows the reader into recalling that this is a fixed form, no matter how natural and relaxed it may sound. The effect here compares to one Browning could have generated, for example, if instead of "My Last Duchess" he had titled his poem "Heroic Couplets." As Browning's poem comes late in the history of its form, so does Bishop's, and both poets understand the literary historical implication of their lateness, namely that they must absorb the technical demands of inherited forms into what appears to be a casual offhandedness, so that the fulfillment of those demands will look like the unplanned side effect of larger intentions. Unlike Browning, however, Bishop explicitly reminds her reader that he or she needs to read with literary historical awareness, a reminder that possibly intimates both her distrust of late twentieth-century readers of verse (the poem first presented itself to the general readership of the *New Yorker*) and her belief that she may have disguised her form too well.

Third, the title "Sestina" really means "Form," and her image of the rigid house and winding pathway represents another aspect of Bishop's fiction of form. Specifically, it represents her solution to the problem of naturalizing the artificial. In verse, the manipulation of lines, stanzas, rhymes, and meters constitutes artifice. By comparison, language itself, no matter how artificial or conventional its structures, represents the natural, the raw material that verse refines. Bishop's image of the rigid and the winding allegorizes the relation of verse scheme to language. Significantly, the image contains no rejection of the rigid in favor of a fiction of organic suppleness. Instead, it insists on the copresence and cooperation of the rigid and the winding, accounting for Bishop's nonalignment with any particular formal ideology.

Fourth, and finally, "Sestina" whispers "Pound," whose "Sestina: Altaforte," published in June 1909, marks the entrance of the form into modernism. Reading Pound's sestina in the light of his subsequent confinement to St. Elizabeths, Bishop could not fail to remark the grim irony of Pound's dramatization of Bertrans de Born, cast by Dante into Hell as "a stirrer up of strife." Published the year before "Visits to St. Elizabeths," Bishop's "Sestina" necessarily associates itself with that poem, both in the timing of its publication and in its placement in *Questions of Travel*. The second of the poems in the "Elsewhere" section of that volume, "Sestina" appears in the context of other poems emerging from Bishop's childhood. Although one may want to resist a reductive biographical reading of the child, the grandmother, and the "man with buttons like tears," whose absence partly motivates the tears in "Sestina," the man is, quite literally, the man of the house that the child draws, and so is a link with Bishop's dead father and with the land where her father died. As "Visits to St. Elizabeths" recalls the house that Jack built, "Sestina" contemplates the house the child draws. In turn, the child's house becomes Bishop's image for her own poem, which binds its meditation on the art of poetry to a meditation on other forces, both foreign and domestic, in the several senses these two words imply. For Bishop, these forces and the discontinuities between them make poetry's sheltering power imperative.

SIX

A. R. AMMONS, OR THE RIGID LINES

OF THE FREE AND EASY

FOR BISHOP the *ars poetica* is a way of escaping apologies and essays; for Ammons it is a characteristic mode. In his long poem "The Ridge Farm," first published in 1983, he turns once again to the idea of form:

> don't think we don't
> know one breaks
> form open because he fears
> its bearing in on him
> (of what, the accusation,
> the shape of his eros, error,
> his guilt he must buy
> costing himself)
> and one hugs form because
> he fears dissolution, openness,
> we know, we know:
> one needs stanzas to take
> sharp interest in and
> one interests the stanza
> down the road to the wilderness:[1]

Nearly thirty years after his claim that the poems of his first volume, *Ommateum* (1955), "suggest and imply and rather grow in the reader's mind than exhaust themselves in completed, external form,"[2] Ammons continues his extensive meditation on poetic shapes and structures.

That thirty-year meditation is neither continuous nor consistent, emerging more prominently, for example, in the early triad of *Expressions of Sea Level* (1964), *Corsons Inlet* (1965), and *Northfield Poems* (1966) than in the later one of *A Coast of Trees* (1981), *Worldly Hopes* (1982), and *Lake Effect Country* (1983). In one book, *Uplands* (1970), the word "form" does not appear at all, although we do find "order," "structure," "shape," and, in the poem "Summer Session 1968," the cognate "formality" ("formality they can define themselves against").[3] Conversely, in the long poems *Tape for the Turn of the Year* (1965),

"Essay on Poetics" and "Hibernaculum" (both in *CP*), *Sphere: The Form of a Motion* (1974), *The Snow Poems* (1977), and *Sumerian Vistas* (1987) comments and observations on poetic form abound. That most, if not all, of Ammons's significant statements about form appear in poems rather than in critical prose is no accident. In his work, the abstraction "form" connotes more than it denotes, charged as it is with Ammons's best fiction-making powers. "The Ridge Farm," "Corsons Inlet," *Sphere*, "Essay on Poetics," and *The Snow Poems* most clearly reveal these powers at work.

The passage from "The Ridge Farm" uses "form" in suggestive ways. Unlike the "completed, external form" Ammons renounces in the foreword to *Ommateum*, where "external" suggests nonorganic rigidity and "completed" implies the kind of autotelic closure Olson, among others, was lobbying against when Ammons wrote his first poems, "form" in the later poem both repels and attracts. In a familiar gesture, the passage opens with Ammons's version of epanalepsis, an enjambed line that begins and ends with the same word: "don't think we don't." Here this self-enclosing pattern, one Ammons uses in different ways throughout his work, is revealed by the conventions of Ammons's lineation rather than by the unaided contours of his syntax. Usually, epanalepsis ("a taking up again") involves a sentence that ends with its opening word or words or a figure in which the same word or clause is repeated after intervening matter.[4] In this opening line, Ammons breaks his syntax against a line to discover a buried repetition, one to which the syntactic pattern alone would not normally call attention. If "one breaks / form open because he fears" it, one also breaks form, such as the form of a syntactic pattern, to reveal other hidden structures.

The humor implicit in this passage arises from its deliberate self-betrayal. Ostensibly, someone speaking on behalf of a group, perhaps of poets, readers of poetry, amateur psychologists, or homespun metaphysicians, claims that "we know, we know" all about form. The tone of mock-weariness may also signal Ammons's acknowledgment that his readers have already heard more than enough about his ambivalence towards form: when form repeats itself without variation, he fears its preempting power, as it becomes a figure of compulsion or obsession, "the accusation, / the shape of his eros, error, / his guilt." The non-etymological, purely auditory association of "eros" with "error" suggests that when human drives lead into patterns repeated for the sake of pattern alone, they necessarily mislead. But when form is all that prevents Ammons from the complete dissolution of self into the alien world of nature ("the wilderness") or poetic autism, or both, as in many of the poems of *Ommateum*, then form is something to be hugged. We know,

we know all this, as we know that "one needs stanzas," as instances of
poetic form, when one strolls down the road into wilderness. Likewise,
we know that because life "is / all one it must be divided / and because
it is / divided it must be all one" (*SV* 28); Ammons has been telling us so
in poem after poem about "the one-many problem" (*Sphere*) or "the
one:many / mechanism" ("The Fairly High Assimilation Rag").[5]

But while the passage extols the stanza, it builds no stanzas, although
other parts of "The Ridge Farm" do. In fact, the passage neither breaks
nor hugs form in any remarkable way. Ammons casts this passage in the
familiar shape of a left-justified stichic column, the lines of which fall
mostly between the lengths of traditional trimeters and tetrameters. In
his *Collected Poems*, this shape appears only twice among poems written between 1951 and 1955 ("Chaos Staggered" and "Bees Stopped"),
but with the poems written between 1966 and 1971, grouped mostly in
Uplands and *Briefings* (1971), it becomes, along with the tercet, one of
his dominant visual patterns. At least once in the passage, the faint trace
of an iambic sequence becomes audible:

> /   /   /   /   /
> because he fears / its bearing in on him

Because Ammons is a self-proclaimed "free-versite,"[6] an occasional
iambic string may seem like a simple accident of language, inhering in
the structure of English. But to argue this is a bit naive, since iambic
forms can be broken, and usually are by Ammons, as easily as they can
be constructed. Furthermore, this particular iambic eddy corresponds
neatly to an expression of formal claustrophobia, one that the next section of "The Ridge Farm" echoes:

> wherever mortality sets up a net
> or responsibility's strictures harden
> I mount into a whirlwind and
> buzz off, clearing a streak
> I spend the night in sonnets but the
> next morning pack my bag with free verse
> the road is my winding song sheet
> the rivers, branches, brooks purl
> my uneasy pleasures.
>
> (*SV* 28–29)

Here the net of mortality and the hardened strictures of responsibility
are both associated with sonnets, in which Ammons spends his nights,
presumably confronted by, among other things, "the shape of his eros,
error, / his guilt," images of which surface from the unconscious in

dreams. But with morning he escapes into free verse, traveling down Whitman's open road, singing himself toward death ("winding song sheet"). Whereas many would associate night with liberation from the conscious mind into dreaming, and so with liberation from sonnets into free verse, Ammons associates night with limitation, as the unconscious mind dominates him until he is released by waking.

At its best, the breaking of form establishes a principle of "uneasy pleasures." The poet breaks to remake to break again. The flight from form is constant, and the refuge in form temporary. Behind the ironic humor of Ammons's know-it-all voice and his stanzaless advertisement for the stanza lies a deep confusion, confusion that vexes not only this passage but also the entire poem "The Ridge Farm" and much of the thirty-year work that precedes it. The confusion is about the relationship of polarities, specifically the polarity of form and formlessness. But confusion has its structures, too, and one structure of confusion is the chiasmus.[7] Significantly, chiasmus structures the second half of the passage from "The Ridge Farm," the first having relied on the parallelism of "one breaks . . . and one hugs." First, Ammons sketches a chiasmus with the sequence "one . . . stanzas . . . interest . . . and / one interests . . . stanza." But then he gives the fully realized, exact inversion in the final four lines:

> life, life: because it is
> all one it must be divided
> and because it is
> divided it must be all one

Parallelism and chiasmus are both rhetorical schemes, and Ammons uses both often. They indicate an acute rhetorical self-consciousness, which despite his apparent nonchalance reveals that even if meter and stanza vanish, language and thought have not collapsed into formlessness. In this particular passage, parallelism yields to chiasmus, so that its overall structure is one of inversion, since chiasmus is the opposite of parallelism. The truth of the passage, then, is that while we say "we know, we know" about the parallel aspects of form (it both threatens and comforts), "we," an imagined group collected around Ammons's speaker, remain deeply confused and uneasy about the polarity of form and formlessness.

One way Ammons manages confusion is with paradox:

> recalcitrance, fluency: these:
> too far with one and the density
> darkens, the mix slows, and bound
> up with hindrance, unyielding, stops:

too far with the other and the bright
spiel of light spins substanceless
descriptions of motion—

always to be held free this way,
staggering, jouncing, testing the
middle mix,
the rigid line of the free and easy.

(SV 5)

In the phrase "the rigid line of the free and easy," confusing opposites
have been reconciled felicitously. By "testing the / middle mix," Ammons moderates extremes, avoiding both darkened density and substanceless spiel. But still one wonders what the rigid line of the free and
easy, with its pun on "line" as both verse line and outline, would look
like. Predictably, as in most of Ammons's work, the line looks like a line
in nature:

but I like the ridge: it was a line
in the minds of hundreds of generations
of cold Indians: and it was there
approximately then what it is now.
five hundred years ago when the white
man was a whisper on the continent:
it is what I come up against:
it regularizes my mind though it has
nothing to do with me intentionally:
the shows that arise in and afflict
nature and man seem papery and
wrong when wind or time tears
through them, they seem not only
unrealistic but unreal: the ridge,
showless, summary beyond the trappings
of coming and going, provides a
measure, almost too much measure,
that nearly blinds away the present's
fragile joys from more durable woes.

(SV 10)

The ridge line combines recalcitrance with fluency, as a few lines earlier
Ammons calls "its rolls my fixed ocean." In pairing the ridge line, a
natural form, with the rigid line of the free and easy, a poetic form,
Ammons continues the tradition of Whitman, who reads Emerson's organic analogies in "The Poet" as prescriptions for substituting natural

for textual forms.[8] Such substitutions appear everywhere in Ammons's work. Winds, waves, brooks, waterfalls, snowfalls, mountains, dunes, elm trees—again and again these natural forms suggest texts to be read in poems attempting to become their figurative analogues.

But, most important for Ammons, the ridge line gives him a limit to "come up against": "it regularizes my mind." Etymologically, *regularize* is related to *rule* and suggests a straight stick or pattern. Psychologically, it suggests a form to hug when the mind, irregular, fears its own dissolution. Still, although the ridge comforts, it also threatens to overwhelm, and confusion hovers:

> the ridge,
> showless, summary beyond the trappings
> of coming and going, provides a
> measure, almost too much measure.

At least two echoes of earlier poems from the volume *Corsons Inlet* sound here. The phrase "the trappings / of coming and going" grafts the opening of "Gravelly Run" ("I don't know somehow it seems sufficient / to see and hear whatever coming and going is") onto the description in "Dunes" of a mound of sand as "a trapping / into shape" (*CP* 55, 158). In "The Ridge Farm" the power of the ridge leads the mind beyond the trappings (both adornments and entrapments) of the coming and going of temporal phenomena. As a geological feature, it transcends human history, specifically the history of the European settlement of North America. As a relatively fixed feature outside that history, it also "provides a / measure, almost too much measure." Once again epanalepsis signals a local rhetorical intensification, as consciousness registers both aspects of the "measure" the ridge provides. The relatively fixed ridge becomes a measure "that nearly blinds away the present's / fragile joys" (again iambic), since those joys depend on the trappings of coming and going. What stands fixed outside human time necessarily denies human joys, as well as human woes. A line that begins and ends with the word "measure" suggests an emblem for the ridge itself: although a part of the continuum, it seals itself off, self-contained and isolated.

Behind this section of "The Ridge Farm," as behind many of Ammons's meditations on form, hovers Williams. Certainly, the influence of Williams is complicated and can be too easily overstated, but Bloom, in what is otherwise a fine essay, surely confesses to deafness when he declares: "I cannot detect in [*Ommateum*] the voice of William Carlos Williams, which indeed I do not hear anywhere in Ammons's work, despite the judgments of several reviewers."[9] Bloom judges rightly when he discounts Williams's voice from *Ommateum*. Its strange, mythic "chants," as Bloom calls them, do not have much in common with Williams's more literal, concrete investigations, nor do the poems of *Om-mateum*, with their long, irregularly indented clusters of lines, some-times stichic, sometimes strophic, suggest the shapes of Williams's art. But from the late fifties or early sixties on, Ammons's work demon-strates an awareness of Williams, whether in its use of the rigorously enjambed, short-line stanza, which is one of Williams's trademarks, or in its deepening commitment to the minimally noted fact—what Bloom calls "Ammonsian literalness"—or in direct quotation and allusion, as in this passage from "Corsons Inlet":

> the possibility of rule as the sum of rulelessness:
> the "field" of action
> with moving, incalculable center:
>
> in the smaller view, order tight with shape:
> blue tiny flowers on a leafless weed: carapace of crab:
> snail shell:
> pulsations of order
> in the bellies of minnows: orders swallowed,
> broken down, transferred through membranes
> to strengthen larger orders: but in the large view, no
> lines or changeless shapes: the working in and out, together
> and against, of millions of events: this,
> so that I make
> no form [of]
> formlessness.[10]
>
> (*CP* 150)

Commenting that "in a difficult transitional passage, the poet associates the phrasal fields of his metric with the 'field' of action on every side of him," Bloom either ignores or does not recognize Ammons's direct ref-erence, signaled by his use of quotation marks, to the title of Williams's important essay "The Poem as a Field of Action" (1948). Among other relevant remarks, that essay argues that "our prosodic values should rightly be seen as only relatively true."[11] Furthermore, if in doubt about the presence of Williams in "Corsons Inlet" and in the period of Am-mons's life from which it comes, one has only to look to the piece that precedes it in the chronologically arranged *Collected Poems*. Titled "WCW," this short poem exults: "What a / way to read / Williams!" Even the most skeptical antagonist of influence theory, let alone its chief formulator, would have a difficult time ignoring these signs.[12]

The transitional passage from "Corsons Inlet" is difficult, but it bears directly on "The Ridge Farm" and on a larger discussion of form. In the lines "this, / so that I make / no form of / formlessness," the antecedent of "this" appears to be "the working in and out," recalling "the coming and going," "of millions of events," each reflecting some degree of order. This working in and out, then, reveals itself to the "I" of the poem, informing and instructing his poetic procedure ("so that I make"). The question is, What do these lines mean? Do they mean that having been instructed by the events of Corsons Inlet, the "I" will not attempt to impose a form on an overall, subsuming formlessness, a kind of undifferentiated plenitude that transcends the polarities of form and no form?[13]

At least one statement from *Sphere* could be enlisted in support of this reading: "The shapes nearest shapelessness awe us most, suggest /the god."[14] Formlessness, then, is an attribute of what is too large and remote to be trapped into shape, call it the god, the Most High, the One, or Unity. But although this reading may persuade locally, it presents two problems for "Corsons Inlet." First, Ammons admits quite explicitly, in terms that suggest his differences with Emerson, that "Overall is beyond me," and "Scope eludes my grasp." In other words, the working in and out of millions of events does not lead Ammons toward the apprehension of transcendent formlessness, even though forms nearest an ideal formlessness may awe him most. Instead, they reveal to him the contours of form in a natural landscape where "terror pervades" because a controlling form appears to be missing. But he refuses to fasten himself to the limited forms he can recognize ("I . . . will / not run to that easy victory"), vowing instead to extrapolate from limited forms to larger, more inclusive ones. Meanwhile, he knows and celebrates the knowledge that no form he discovers can be all-inclusive.

Second, if it is true that for Ammons formlessness is an attribute of overall Unity, then there must be two kinds of formlessness with which he concerns himself. Like Stevens's two versions of nothing in "The Snow Man," Ammons's versions of formlessness imply both a condition to be aspired to and a condition to be escaped from. When he explains in "The Ridge Farm" that "one hugs form because / he fears dissolution, openness," he cannot mean that formlessness offers him order or stasis, which some would consider attributes of Unity. He means that form defends him against extreme randomness, chaos, and disintegration. The declaration of mental independence in "Corsons Inlet," "I was released from forms," is deceptive. It does not mean that the speaker now enjoys an Emersonian transparency, as he becomes one with formless Unity. It means that having shed preemptive, a priori forms of thought, he must discover or invent new forms to ward off the terror of dissolution. The search for new form is every bit as urgent as the flight from old, and it is this urgency, and the preoccupation with form it engenders, that links Ammons so closely with Williams.

"Measure" is Williams's word. In "The Poem as a Field of Action," he announces, "The only reality that we can know is MEASURE" (*SE* 283). To Williams the all-inclusive reality of measure meant many things, including both prosodic form and the mental processes prosodic form can signify. When Ammons admits that the ridge line "provides a / measure, almost too much measure," we cannot help but hear Williams's voice, as in the passage from *Paterson*, book 2, in which Williams answers Pound's canto 45:

> Without invention nothing is well spaced,
> unless the mind change, unless
> the stars are new measured, according
> to their relative positions, the
> line will not change, the necessity
> will not matriculate: unless there is
> a new mind there cannot be a new
> line, the old will go on
> repeating itself with recurring
> deadliness.[15]

In addition to the word "measured" and Williams's own use of epanalepsis ("unless the mind change, unless"), this passage has in common with Ammons's "The Ridge Farm," as with "Corsons Inlet," a preoccupation with lines: lines of verse, the outlines of shape, and the conceptual lines of mental connection.

Ammons's most important sustained consideration of lines, measure, and form occurs in *Sphere: The Form of a Motion*. A question in the earlier "Hibernaculum" anticipates this title: "Are there any concepts to circulate: can / anyone form a motion:" (*CP* 366–67). Can anyone take the working in and out of millions of events, the continual change of coming and going, and give it conceptual and poetic form that will not destroy it? In the language of the foreword to *Ommateum*, published nineteen years before *Sphere*, can one make poems that do not exhaust themselves in completed, external form? In "Summer Session," Ammons formulates his dilemma succinctly: "The problem is / how / to keep shape and flow" (*CP* 248). The ambiguity of whether *flow* is part of the direct object or part of the infinitive exemplifies the kind of shifting play of significance, the continual metamorphosis of meaning, that Ammons cultivates and wants to protect against overdetermining forms. But "the form of a motion" may also have another meaning for him. Williams's poem "The Wind Increases," first collected in the "Della Primavera Trasportata" sequence (1930) and later included in his *An Early Martyr* (1935), poses the question "Good Christ what is / a poet—if any / exists?" then answers:

a man
whose words will
bite
their way
home—being actual
having the form
of motion[16]

Here Williams experiments with typographic simulations of motion, as Ammons does most adventurously in "Corsons Inlet." Both poets attempt to bring their printed words and lines as close to forms of motion as they can in the frozen world of the typesetter.

In *Sphere*, however, words and lines do not simulate motion. In fact, they do the opposite, simulating the completed, external forms of tercets, four to a numbered section, of lines the length of Blake's fourteeners. One reader has even suggested that *Sphere* is metrical, its lines organized by a seven-stress accentual norm.[17] But the norm is actually typographic, the five, six, seven, or more major stresses merely reflecting the accentual nature of English in long lines; and yet other consciously manipulated structures give the verse of *Sphere* a dense auditory texture:

this measure, maw, can grind
up cancers and flourish scarfs of dandelions, manage the
pulp of hung ticks and be the log the stream flows against

for a whole year: its mesh can widen to let everything
breeze through except the invisible: it can float the
heaviest-blooded scalding dream and sail it into the high

blue loops of possibility: it can comprise the dull
continuum of the omnium-gatherum, wait and wait, without
the alarm of waiting, getting as much being out of motion

as motion out of being: multiple and embracing, sweet
ingestion, the world bloat, extension pushed to the popped
blossoming of space, the taking of due proportion's scope.

(*S* 28–29)

The engine of this verse is repetition. In *Sphere* Ammons does not say only once something he can say several times, running it instead through permutations of extended qualification, variation, and apposition. This richly self-reflexive passage both describes and exemplifies Ammons's measure. Auditory repetitions bind words and associate meanings. Alliteration, a recurrent device in *Sphere*, links "measure," "maw," "manage," and "mesh," all words that suggest the control and enclosure of form. In other phrases, a thick intertwining of consonants and vowels gives Ammons's language a tautness that belies his casual tone. Examples here are the various incarnations of the phonemes /k/, /ʌ/ ("short" *u*), /ə/, and /m/ in "it can comprise the dull / continuum of the omnium-gatherum" or of /p/, /s/, /bl/ and assorted shadings of sounds represented by the letter *o* in "the world bloat, extension pushed to the popped / blossoming of space, the taking of due proportion's scope."

Parallelism shapes the passage syntactically, as all its finite verbs ("can grind . . . manage," "can widen," "can float," "can comprise") establish the rhythm of anaphora. Unlike Whitman, however, Ammons does not align the beginnings of parallel clauses at the left margin, choosing instead to coil them irregularly around lines and stanzas. Among his short lyrics, "The City Limits," the closing poem of *Briefings* (1971), uses the same technique. Grouped in the same section of *Collected Poems* as "Essay on Poetics" and "Hibernaculum," which also use long-line tercets, "The City Limits," more than any other short poem, foreshadows the technique of *Sphere*. Next, as in "The Ridge Farm," the parallel movement ends in chiasmus, a figure that recurs throughout *Sphere*: "Getting as much being out of motion / as motion out of being." Once again, it cannot be simple coincidence that this figure of confusion appears in a passage about poetic form. One might argue that the neat verbal flourish of chiasmus reflects anything but confusion, since it deftly snaps contraries into a satisfying balance. But this deftness is precisely the point. Chiasmus, as Ammons uses it here, is a trick of language, one that allows him to tie off a rapidly extending, open-ended line of thought, imposing an apparent aphoristic certainty where none can exist. Being and motion, like shape and flow, stasis and change, form and formlessness are remote, conceptually difficult abstractions. They resist reductive formulation, and yet reductive formulation is what chiasmus offers. Chiasmus, in its extreme overstatement, banishes shadings and overlappings. Significantly in this passage, the lines following the chiasmus are about extension and overextension "pushed to the popped / blossoming of space," an image of the formlessness, dissolution, and openness that chiasmus defends against.

Still, what is most remarkable about this passage is not the compulsive gathering of auditory and syntactic patterns into its "maw," but rather its sudden closure. End-stopped sections are rare in *Sphere*. There are only 32 out of 155. Enjambment dominates Ammons's poem. One way to describe *Sphere*, and by extension all those poems, short and long, in which Ammons uses regular stanzas as purely graphic groupings divorced from their auditory origins, is to say that the three-line stanzas and the four-stanza sections are Ammons's tropes of form, shape, and fixity, while enjambment is his trope of motion, flow, flux. The real measure of *Sphere* lies in neither the mere stanza nor the perpetual enjambment but in Ammons's manipulation of the alignment between the two. With only thirty-two of its sections closed, *Sphere* works broadly across intervals of openness and closure.

Through the first eighteen sections, intervals between closed sections are minimal. If a numbered section does not end with a closing colon, then the next one will. Alignment between section and conceptual movement is relatively high. But with section 19 and its gestures toward Emersonianism ("oh, it's spring, and I'm more transparent than ever: / ... my idealism's as thin as the sprinkled / sky and nearly as expansive:"), the intervals between closed sections grow, and conceptual movements begin to expand. For the rest of the poem, Ammons's measure grows out of the rhythm of expansion and contraction, as intervals between closed sections increase and diminish. Most striking and significant is the longest interval in *Sphere*, which falls between the end of section 122 and section 150. In its expansiveness, this interval corresponds to the longest section of "Song of Myself," number 33 in Whitman's death-bed edition. In this section, with its long catalogues, Whitman is afoot with his vision, "speeding through space . . . . speeding through heaven and the stars" (*CP* 63). His expansion includes not only a cosmic vision of our universe but also an empathetic vision of human suffering, which Whitman associates with "walking the old hills of Judea with the beautiful gentle god by my side" (*CP* 62). Not surprisingly, Ammons's interval of expansion also culminates in a view of earth under the aspect of eternity:

> from other planets,
> as with other planets from here, we rise and set, our presence,
> reduced to light, noticeable in the dark when the sun is
>
> away: reduced and distanced into light, our brotherhood
> constituted into shining, our landforms, seas, colors
> subsumed to bright announcement: we are alone in a sea that

> 150
> shows itself nowhere in a falling surf but if it does not
> go on forever folds back into a further motion of itself:
> the plenitude of nothingness! planets seeds in a coronal
>
> weaving so scant the fabric is the cloth of nakedness:
> Pluto our very distant friend skims a gulf so fine and far
> millions and thousands of millions of years mean little to—

how far lost we are, if saving is anywhere else: but light,
from any distance or point we've met it, shines with a similar
summation, margin affirmational, so we can see edges to the

black roils in central radiances, galaxies colliding in
million-year meetings, others sprung loose into spiral
unwindings: fire, cold space, black concentration.

(*S* 77)

This grand passage with its crucial realization, "how far lost we are, if
saving is anywhere else," closes a movement that begins twenty-eight
sections earlier with the introduction of—not coincidentally—Whitman: "I'm just, like Whitman, trying to keep things / half straight about
my country" (*S* 65).

In the course of *Sphere*'s greatest expansive movement, after which its
intervals contract to one of four sections and then the final, self-contained section, Ammons meditates again on measure:

seek the whole measure that is ease
and ramble around without constriction or distortion
(debilitating exclusion) until the big sky opens the freedom

between design and designed airiness.

(*S* 71)

The phrase "the whole measure that is ease" recalls "the rigid line of the
free and easy." Another paradox, it is most fully illuminated by Ammons's earlier *ars poetica*, "Corsons Inlet." There he asserts that he recognizes only "transitions":

by transitions the land falls from grassy dunes to creek
to undercreek: but there are no lines, though
    change in that transition is clear
    as any sharpness: but "sharpness" spread out,
allowed to occur over a wider range
than mental lines can keep.

(*CP* 149)

This description of the natural continuities of an inlet also describes
Ammons's own poetic practice, as in *Sphere* in which form realizes itself
"over a wider range than mental lines can keep," if mental lines are
drawn according to local line-to-line, stanza-to-stanza readings. Because the important patterns in *Sphere* take place across 155 sections, it
is easy to miss them. Only when one reads the poem trying "to fasten
into order enlarging grasps of disorder, widening / scope" (*CP* 151)
does the operation of its form emerge.

2

Although Ammons shares with Williams both the word "measure" and the preoccupation with breaking and making form it signifies, there is also something important the two poets do not share. Whereas one generated reams of critical and theoretical writing intended to explain what he thought he was doing, the other has produced almost none. With the exceptions of the two-page "Note on Prosody" (1963) and the two-page "Inside Out" (1983),[18] Ammons's comments on poetic form outside his poems remain limited to occasional brief notes and remarks in various interviews:

> I've done a good many kinds of experiments, right? Some of them look like purposely regular stanzas and some don't. In some, the indentations correspond from stanza to stanza, the same line by line. But in some of them there is the random. I usually feel that I don't have anything to say of my own until I have tripped the regular world, until I have thrown the Western mind itself somehow off, and I think that's what those—if I began to write a sonnet, for example, I think I would be stultified and silenced by that form, because it's my nature to want to trip that form out of existence as a way of making room for myself to speak and act.[19]

Here Ammons shares with Williams a distrust of the sonnet, although he finds it merely stultifying, whereas Williams, in a characteristic overstatement, calls it "fascistic" (*SE* 236).[20] But while these remarks gesture toward an aesthetic ideology and interest any devoted reader of Ammons, they add relatively little to discussions of form found in his poems. Passages in "Corsons Inlet," *Sphere*, and "The Ridge Farm" do not necessarily deepen or unfold just because one knows Ammons has read Lao-tse and wants to unsettle the Western mind.

More complex are his comments in "A Note on Prosody." First quoting the fourth through eleventh lines of "Close-Up," a poem placed in the 1956–60 section of *Collected Poems* and included in *Expressions of Sea Level* (1964), Ammons explains: "Here the box-like structure of rhymed, measured verse is pretty well shot. The emphasis has shifted from the ends of the lines (see German sentence structure, see the concluding emphasis that rhyme itself imposes) toward the lefthand margin" (202). The shifting of "emphasis" toward the left margin corresponds to enjambment, although Ammons does not use that term. Instead, he turns to figurative elaboration: "What I think is illustrated by so tiny a fragment of verse is that both ends are being played against a middle. The center of gravity is an imaginary point existing between the two points of beginning and end, so that a downward pull is created that gives a certain downward rush to the movement, something like a waterfall glancing in turn off opposite sides of the canyon, something like the right and left turns of a river" (202–3). Finally, having identified "a downward pull" and considered the use of the caesura in traditional couplets, he concludes: "I think the quoted fragment and these thoughts suggest that a non-linear movement is possible which uses both the beginning and the end of the line as glancing-off points, so that the movement is not across the page but actually, centrally down the page" (203).

Several points are significant here. First, the conclusion that "a non-linear movement is possible . . . centrally down the page" is true, as "Close-Up" shows, but that downward movement owes more to the extreme brevity of most of the lines than it does to enjambment. Second, the modesty of wondering whether or not "a few things" in his verse "reflect important little real things that are happening to poetry" (202) is attractive but also misleading. The things he notices in his verse do indeed reflect important little real things that are happening in poetry, since they reflect the technique Williams developed over fifty years and left to contemporary poets as his legacy. Although Bloom is right in arguing that Williams's voice contributes little to Ammons's many mountain fables, he would be wrong if he tried to maintain that Ammons could have given this poem its downward pull without the example of Williams.

But third, and most important, Ammons's discussion of poetic form turns here, as it does throughout his poems, on the figurative use of a natural image, the waterfall. In turning to nature for his emblem, Ammons not only confirms his affinity with Whitman and the post-Emersonian habit of interchanging the natural and the textual, but he also reveals the habit of his poetic imagination that makes the writing of critical pieces like "A Note on Prosody" unnecessary. For Ammons the natural and the textual remain inseparable. Each figures the other completely. One of his poems about a detail in nature is also about itself, not in a crudely allegorical way, in which natural phenomena are reduced to mere signs for poetic processes, but in a richly figurative one that demonstrates how the operations of nature instruct and replicate themselves in the operations of poetic imagination, which in turn informs the perception of nature. In this way, Ammons differs greatly from Williams. Unlike his modernist predecessor, he does not interest himself in trying to argue that the breaking and making of poetic form reflects a shift in scientific paradigms toward Einsteinian relativity, that it demonstrates the linguistic realities of an American idiom, or that it represents a new way of counting and keeping time in verse. Each of these arguments literalizes poetic form in a way that Ammons seeks to avoid. His preoccupation with form derives from an unswerving attention to the way his own mind works, confronting itself and nature. How are perceptions received? How do perceptions inform concepts? How do concepts knit themselves into patterns that influence perception?

For Ammons, then, the word "form" often signifies poetic form and leads him to some image from nature: a log against a stream, the line of a ridge, a waterfall, an inlet. But the word "form" also signifies the abstract structures of cognition. The poem about nature, then, is both about poetic style and about mind. In *Tape for the Turn of the Year* (1965), Ammons describes these interrelating forms:

> I feel ideas—as forms of
> beauty: I describe
>   the form as
> you describe a pear's
> shape:
>   not idea as ideal—
> ideas are human products,
>   temporal & full of
>   process:
>   but
> idea as perception of form,
> outside form that
>   corresponds
> to inner form, & inner to
> outer.[21]

The statement "I feel ideas—as forms of beauty" would seem to point to the Platonic abstraction of form as essence; yet Ammons moves quickly to dissociate himself from Platonism: "not idea as ideal" because "ideas are human products, / temporal & full of / process." Instead, by "idea" he means the recognition and registration by the mind of an external shape or structure in the world ("outside form"), not as an earthly copy of a Platonic essence, but as the natural analogue of mental shape and structure. The chiastic pattern of "outside form that / corresponds / to inner form, & inner to / outer" only relates structures in nature to structures in the mind. A statement of philosophy rather than aesthetics, it tells nothing about the poem. But the self-description emerges earlier with "I describe / the form as / you describe a pear's / shape." In other words, once the correspondence between inner and outer structures registers, the poet attempts to describe that correspondence with the same immediacy and specificity one might use to describe a pear or other concrete physical object.

For Ammons, then, poetic form mediates between abstract mental forms and concrete physical ones. Most of his poems ground themselves in natural physicality to authenticate his abstractions. A good example comes from the first section of "Four Motions for the Pea Vines," the ninth poem in the 1961–65 section of *Collected Poems* and included in *Corsons Inlet*:

> the rhythm is
>   diffusion and concentration:
> in and out:
>   expansion and
> contraction: the unfolding,
>   furling: . . .
>   the rhythm is
>   out and
>   in,
>   diffusion and concentration:
>
>   the dry pea from the
>   ground
>   expands to vines and leaves,
>   harvests sun and water
>   into
>   baby-white new peas:
>
> the forms that exist
> in this rhythm! the whirling
>   forms!
>   grief and glory of
> this rhythm:
> the rhythm is.

(CP 130–31)

The question prompted by the thrice-repeated line "the rhythm is" is "What rhythm?" The rhythm of the pea vines? The poem? The mind? The answer is all three. On one level, the poem sets out to describe the physical motions of pea vines growing: "expansion and / contraction: the unfolding, / furling." But with the word "rhythm," the poem abstracts the repeated motions of the pea vines into figurative status: the rhythm of the pea vines also corresponds to the rhythm of the mind, or a least Ammons's mind. The phrase "diffusion and concentration" accurately describes the way the shapes of his poems represent that mind, as they alternate loose, easy chat with hard compressed formulation. Also, the rhythm "in and out / . . . out and / in" corresponds to Ammons's habit of alternating mental with natural realities. But then there is also the very real way in which the rhythm of the pea vines corresponds not only to the overall poetic shape Ammons gives his meditative pattern but also to the prosodic structure of the verse itself: "the

lines of winding-up, / loosening, depositing, / dissolving: / the vehicles!"
The clearest example of self-description comes when Ammons reverses
"in and out" to "out and / in":

> the rhythm is
> out and
> in,
> diffusion and concentration.

Here the word "in," isolated at an indented left margin, becomes an
image of inwardness and concentration, as it roughly centers itself on
the page.[22] This moment of local self-description corresponds to another a few lines earlier: "light, the vehicle of itself, light / surrounding."
An example of epanalepsis, the longer line becomes an emblem of its
own surroundedness, bounded on either end by the word "light" as we
are surrounded by the natural phenomena of light, "the vehicle of itself." In a larger way, the first section of "Four Motions for the Pea
Vines" is likewise surrounded by the refrain "the rhythm is." The poem
considers, among other things, the "grief and glory" of a rhythm that,
no matter how far it diffuses, expands, and unfolds, is inevitably com-
pelled to circle back on itself, effecting its own confinement.

The three-way identity of natural form, mental form, and poetic form
(meaning both imaginative shape and prosodic structure) cannot help
but suggest the Romantic myth of organicism, particularly the boldly
hyperbolic American versions initiated by Whitman. As Hollander comments on the fulfillment of Emersonian prophecy in "The Poet" by
Leaves of Grass, "Organic form is to be the emblem, then, of the au-
thenticity of the text, although the precise nature of the form is not
made clear." In fact, the imprecise nature of what poetic form has to do
to be considered "organic" harasses many discussions. Is organicism a
condition the poem aspires to in its imaginative movement but not necessarily in its prosody? In its prosody only? In both? Wesling's definition of organic form is helpfully clear and usefully concise: "This, or the
illusion of it, is what the successful poem has when it justifies the arbitrariness of its technique; and what the failed poem lacks, when its technique seems obtrusively imposed. . . . I would define organic form as
convention in its innovative guise."[23] Although Wesling singles out
rhyme to stand for technique and convention, other techniques and conventions also work with this definition.

In Ammons's case, the myth of organicism embodies itself in subtle
and complex ways, although Waggoner is not alone in taking Ammons's organicism at face value: "Ammons, like most of his best contemporaries, has moved all the way toward practicing the theory announced in 'The Poet' and elaborated in 'Poetry and Imagination.'"[24]

But for someone who "has moved all the way" toward practicing Emersonian theory, Ammons has much to say on the subject of artifice and artificiality in poetry, and in his poetry in particular. In *Tape*, for example, he states baldly: "poetry is art & is / artificial: but it / realizes reality's / potentials" (*T* 177–78). In "Extremes and Moderations," he adds:

> everything, they say, is artificial: nature's the
> artwork of the Lord: but your work, city, is aimed unnaturally
> against time: your artifice confronts the Artifice.
>
> (CP 335)

And in "Hibernaculum," he ponders artifice in the context of the promotion of art over nature Oscar Wilde preaches, for example, in his essay "The Decay of Lying" (*CP* 381–82).

Predictably, Ammons's only explicit commentary on organicism comes in the course of a poem, the long "Essay on Poetics," originally published in 1970. The earliest of the longer poems that use the long-line tercet ("Hibernaculum," *Sphere*, and "Summer Place" are the others), "Essay on Poetics" maintains a relentless loyalty to its own stanzaic regularity, even as it interpolates into the midsts of various stanzas three shorter poems, three long quotations from scientific texts, and one column of words. After each of these interruptions, the respective stanzas pick up where they left off, often in the middles of lines. Ostensibly a meditation on the nature of the lyric versus its own longer "linear mode," Ammons's "Essay" at one point reads Williams's dictum "no ideas but in things" into various alternatives: "'No things but in ideas,' / 'no ideas but in ideas,' and 'no things but in things'" (*CP* 308). These revisions of the famous refrain of *Paterson* lead to an extended figuring of different poetic modes in terms of the stages of water flowing, as it goes from snow-melt to brook-rapids, to slow river, and finally to sea:

> genius, and
>
> the greatest poetry, is the sea, settled, contained before the first
> current stirs but implying in its every motion adjustments
> throughout the measure.
>
> (CP 309)

Both the word "measure" and the image of a river running to the sea suggest that the dialogue with Williams and *Paterson* continues throughout this section. Holder contends that here Ammons is pointing up "the inadequacy of William Carlos Williams' famous prescription for the poet."[25] Certainly, Ammons is examining that prescription critically ("one thing / always to keep in mind is that there are a number of possibilities"); yet in the adoption of Williams's image of the river running to the sea, an image that despite his own brooks and falls he does not use often, Ammons may also be making his pact with Williams, who in his own way challenges the organicist label applied to him.

As Henry Sayre has argued convincingly, Williams's "notoriously inadequate explanations of the so-called variable foot are most usefully seen as efforts to defend as organic what through the 1940s and 1950s is more and more evidently a formally mechanical and arbitrary practice."[26] Like Williams, Ammons invents a three-line stanza that is mechanical (in Schlegel's sense of the word), arbitrary, and artificial. But unlike Williams, Ammons does not try to defend that artificiality with a rhetoric of traditional organicism. Instead, the exact opposite is true. He challenges the rhetoric of traditional organicism and flaunts the artificiality of his form. The challenge to organicism, or more precisely, literary organicism, comes near the end of "Essay on Poetics" in a long passage that begins

> the point of change, though,
> brings me to a consideration of the adequacy of the transcendental
> vegetative analogy: the analogy is so appealing, so swept with
>
> conviction, that I hardly ever have the strength to question it.
>
> (CP 315)

In his "consideration of the adequacy of the transcendental / vegetative analogy," Ammons subverts the literary rhetoric of organicism by confronting it with scientific literalism. As this passage argues, it is naive to think that a particular tree realizes itself according to innate individual laws. In fact, what is innate in a particular tree is not its own uniqueness, but quite the opposite, its preordained genetic code, which nature protects against "haphazard change." The uniqueness of a given tree, then, results when its genetic "print-out" is modified from outside by "the bleak periphery of possibility," which includes "variables of weather, soil, etc."

Ammons's revised organicism has important implications for his poetics. If a tree develops according to a code that is genetically preordained and a given tree varies only according to local external modifications, then a truly organic poem is one that figuratively does the same. A truly organic poem reflects both the predetermination of structures it cannot change and the local variation of those structures where other conditions modify them. In Wesling's terms, Ammons's poem justifies the arbitrariness of its stanzaic regularity by letting that arbitrariness stand for predetermination, the poetic analogue of a locked-in genetic code. Each stanza is a printout of the predetermined pattern; and yet, like a given tree, a given stanza varies according to local effects—effects, in its case, of syntax, diction, rhythm, enjambment, and typography. Ammons multiplies organic analogies by quoting passages of prose, as Williams does in *Paterson*. One passage celebrates "a good worm" that has "developed segmentation or reduplication of parts, permitting increase in size with completely coordinated function," an apt self-description of "Essay on Poetics." Another passage describes "the molecular bricks out of which living matter is made," adding that "a mere random pile of such bricks does not make a living structure, any more than a mere pile of real bricks makes a house" (*CP* 314). By analogy, this statement also describes Ammons's own poem, as its stanzas are the brick-shaped blocks that attempt to build a living structure instead of a mere pile.

"Essay on Poetics" provides a key to Ammons's formal intentions, especially in those poems that seem at first to organize themselves arbitrarily around regular typographic patterns, such as stanzas or indentations. In those poems, short and long, arbitrary regularity is the artifice by means of which Ammons, as he explains in *Tape*, "realizes reality's / potentials." Although what nature predetermines for a white oak evolves through a series of favorable mutations, and so is not arbitrary in the way the selection of a stanza shape may be arbitrary, the stanza shape nevertheless represents the given, whether it be the organic given of a genetic pattern, the mental given of binary concepts, the linguistic given of modern American English, or the literary given of poetic tradition. One does not invent these; one inherits them. When Ammons closes "Hibernaculum" with the outrageously flippant stanza

> I'm reading Xenophon's *Oeconomicus* "with
> considerable pleasure and enlightenment" and with
> appreciation that saying so fills this stanza nicely.
>
> (*CP* 388)

he tweaks the noses of both the traditional formalist for whom the stanza is necessarily a metrical and auditory reality, never merely a typographic one, and the naive organicist who believes that a poem should never compromise content to fulfill the demands of a predetermined form. But beneath the humor lies more serious meaning. Disciple of Socrates, military leader, and historian, Xenophon presides over the close of "Hibernaculum" as a representative of the accumulated weight of a philosophical, historical, and literary past. His *Oeconomicus*, undoubtedly a model for the chapter "Economy" in Thoreau's *Walden*, casts Socrates in a dialogue on household management and married life, two subjects the domestically hibernating Ammons contemplates in

"Hibernaculum" and elsewhere. In its casual way, Ammons's final stanza is about demands and expectations generated by the past, demands and expectations he did not create but still must meet. These exert a pressure on him that shapes his utterances.

"Extremes and Moderations," which falls between "Essay on Poetics" and "Hibernaculum" in the 1966–71 section of *Collected Poems*, opens and closes with remarks on its own four-line stanza, unique among Ammons's longer poems. The introduction of the stanza again recalls Wesling's formulation that successful organicism involves the justification of arbitrary technique:

> constructing the stanza is not in my case exceedingly
> difficult, variably invariable, permitting maximum change
> within maximum stability, the flow-breaking four-liner, lattice
>
> of the satisfactory fall, grid seepage, currents distracted
> to side flow, multiple laterals that at some extreme spill
> a shelf, ease back, hit the jolt of the central impulse.
>
> (CP 329)

The admission that the construction of stanzas "is not in my case exceedingly difficult" anticipates the end of "Hibernaculum" in its unabashed acknowledgment of an artificiality that neither the traditional formalist nor the naive organicist could justify. Meanwhile, the description of the stanza as "variably invariable" continues the argument from "Essay on Poetics," abstracting it from the realm of white oaks and genetic printouts, yet preserving the conjunction of general predetermination with specific modification. Although "variably invariable" takes the rhetorical shape of oxymoron, Ammons's version of organicism demonstrates the necessary congruity of the variable and invariable. Images of water flowing through the stanza, "the flowbreaking four-liner, lattice / of the satisfactory fall, grid seepage, currents distracted / to side flow," prefigure images of form in *Sphere*. In both poems, Ammons's images of flowing water recall the etymological meaning of *rhythm* (Greek *rhein*: to flow), while his images of the stanza as "lattice," "grid," "log the stream flows against," and "mesh" describe the phenomenology of verse structure in new terms. Etymologically, a *stanza* is a stopping place, a place to stand. The word suggests a phenomenology of writing and reading that involves a series of stops between which one crosses white space or silence to get to the next stop. More recently in poetic tradition, occasional enjambment between stanzas may vary the stop-and-go pattern; yet such enjambment remains exceptional in most verse and should remain exceptional, according to those, such as Paul Fussell, who place high value on stanzaic integrity.[27] The stanzaic repetition of stops and starts reflects the origin of stanzas in the strophic divisions of song, divisions that allow a singer to sing new verses to a recycled tune.[28] As verse becomes more removed from its historical origins in song, structures that originated as auditory modes become increasingly visual. In Ammons's stanzas the removal from auditory origins is complete, his various images of the stanza implying a different model for writing and reading. Instead of a phenomenology of stopping and going, his stanzas generate one of speeding and slowing. If going ever stops, it stops only partially with a colon, and even then, as *Sphere* demonstrates, it stops much less than it continues.

The speeding and slowing of perpetual going, the presentation of some resistance or channel that flow must overcome or follow, revises another Romantic metaphor, that of the Aeolian harp. Although that image runs on wind and Ammons's on water, they share the fiction of an essential passivity. For Shelley in "Ode to the West Wind," the desire for inspiration leads to the petition "make me thy lyre," while for Coleridge in "The Eolian Harp," the image leads him to ask whether "all of animated nature," himself included, "be but organic Harps diversely fram'd" over which "sweeps / Plastic and vast, one intellectual breeze, / At once the Soul of each, and God of all?"

At the close of "Extremes and Moderations," written about the time that, as Bloom points out, "the motions of water . . . replaced the earlier guiding movements of wind" in Ammons's poetry,[29] the Romantic metaphor surfaces in final remarks on the stanza:

> it's Sunday
>
> morning accounts for such preachments, exhortations, and
> solemnities: the cumulative vent of our primal energies is now and
> always has been sufficient to blow us up: I have my ventilator
> here, my interminable stanza, my lattice work that lets the world
>
> breeze unobstructed through: we could use more such harmless
> devices.
>
> (*CP* 340–41)

Punning on the Latin for wind (*ventus*), Ammons describes his ventilating stanza as both a device for passively letting the world breeze through and for venting his prophetic anger over human uses and abuses of nature. Whether he describes the stanza in terms of wind or water, it remains his typographic version of the Romantic harp. In each case, the image of sweeping over or breezing through functions to naturalize poetic artifice. If the poetic imagination simply presents itself in the form of a harp or stanza to be acted upon by a wind or a stream, then that imagination cannot be held responsible for what results. The burden of structuring the poem shifts away from the poet, so that, at least in Ammons's case, he escapes having to account fully for his form. Whereas Ammons's revision of organicism allows him to justify arbitrariness by redefining "organic" in terms of scientific literalism, his version of the Aeolian harp allows him to do so by trivializing his own role as maker of "harmless / devices."

Nowhere in Ammons's work have issues of form and formlessness, arbitrariness and organicism, poet as artificer and poet as innocent bystander caused more disagreement and more misunderstanding than in *The Snow Poems* (1977). Waggoner pronounces the volume "a thick book of dull, tired poems that prompt us to wonder, does Ammons write too much?"[30] *The Snow Poems* appeared too late for consideration by Holder, which is unfortunate, since the ways in which his judgments differ from Waggoner's represent a larger critical disagreement over Ammons's work.[31] Amidst a swirl of negative reviews, such as Hayden Carruth's ("a dull, dull book"),[32] Bloom has remained determinedly silent, while Helen Vendler has given the book limited but sympathetic attention: "Ammons has delineated that landscape and that climate [of Ithaca, New York] for good and all, with an Emersonian wintriness of voice diluting the ebullience he inherited from Williams."[33]

But most interesting is the welcome reappraisal of *The Snow Poems* made by Michael McFee after the appearance of *A Coast of Trees* signaled Ammons's return to the short lyric. Arguing against what he calls the "popular critical pacifier, as manufactured by Bloom and others, . . . that Ammons had come into the world to fulfill the Romantic Transcendental heritage, to realize the promise of Organic Form," McFee makes two significant points. The first is that "as Ammons became more prominent, the form of his poetry became more conservative, taking on a more orderly and regular appearance." The second is that "the heart of *The Snow Poems*" is "Ammons's deep anti-formalism."[34] Both points raise important questions that need further consideration.

The argument that Ammons's form becomes more conservative as it takes on the orderly and regular appearance of uniform stanzas has two problems. The first is that it reduces poetic form to mere format, or the typographic shape of a poem on the page. Williams often veered dangerously close to the same error, sometimes even committing it, but Ammons never does. For Ammons, "form" is far too large and suggestive a term to let itself be contained within the boundaries of a stanza shape. Any account of his poetic forms must also reckon with rich phonemic configurations, syntactic patterns, rhetorical figures, and occasional metricality, as well as with the larger contours of his characteristic meditative habits. The second problem is that the term "conservative" does not accurately describe what appears to be Ammons's devoted guardianship of the traditional stanza. In Ammons's hands, the stanza format is an instrument of humor, parody, playfulness, figuration, self-description, and poetic revision. The irreverent liberties he takes with his stanzas should disabuse his readers of any notion that his growing fame has caused him to think twice about formal experimentalism. As Ammons's more recent work has shown, especially "The Ridge Farm," he can take or leave the stanza with no trouble at all.

But the second point, that the heart of *The Snow Poems* is a deep antiformalism, leads to a larger debate about Ammons's work. To support his contention, McFee quotes part of the poem "One at One with His Desire":

> this stanza compels
> its way along: a
> break will humble it:
>
> form consumes:
> form eliminates:
> form forms the form
> that extracts of the elixir from
> the passage of change:
> well, we mustn't let this
> form reverse itself
> into an opposite
> though parallel
> largely similar insistence:
> must we?
>
> (SP 169)

McFee then concludes that Ammons "endorses the 'hellish paradise' susceptible to shit and wind change, not the artificial order of a stanza." Yes, a break will humble the stanzaic compulsion to repeat and rescue Ammons from the fear of overbearing form he expresses in "The Ridge Farm." But the subsequent lines about form consuming, eliminating, and extracting do not necessarily mean only that form constructs "inflexible structures which drain the elixir vitae of motion."[35] The sequence of consumption, elimination, and extraction also suggests the digestive processes of an organism. In other words, although form may threaten to assume an autonomy of its own, and so must be humbled if creator is to retain control over creation, still that form does have a life of its own. In fact, "the form / that extracts of the elixir from / the passages of change" performs a kind of alchemy, as it rescues from the rush of impermanence and dissolution a precious essence that remains. When this passage joins with a long one preceding it, the full complexity and pathos of Ammons's ambivalence toward his stanza, and toward abstractions of form it represents, emerges:

> art's
> nonbeing's
>
> dark consolation:
> what a nice stanza! imagine just going
> on: I think I've invented
>   rooms to walk through
>   or stand amazed
>   or lie sleepy in:
> it is no place, though,
> to rehearse the flesh
> of the beloved,
>   it is no place to touch
>   or taste
>   enter or leave:
>
> it is dry delight, whatever
> service remains when
> the church closes:
>   the sweepstakes of
>   no desire
>   whole as fulfillment:
> the sweetest passer of time
> scheduled for emptiness:
> the drug that makes erasure
>   bliss: an illusion some
>   of the uneasy can cover
>   misery with:
>
> still when you think of the
> nourishment of such delight as
> over starvation,
>   what a numb pale
>   paradise! how constant
>   the music
> dwelling among the constant
> bushes, the deathlessness only
> lifelessness can know
>   one not at one with his
>   desire still has to desire
>   so much more than nothing.

(SP 168–69)

This is not the voice of one who hates form. Instead, it is the deep, moving confession of a man who realizes that he finds himself shut out from rooms where life goes on immediately and unconsciously, shut out from the places where his desire can be fulfilled. As a result, the rooms that stanzas build, and the poems for which they stand as synecdoches, provide the only places for him to dwell. He is fully, radically disillusioned about the "numb pale / paradise!" form encloses, its druglike power that makes erasure bliss, or the misery "the uneasy" use it to cover. This last phrase recalls the "uneasy pleasures" Ammons identifies in the passage about sonnets and free verse in "The Ridge Farm." But he sees no alternative. Life may be preferable to form, but form is the dark consolation of lifelessness. Against the background of these stark choices, the familiar figure of epanalepsis, "desire still has to desire," looms with uncanny power. Like the line below it, "form forms the form," in which repetition threatens to hollow "form" of its substance and meaning, this self-enclosed, self-mirroring line figures both the entrapment of desire and the poetic self-consciousness that gives desire form, if not fulfillment. Ammons gives the repetition of *desire* a twist, as he uses the word first as a noun and second as an infinitive, binding a state or condition to the process that generates it. These nuances may not be much, but they are so much more than nothing.

3

If stanzas, form, and poetry amount to a dark consolation for Ammons's sense of exclusion, that sense of exclusion also has its national dimension. When it comes to America, there are two Ammonses. The first, more familiar to readers who know his work primarily through anthologized selections, appears to be a man without, or beyond, a country. In his compressed fables or his careful annotations of natural phenomena, the operations of history, the pressures of politics, and the awareness of actual America play almost no part. This apparent reticence about, or repression of, America and Americanism associates Ammons with Dickinson and Bishop, or at least with the versions of Dickinson and Bishop that have emerged in much critical writing about their work. But if one comes away from a narrow sampling of Ammons's work with the sense that he has denied, escaped, or transcended nationality, the anthologizers are not entirely to blame, for, as the three editions of his *Selected Poems* make clear, Ammons has chosen to turn this side of himself to the light.[36]

Meanwhile, another Ammons lives in the longer poems, especially in poems that are out of print (*Sphere*) or uncollected ("Summer Place" [1977]). This Ammons explicitly identifies himself with America, alter-

natingly celebrating and scolding his country in ways that associate him
more with Whitman and Pound than with Dickinson and Bishop. This
duality in Ammons's work mediates between extremes in both contemporary American poetry and contemporary American criticism. It also
corresponds to a duality in Ammons's formalism, which mediates between the prescriptive fictions of poets like Whitman or Pound and the
more internalized fictions of poets like Dickinson or Bishop.

In *Sphere* Ammons considers the nature of his own Americanism in
the self-justifying tone of an *apologia* responding to his readers:

> I can't understand my readers:
> they complain of my abstractions as if the United States of America
> were a form of vanity: they ask why I'm so big on the
>
> one:many problem, they never saw one: my readers: what do they
> expect from a man born and raised in a country whose motto is *E*
> *pluribus unum*: I'm just, like Whitman, trying to keep things
>
> half straight about my country: my readers say, what's all
> this change and continuity: when we have a two-party system,
> one party devoted to reform and the other to consolidation:
>
> 123
> and both trying to grab a chunk out of the middle: either we
> reconcile opposites or we suspend half the country into
> disaffection and alienation: they want to know, what do I
>
> mean *quadrants*, when we have a Southeast, Northeast, Southwest,
> and Northwest and those cut into pairs by the splitting
> Mississippi and the Mason-Dixon line: I figure I'm the exact
>
> poet of the concrete *par excellence*, as Whitman might say:
> they ask me, my readers, when I'm going to go politicized or
> radicalized or public when I've sat here for years singing
>
> unattended the off-songs of the territories and the midland
> coordinates of Cleveland or Cincinnati.
>
> (*S* 65)

In its assertion of nationality and its association of aesthetic ideology
with political ideology, this passage foreshadows the dedication of *The
Snow Poems*, published three years after *Sphere*: "for my country." On
one level, Ammons is fooling around here, easing his sense of isolation
by staging a debate between himself and an imagined readership. That
the debate represents a piece of ventriloquism becomes apparent when
he admits that he has been "for years singing / unattended the off-songs
of the territories." If he is truly unattended, then he has no readers, a

possibility he considers a few lines later: "My readers are baffling and / uncommunicative (if actual)" (*S* 65).

But on another level, the debate is a profoundly serious one, for it amounts to a psychomachia between two sides of Ammons's consciousness. One side tells him that his poems have national significance and political implications; the other side, displaced onto his imagined readers, taunts him with evading social and political responsibilities. Parts of *Sphere* were published in 1973, the year the United States formally committed itself to removal from Vietnam, and the entire poem appeared in 1974, amidst the Watergate hearings and the resignation of Richard Nixon. Against this background, the lines "they ask me, my readers, when I'm going to go politicized or / radicalized or public" suggest a troublesome anxiety on Ammons's part, one that recalls the experience of many American writers during the thirties, when a public political commitment appeared both appropriate and fashionable.

Ammons negotiates his way out of this impasse by allegorizing his own aesthetics in political terms and by appealing to Whitman, who often does the same. The "one:many problem," the cornerstone of Ammons's ontological musings, aligns itself with the American motto "*E / pluribus unum*," an enjambment that frames the Latin words for "many" and "one" at the same time that it disrupts the continuity Ammons is asserting. Meanwhile, the passage maps the principles of change and continuity, by means of which Ammons habitually reconciles the impermanence of physical phenomena with his own religious impulse toward what he names the Most High throughout *Sphere*, onto the American political system, identifying the former with the Democratic party and the latter with the Republican. This last strategy recalls the description of the two-party system in Emerson's "Politics" (1844): "Of the two great parties which at this hour almost share the nation between them, I should say that one has the best cause, and the other contains the best men" (*W* 3:209). In its historical context, Emerson's oversimplification allows him both to affirm the reformist impulses he associates with the Democratic party and to distance himself from the "destructive and aimless" radicalism he associates with Jacksonianism and its aftermath (*W* 3:210). Like Emerson's, Ammons's formulation effectively neutralizes the differences between the two parties by presenting them as necessary complements of one another.

Whitman provides Ammons with an alternative to what he sees as the limitations of commitment and partisanship (although, particularly in his early career, Whitman was a staunchly loyal Jacksonian Democrat). Admittedly, Ammons's presentation of Whitman in *Sphere* is not without its ironies and implicit criticisms. The statement "I figure I'm the exact poet of the concrete *par excellence*, as Whitman might say" pokes fun at Whitman's penchant for Gallicisms such as embouchure, en masse, and ensemble, while a subsequent mock-exhortation, "O comrades! of the / seemly seeming" (*S* 67), parodies Whitman's compulsive apostrophizing. Furthermore, in an ambiguous moment, Ammons claims, "I want, like Whitman, to found / a federation of loveship, not of queers but of poets, where / there's a difference" (*S* 66), affirming Whitman's vision of a nation welded by adhesiveness but also qualifying that affirmation in language some might reject.

Nevertheless, Whitman's example provides the precedent Ammons needs, as it shuttles him between potentially divisive oppositions: oppositions between parties, oppositions between the politically committed and uncommitted, and oppositions between those in power and those suspended in "disaffection and alienation." This last group, the disaffected and alienated, Ammons, like Whitman, is particularly anxious to incorporate into his vision of America, for the existence of disaffection and alienation threatens to subvert his dream of national balance and inclusiveness, represented here in terms of the fourfold symmetry of American geography. Another of the conceptual pairings Ammons establishes early in *Sphere* is that of center and periphery (*S* 12), and it serves him in this context, along with those of one-many and change-continuity: "When I identify my self, my work, and my country, you may / think I've finally got the grandeurs: but to test the center / you have to go all the way both ways" (*S* 66). On the periphery, figured geographically as the "territories" (a Whitmanian archaism for a poet in the late twentieth century), are the disaffected and alienated; if Ammons can link them to the center, as Whitman attempts to link a prostitute with a president, he can identify himself with America in good conscience and, he hopes, without a debilitating egotism.

But disaffection and alienation prove to be more difficult for Ammons than the passage from *Sphere* suggests. In "Summer Place," first published in the *Hudson Review* in the summer of 1977, he looks back at *Sphere*, "my last fallacy of imitative form, my book on / roundness," and admits that it "disappointed me some (oh, yes, it did)."[37] Ammons's disappointment in the earlier poem, which won him the Bollingen Prize and which "a lot of people have / bought . . . reading it or not" (*SPl* 173), arises from his wanting to write a poem "standing recalcitrant in its own nasty massiveness, / bowing to no one, nonpatronizing and ungrateful" (*SPl* 173). Although one might question Ammons's disappointment in *Sphere*, he is right; it is not a recalcitrant, nasty, massive, unbowed, nonpatronizing, and ungrateful poem. But in a passage that Ammons is echoing here at the opening of "Summer Place," *Sphere* contemplates such a poem:

>   I don't know about you,
> but I'm sick of good poems, all those little rondures
> splendidly brought off, painted gourds on a shelf: give me
>
> the dumb, debilitated, nasty, and massive, if that's the
> alternative: touch the universe anywhere you touch it
> everywhere.
>
>   (S 72)

This passage, published in 1974, prophesies the changes to come in the writing of 1975–76. According to internal evidence, Ammons composed "Summer Place" between July 4 and July 21, 1975, on the New Jersey coast near Corsons Inlet. The poem did not appear, however, until two years later, by which time Ammons had also composed and published *The Snow Poems*, which follows "Summer Place" in the order of composition but precedes it in the order of publication.

Although in many ways *The Snow Poems* fulfills Ammons's vision of a nasty and massive poem, one from which both he and his critics appear subsequently to have retreated, "Summer Place" represents the transition between the neat tercets of *Sphere* and the nastiness of *The Snow Poems*. It embodies Ammons's urge to write "a / complaining poem" and "a big gritty poem that would just stand / there and spit" (*SPl* 174). Of course, Ammons realizes that "nothing turns people off like complaining, they get / enough of it doing their own" (*SPl* 174), a realization that may explain his decision not to include "Summer Place" in any of his subsequent volumes, including *Selected Longer Poems* (1980), which contains a chronological list of Ammons's longer poems revealing that "Summer Place," although about the same length as "Hibernaculum," is the one long poem under book-length he chose to omit.[38]

Both "Summer Place" and *The Snow Poems* come out of a difficult period in Ammons's career, one during which he seems to have been struggling with the ambiguous aspects of his success as a poet (the Bollingen Prize was preceded in 1973 by a National Book Award for *Complete Poems*). "Summer Place" contains numerous complaints about the chores and burdens of being famous in America, or at least famous among American poets: the letters of recommendation to be written, the manuscripts sent by unknown poets hoping for encouragement and advice, the appeal from a bookstore owner in Arkansas who wants Ammons to sign a stack of bookplates to help move her stock, a review that compares him unfavorably with Stevens. It also contains many statements about how meager and qualified the rewards for poetic fame and power are compared to other kinds of fame and power in America:

> thank goodness, I'm the very
> peakstone of something, a mt [mountain], though I don't know how high
>
> it is: it is not as high as General Motors or even
> Anaconda Copper or Kennecott: it's about as high as
> up to here: anyhow, I'm sitting on it: it feels good:
>
> bowling champions make twelve times as much as poetry
> champions: pool sharks about ten: tennis, fifty, etc:
> poetry is a range of ridges which, however, rises.
>
> (*SPl* 185)

In addition to these complaints about money and the uncharacteristic references to corporate America, "Summer Place" contains many complaints about desire and the paucity of opportunities for satisfying it, complaints that fill the poem with the same kind of erotic bitterness Stevens wrestles with in "Notes toward a Supreme Fiction."

Although the complaint is an ancient and venerable subcategory of poetry, many readers, as Ammons apparently realized, may have limited patience with the griping of a forty-nine-year-old man who only a few years after the publication of "Summer Place" became one of the first recipients of the lucrative MacArthur Fellowships. But to read "Summer Place" as nothing more than the venting of crankiness is to miss its larger ambitions:

> I guess I
> should forget the grandiose, and all distant approaches
> to it, and just say how I feel: well, I feel lousy:
>
> I feel lousy, though, mainly because I can't get through
> to do anything good for my country: it matters how
> your relations with your wife are holding up, how great a
>
> father you are, whether you're making progress with
> the oedipal situation or learning how to mosey with
> your peers: but the local effect does not suffice:
>
> profound emotions of allegiance and patriotism (the most
> profoundly selfless emotion, probably) are with us,
> if not now much in the wear.
>
> (*SPl* 197)

Not only a personal complaint, "Summer Place" is also an American jeremiad. Begun on the fourth of July, the poem meditates on America not, as in *Sphere*, from the perspective of one who identifies himself with his country, but rather from the perspective of one who finds himself, in spite of his successes, among the disaffected and alienated. In fact, if anything, his successes irritate Ammons, for instead of bringing him the influence and power necessary to improve his country, they merely confirm his own social and political impotence:

> what *is* it I want to do for my country: I mean, as a
> poet: that is, if I could get anybody to read the
> stuff: as if reading about something would make it come
>
> true: that is, if I could come up with something worth
> coming true: Dean Martin has more effect on this
> country in a minute than I have in a lifetime.
>
> (*SPI* 196)

But Ammons does not limit his criticism of America to resenting that the country does not listen to its famous poets. Instead, he embarks on the more ambitious project of describing why the America he loves "is hardly / in prevalent view":

>   yesterday
> was Independence Day: someday we will have to call a
>
> Day Interdependence Day: neither sincere nor serious,
> I hesitate to engage anything above the level of a
> broken bottle for fear of being, in a free state,
>
> misunderstood or investigated: questioned closely, I
> would have to admit that the America I love is hardly
> in prevalent view so it must be somewhere hiding around
>
> weeds, fencerows, windowboxes, railsidings, and abandoned
> roads.
>
> (*SPI* 184)

The distinction between independence and interdependence recalls Ammons's pairing of the one and the many. Independence guarantees the individual's right to life, liberty, and the pursuit of happiness, whereas interdependence entails the recognition that each individual's independence qualifies and compromises the independence of all other individuals. Appropriately, Ammons sets his meditation on interdependence not in the isolated natural scenes most of his readers will associate with him but rather in the hot, crowded, noisy streets of Ocean City, New Jersey, a locus of American democracy at its most vivid and concrete.

In formulating a distinction between independence and interdependence, and in arguing that the former without the latter is incomplete, Ammons restates Whitman's version of what he calls in a late note "An American Problem" (*Specimen Days and Collect* [1882]):

One of the problems presented in America these times is, how to combine one's duty and policy as a member of associations, societies, brotherhoods or what not, and one's obligations to the State and Nation, with essential freedom as an individual personality, without which freedom a man cannot grow or expand, or be full, modern, heroic, democratic, American. With all the necessities and benefits of association, (and the world cannot get along without it,) the true nobility and satisfaction of a man consist in his thinking and acting for himself. The problem, I say, is to combine the two, so as not to ignore either. (*PW* 2:540)

It is no less a problem for Ammons in the 1970s than for Whitman in the 1870s, and in coming to understand that the America he loves, an America that acknowledges interdependence as much as independence, is not in prevalent view because it has been pushed toward a peripheral realm of weeds and abandoned roads, the later poet retraces a pattern inscribed by the earlier.

Ammons may be thinking of Whitman's dismissal from the Bureau of Indian Affairs by Secretary of the Interior James Harlan (1865), as of Pound's indictment for treason (1943) or Williams's investigation by the Civil Service Commission, the Federal Bureau of Investigation, and the Library of Congress Loyalty Board (1952–53), when he admits the "fear of being, in a free state, / misunderstood or investigated." Nevertheless, despite disclaimers such as "neither sincere nor serious," "my pure country trash platitudes" (*SPl* 193), and "my trouble as a propagandist" (*SPl* 194), he proceeds to engage a good deal "above the level of a / broken bottle," this last image recalling the broken bottle of Williams's short poem "Between Walls" (1938).

Specifically, Ammons identifies himself with the American periphery, claiming that on the beach surrounded "by all the bathing beauties and bathing boys, / and by the older folks in good houses, . . . I feel like / a bit of country trash" (*SPl* 181). After a trip to the local "library to / look up *trash* in the unabridged . . . / . . . including the *white*" (*SPl* 191), he moves beyond his own rural North Carolina origins and expands his feelings of trashiness into a larger vision of the disaffected and alienated in America:

> take the old geezers and other rest-home spindly drifts of
> flesh: now, that's *trash*: or how about all
> the mentally retarded or disturbed children or old folks:
>
> lesbians and queers of all varieties: migrant workers,
> not getting anywhere: strung-out guitar pickers at
> hopeless junction so and so: aging hookers and johns who
>
> helped with the tide: retired persons: little old
> ladies floated up in Florida, no husband, no home
> no children who want them, and not enough to eat:

we should call this The Republic of Barrels of Trash: we could
now be entering the bicentennial year of The United States of
Barreling Trash: "pretty soon the people on welfare gone

be richer than working people": The United States of
Shining Garbage from Sea to Greasy Sea: the litter
glitter: all that remains of free enterprise is if

you fail you deserve it: the land of the hopeless case:
the land of the biggest lobby: we know what is right:
when are we going to make it right.

(SPI 192–93)

Many of the figures in Ammons's grim catalogue appear at various
points in Whitman's poetic inventories and prose memoranda, but nowhere in Whitman's *Leaves of Grass* (1891–92) or *Complete Prose
Works* (1892) are they concentrated into such an unmitigated vision of
American social and economic failure. This is the nadir of Ammons's
meditation on interdependence, and it contrasts sharply with the passage about America in *Sphere*. "Summer Place" attempts to modulate
the harshness of this vision by adopting the optative mood ("we need to
sustain the / fallen and extend opportunity to the fallen who can / rise"
[*SPI* 193]), but the poem has arrived at a verdict which it cannot unsay:
"it is not a great country that grinds along on / the spills and breakage
of the weak" (*SPI* 193).

Whether or not Ammons will return to such direct scrutinies of
America remains to be seen, but for the moment he has shifted away
from them toward more familiar apolitical ground.[39] This shifting has
met with considerable approval (*A Coast of Trees* won the 1981 National Book Critics Circle Award for Poetry), approval that, in its contrast to the reception of *The Snow Poems*, may keep Ammons away
from the long complaint or jeremiad. Still, America may not have van-
ished entirely from his poems, as this poem from *Sumerian Vistas*
(1987) suggests:

> Another day promised for forty
> come and gone, and we're
> still below freezing: but, at least,
> the trees heavy with ice, it's
> been calm: now, the gray deep
> afternoon is turning windy, and
>
> the thicket snaps like a fire,
> ice creaking and jamming but
> holding, an occasional splinter

at a crack flicking free:
another night enameled ghostly!
yesterday afternoon the sun broke

out late and the trees, perpendicular
to the light, lit up strict white
ice-lights at the fractures: tiny
stirs winked some: others held, red, blue
glows, water-clear: tonight, we
have nothing to go on but continuance.

(SV 61)

This poem reads like so many of Ammons's observations of natural phenomena, which begin in literal description of the mundane, detach themselves into figurative possibility or parable, and conclude with a statement that is at once banal and prophetic. After the deliberately flattened weather summary, the shimmering into metaphor begins with the enjambment "the gray deep / afternoon," which renders "deep" momentarily nominal and throws the poem toward a vast, wintry abyss that is at once physical and metaphysical, external and internal. The second stanza unleashes a wind as an agent of apocalyptic violence, both destructive and liberating, and the third follows with a sudden illumination, or rather the memory of sudden illumination, that ignites the depressingly gray deep and constitutes the kind of intermittent epiphany that, the poem suggests, rewards and justifies the grim stoicism of the final lines.

But then there remains the matter of the titling, both of poem and of volume. Ammons titles this poem "20 January," a title that pushes the poem toward the mode of the poetic journal and recalls his *Tape for the Turn of the Year* (1965), which begins with "6 Dec:" and ends two hundred pages later with "10 Jan:." Ammons's use of a date as title here may simply represent an intention to associate the later poem with its earlier precedents. But "20 January" is the only date-title in *Sumerian Vistas* or in any of the four books following *The Snow Poems*, which contains a poem called "It's April I." Furthermore, since the Twentieth Amendment to the Constitution was ratified in 1933, the twentieth of January has become a fixture of the American political calendar: "The terms of the President and Vice President shall end at noon on the 20th day of January . . . and the terms of their successors shall then begin." Both January 20 and July 4 mark inaugurations, but the latter marks an inauguration of political change, whereas the former marks an inauguration contained within political continuity.

In this context, Ammons's nature poem, and its final statement "Tonight, we / have nothing to go on but continuance," gather new meaning. Other details in the poem hint at the national resonances of "20 January." First, Ammons's use of "we," rather than the far more prevalent "I," involves a wider community and acknowledges if not interdependence, at least interrelatedness. Second, like Whitman, Dickinson, Pound, and Bishop, Ammons narrows that interrelatedness to a community that has special associations with the colors red, white, and blue, all three of which are hung out at the ends of lines in the third stanza, associating them typographically with "we" and "continuance."

As a political fable, "20 January" moves toward a middle ground somewhere between the positive vision of *Sphere* and the negative vision of "Summer Place." Although Ammons may have written the poem long before its book publication, the timing of its appearance in print would link it to either, or both, of the inaugurations in 1981 and 1985. The phrase "the gray deep / afternoon" recalls the commencement of the new presidential term at noon on January 20 at the same time that it suggests a metaphor for America in the eighties. The violent imagery of the second stanza doubles as both a prophecy of and a wish for radical change. The remembered illumination of the third stanza, and the implicit wait for its return, fulfills Ammons's statement in "Summer Place" that "if one cannot improve things, one must improve one's / view of things" (*SPl* 200). Somewhere between the confidence of *Sphere* and the despair of "Summer Place," Ammons realizes that the only chance for either improvement or an improved view of the unimproving lies in simple continuation.

The act of viewing is implicit in the title *Sumerian Vistas*, which returns Ammons to his earliest poems, several of which are set in Sumer, an ancient country of Mesopotamia.[40] The remoteness in time and place of Sumerian culture would appear to distance Ammons from the actual America of the late twentieth century, as it does distance him in the early Sumerian poems; yet the title of his volume inevitably recalls Whitman's *Democratic Vistas* and intimates that by way of Sumer Ammons may be taking the long view of his own time and place. In any event, "20 January" also has Whitmanian resonance, as it recalls "November 8, '76," the only note of *Specimen Days* that takes the date of a particular day as its title: "The forenoon leaden and cloudy, not cold or wet, but indicating both. As I hobble down here and sit by the silent pond, how different from the excitement amid which, in the cities, millions of people are now waiting news of yesterday's Presidential election, or receiving and discussing the result—in this secluded place uncared-for, unknown" (*PW* 1:135). The ambiguity of this passage, which opens with a description of weather similar to that of "20 January," resides in the afterthought following the dash. Is it the natural setting of Timber Creek that is indifferent to the contest between Rutherford B. Hayes and

Samuel Tilden, which led to the disputed Compromise of 1877 and the election of Hayes, or is it Whitman himself? Is Whitman aligning himself with the indifference of nature or contrasting the indifference of nature with his own inescapable interest, an interest without which he would never have written this note?

Either way, Whitman, who despite the notes from Timber Creek is not a nature poet in the same way as Ammons, uses the distinct realms of natural phenomena and American politics much differently from the way Ammons does. To Whitman, they are completely separate; to Ammons, they are images of one another. For this reason, reading "20 January" in a national context does not exclude reading it in a natural one. Furthermore, both the political and the apolitical readings accommodate a third and final reading, one that takes the poem as yet another *ars poetica*. In this context, the key word is "continuance," which pertains simultaneously to the succession of the seasons, the duration of human life, the persistence of actual America, and the perpetually extended movement of Ammons's verse, regulated by the colon, a mark he has made his as Dickinson made the dash hers and Whitman, at least in the 1855 *Leaves of Grass*, made the ellipsis his. Like Ammons's inclusive vista, the colon connects, joins, and splices what at first appear to be separate phenomena, all the while insisting that closure, or the approximation of closure, be suspended until the genuine end.

ENVOI

WHITMAN HAS been dead one hundred years, yet the controversies generated by his writing thrive. When Henry James's 1865 review of *Drum-Taps* described the "melancholy task" of reading that book, charging that the "frequent capitals are the only marks of verse in Mr. Whitman's writing," it established both the terms and the tone of much of the argument to follow.[1] Two recent studies show clearly that the two sides of this argument remain unreconciled, one contending that postmodern verse suffers because of its metrical deficiencies, the other prophesying that postmodern poets who attempt to revive traditional forms will produce verse that is only stagnant and derivative.[2]

In examining a range of poets, poems, and attitudes toward poetic form, I have been attempting to demonstrate the limitations of both these positions, as of the general inclination toward critical side-taking in the debate Whitman left to readers and writers of poetry in America. But in doing so, I have not hoped merely to fill the tepid role of mediator, coaxing recalcitrant disputants to the negotiating table. Readers of American poetry need not aspire to a golden future in which New Formalists and Language Poets stroll arm in arm in poetic comradeship. Although such an image might partially fulfill Whitman's vision of adhesiveness, it does not correspond at all to the temper of American poetry as many have come to know and need it, a temper best described by a very different word, one that Whitman used to sum up not only the Civil War years but also his written reminiscences of those years: convulsiveness.

American poetry without convulsiveness would not be American poetry. To wish for a more tranquil tradition, one in which factions have settled their differences or a particular faction has displaced all others, is to wish American poetry out of existence. But my larger point is that nothing has convulsed, and continues to convulse, American poetry as violently as arguments about poetic form. In a period when many are suspicious of, or hostile to, the adjective "essential," safety lies in using the plural to speak of traditions, modernisms, poetries, even Americas. Nevertheless, a preoccupation with issues of form, style, and technique does not drive only one group of American poets. Whitman, Dickinson, Pound, Bishop, and Ammons are white, but in 1950, the year of Charles Olson's manifesto "Projective Verse," Gwendolyn Brooks published the brief exhortation "Poets Who Are Negroes," which closes with the dictum, "The Negro poet's most urgent duty, at present, is to polish his technique, his way of presenting his truths and his beauties, that these may be more insinuating, and, therefore, more overwhelming."[3] Except for the word "Negro," this statement could have been made by the young Ezra Pound.

But most good poets emphasize technique, not just American ones. The sentence from Brooks follows another that makes exactly this point: "But no real artist is going to be content with offering raw materials." If this statement is true, then how can one argue that a preoccupation with form, style, and technique characterizes American poetry in particular? In modern Greek poetry, for example, the preoccupying, convulsing issue is one of diction, as poets choose between so-called purist and demotic forms. Furthermore, this feature of poetic technique has convulsed more than just Greek poetry. Riots broke out in Athens in 1901 when Alexander Pallis's demotic translation of the New Testament appeared and in 1903 with the presentation in the demotic of the trilogy of Aeschylus.[4] It is hard, if not impossible, to imagine riots breaking out in New York over Whitman's 1855 *Leaves of Grass* or in Boston over the 1955 edition of Dickinson's *Poems*.

Even if the preoccupation with form is not uniquely American, American formalism may still have a distinctly American component. Yes, one might quip, the American component is irrelevance, since in early twentieth-century Athens people took these matters seriously, but in America a poet who breaks a line abruptly is unlikely to disturb the peace. In fact, this line of argument might continue, American poets occupy themselves with formal issues, and with spinning out these bothersome fictions of form meditating on those issues, because few people pay attention to them, so they need to convince themselves that their endeavors matter. Their exaggerated formalism simply testifies to their social inefficacy.

But social efficacy, putative or actual, proves nothing. It offers one standard of measurement among many. Arguing that poets do not matter because few people read them is like arguing that Antarctica is irrelevant because few people live there. The various ecological systems of the South Pole continue to operate, witnessed or unwitnessed. If the operations of those systems have no meaning for most people, they do not necessarily have no meaning. What does the formalism found in American poetry mean? How can it mean anything?

This second question would be hard enough at any time, but it has become more complicated with the rise of philosophical and critical methods that question the power of anything to function as a sign of anything else in a fixed and stable system of reference. To say, for example, that the formal structures of poems carry out various symbolic actions, attractive as this formulation still may be, is to risk sounding hopelessly quaint. Likewise, even a moderate dose of skepticism, whether Socratic or poststructuralist, makes the turning of poetic forms into political allegories a troubled enterprise. Even if we grant that poetic forms, or their accompanying fictions of form, signify political impulses, we have gotten nowhere, since we cannot avoid asking then what political impulses signify. Survival impulses? Sexual impulses? Religious impulses? Which, if any, is sign? Which signified?

One way out of this impasse is to set aside the question of signification for a moment to concentrate instead on the American component of American formalism. Recalling Auden's assessment of American poetry, quoted earlier, leads back to the question, What does the formalism of American poetry mean? "The prose of Emerson and Thoreau is superior to their verse, because verse in its formal nature protests against protesting; it demands that to some degree we accept things as they are not for any rational or moral reason, but simply because they happen to be that way; it implies an element of frivolity in the creation." *Things as they are.* The echo of "The Man with the Blue Guitar" suggests several possibilities (Auden's essay first appeared the year Stevens died), but even without it Auden's phrase points to a crucial distinction. Someone from a country that has no identifiable beginning (the Celts? the Anglo-Saxons? the reign of Edgar?) must understand "things as they are" altogether differently from someone whose country came into being with a document written in 1776. Why should an American accept things as they are "simply because they happen to be that way"? For all he or she knows, another document or a change in existing documents could drastically change things as they are. For an American, things as they are merge with things as they are *made.*

The power to make with words is *poiesis,* the power of the poet. If that poet happens to be from America, a country made with words, the activity of making with words will carry double significance, significance that may make it harder to acknowledge, let alone to celebrate, an element of frivolity in the creation. To make this statement is not to say that American formalism necessarily signifies (or represents or reflects or mimes or mirrors or tropes or figures) the authoring of the country, although in fact this claim may be true. But it is to say that if the formalism of American poetry signifies anything, it signifies an unusually vivid sense of the power of words, in both their composing and their unsettling capacities, which many experience occasionally and some continually. When Williams warns in the third book of *Paterson,* "A chance word, upon paper, may destroy the world," his hyperbole is both idiosyncratic and typical. In a country made by words, it is no wonder that people generally live indifferent to men and women who labor under this vivid sense. Tocqueville, Emerson, and others have assumed that the indifference to poets, and literature in general, indicates the obtuseness of American materialism, but exactly the opposite may be true. It may be that what appears to be indifference reveals instead a shrewd estimate of, and a pragmatic defense against, the power of words. It is not that poetry makes nothing happen, but that it could make something happen, something unpredictable and unpragmatic. To open oneself wholly to poets, or to the power they conduct, is to gamble that something could happen, that the unknown could be made and the known unmade.

NOTES

CHAPTER ONE

1. Alexis de Tocqueville, *Democracy in America*, ed. Phillips Bradley (New York: Alfred A. Knopf, 1945), 2:56. Subsequent page references to this edition will appear in the text.

2. Walt Whitman, *Leaves of Grass: Comprehensive Reader's Edition*, ed. Harold W. Blodgett and Sculley Bradley (New York: New York University Press, 1965), 709. Subsequent page references to this edition will appear in the text as *CRE*.

3. Antony Easthope, *Poetry as Discourse* (London: Methuen, 1983), 16. Easthope's formulation owes much to Roman Jakobson's description of the poetic function of language in "Closing Statement: Linguistics and Poetics," *Style in Language*, ed. Thomas A. Sebeok (Cambridge, Mass.: Massachusetts Institute of Technology Press, 1960), 358: "*The poetic function projects the principle of equivalence from the axis of selection into the axis of combination.*"

4. *On the Poet and His Craft: Selected Prose of Theodore Roethke*, ed. Ralph J. Mills, Jr. (Seattle: University of Washington Press, 1965), 83.

5. In his study *Poetry in America: Expression and Its Values in the Times of Bryant, Whitman, and Pound* (Durham, N.C.: Duke University Press, 1978), Bernard Duffey also uses the term *fiction* to describe two of the three phases into which he divides American poetry from the early-nineteenth to the mid-twentieth century. Duffey defines *poetic fiction* as "the context of feelings and ideas resorted to by the largest number of poets within an epoch, contexts of poetic expression that are assumed to be real but that have no necessary reality outside of poetry itself" (xii). Used this way, *fiction* seems to be a synonym for *world view* or *Zeitgeist*, that is, a shared, common perspective. In this study, I use the term *fictions* to refer to the larger myths or images poets invent, myths or images based on particular features or statements in their own verse or prose. For Duffey, a fiction is something public that poets and poems reflect, whereas I think of it as something individual that poets and poems make.

6. Harold Bloom and David Bromwich, "American Poetic Schools and Techniques (Contemporary)," *Princeton Encyclopedia of Poetry and Poetics*, ed. Alex Preminger, Frank Warnke, and O. B. Hardison, Jr., enlarged ed. (Princeton: Princeton University Press, 1974), 916, 919.

7. Ibid., 919; "The Poet," *The Complete Works of Ralph Waldo Emerson*, ed. Edward Waldo Emerson, centenary ed. (Boston: Houghton Mifflin, 1903–4), 3:9. Subsequent references to this edition will appear in the text as *W*.

8. Bloom and Bromwich, "American Poetic Schools," 917.

9. Ibid., 916.

10. Roy Harvey Pearce, *The Continuity of American Poetry* (Princeton: Princeton University Press, 1961), 4.

11. Edwin Fussell, *Lucifer in Harness: American Meter, Metaphor, and Diction* (Princeton: Princeton University Press, 1973), 4.

12. John Hollander, *Vision and Resonance: Two Senses of Poetic Form*, 2d ed. (New Haven: Yale University Press, 1985), 235, 189.

13. Daniel Hoffman, *Harvard Guide to Contemporary American Writing* (Cambridge, Mass.: Belknap Press, 1979), 497.

14. Ibid.

15. W. H. Auden, *The Dyer's Hand and Other Essays* (New York: Vintage, 1968), 355, 366, 364. "American Poetry" was first printed under the title "The Anglo-American Difference: Two Views" by D. Daiches and W. H. Auden in *Anchor Review* 1 (1955): 205–19. Subsequently, it was reprinted as Auden's introduction to his edition of *The Faber Book of Modern American Verse* (London: Faber and Faber, 1956), 9–21.

16. Robert Graves, "Harp, Anvil, Oar," *The Crowning Privilege* (London: Cassell, 1955), 93, 94. Although Graves cites him as an exception, even Frost links his fiction of "the sound of sense" to America: "I have even read that our American Indians possessed, besides a picture-language, a means of communication (though it was not said how far it was developed) by the sound of sense." *Robert Frost: Poetry and Prose*, ed. Edward Connery Lathem and Lawrance Thompson (New York: Henry Holt, 1972), 262. I am grateful to Tyler Hoffman for pointing out this passage to me.

17. In addition to the other studies cited here, an earlier attempt to define the Americanness of American poetry is Henry Wells's *The American Way of Poetry* (New York: Columbia University Press, 1943). Wells "aims to define whatever is truly indigenous and unique in the American tradition itself" (1) and reaches the general conclusion that American poetry stresses "intimate ties with human life rather than smoothness and perfection of form" (229), a statement that agrees with Tocqueville's observations and predictions.

18. Pearce, *Continuity*, 5; Hyatt Waggoner, *American Poets from the Puritans to the Present*, rev. ed. (Baton Rouge: Louisiana State University Press, 1984), xvii.

19. Fussell, *Lucifer in Harness*, 8, 15; Albert Gelpi, *The Tenth Muse: The Psyche of the American Poet* (Cambridge, Mass.: Harvard University Press, 1975), xii. Gelpi extends his study of American poetry in *A Coherent Splendor: The American Poetic Renaissance, 1910–1950* (Cambridge: Cambridge University Press, 1987).

20. Hoffman, *Harvard Guide*, 497–98; Harold Bloom, *Agon: Towards a Theory of Revisionism* (New York: Oxford University Press, 1982), 332.

21. Fussell, *Lucifer in Harness*, 8; Bloom and Bromwich, "American Poetic Schools," 917.

22. Wyatt Prunty discusses some of the problems surrounding the name "New Formalism" and concludes, quite sensibly, that "Formalism is neither new nor renewed." Nevertheless, he uses the term grudgingly in the subtitle of his study *"Fallen from the Symboled World": Precedents for the New Formalism* (New York: Oxford University Press, 1990). See 5–7.

23. Denis Donoghue, *Connoisseurs of Chaos: Ideas of Order in Modern American Poetry*, 2d ed. (New York: Columbia University Press, 1984), 7.

24. James Breslin, *From Modern to Contemporary: American Poetry, 1945–1965* (Chicago: University of Chicago Press, 1984), 29.

25. Stephen Cushman, *William Carlos Williams and the Meanings of Measure* (New Haven: Yale University Press, 1985).

26. Wallace Stevens, "Two of Three Ideas," *Opus Posthumous*, ed. Samuel French Morse (New York: Knopf, 1975), 204.

27. See Marjorie Perloff's chapter "Pound/Stevens: Whose Era?" in *The Dance of the Intellect: Studies in the Poetry of the Pound Tradition* (Cambridge: Cambridge University Press, 1985), 8.

28. In this context, consider Patricia Parker's claim that "much of poststructuralist criticism of the lyric has paid remarkably little attention to prosodic analysis. . . . A similar omission characterizes much of the criticism interested in wider social or historical questions." Introduction to *Lyric Poetry: Beyond New Criticism*, ed. Chaviva Hošek and Patricia Parker (Ithaca: Cornell University Press, 1985), 27. For a persuasive discussion of poststructuralism and its limitations with respect to prosody, see William Wenthe, " 'Beyond Formulated Language': Self, Prosody, and Theory," *Western Humanities Review* 46, no. 1 (Spring 1992): 94–114.

29. Breslin, *From Modern to Contemporary*, xiv.

30. Geoffrey Hartman, *Beyond Formalism: Literary Essays 1958–1970* (New Haven: Yale University Press, 1970), 42.

31. "The Art of Poetry: Robert Lowell," *Robert Lowell: A Collection of Critical Essays*, ed. Thomas Parkinson (Englewood Cliffs, N.J.: Prentice-Hall, 1968), 19.

32. Hartman, "Beyond Formalism," 56; Victor Erlich, "Russian Formalism," *Princeton Encyclopedia of Poetry and Poetics*, 727.

33. Terry Eagleton, *Marxism and Literary Criticism* (Berkeley: University of California Press, 1976), 20, 24.

34. John Hollander, *Melodious Guile: Fictive Pattern in Poetic Language* (New Haven: Yale University Press, 1988), 15.

35. F. O. Matthiessen, *American Renaissance: Art and Expression in the Age of Emerson and Whitman* (New York: Oxford University Press, 1941), 25.

36. *Journals and Miscellaneous Notebooks of Ralph Waldo Emerson*, ed. Merton M. Sealts, Jr. (Cambridge, Mass.: Belknap Press, 1965), 5:336.

37. Matthiessen, *American Renaissance*, 26.

38. For claims that Emerson is antinomian, see Pearce, *Continuity*, 5; Waggoner, *American Poets*, xvii; Bloom, *Agon*, 331.

39. Sacvan Bercovitch, *The Puritan Origins of the American Self* (New Haven: Yale University Press, 1975), 174.

40. Consider, for example, Whitman's statement in the prose note "Freedom," published in *Specimen Days and Collect* (1882): "The shallow, as intimated, consider liberty a release from all law, from every constraint. The wise see in it, on the contrary, the potent Law of Laws." *Prose Works 1892*, ed. Floyd Stovall (New York: New York University Press, 1964), 2:538; subsequent references to this edition will appear in the text as *PW*.

41. Bercovitch, *Puritan Origins*, 175.

42. Fussell, *Lucifer in Harness*, 6.

43. Wallace Stevens, *The Necessary Angel: Essays on Reality and the Imagination* (New York: Vintage, 1951), 26–27, 28.

J

44. For the 1855 text of "Song of Myself," which despite Whitman's final wishes I find the most effective version of the poem, I have used *Complete Poetry and Collected Prose*, ed. Justin Kaplan (New York: Library of America, 1982), 67. Subsequent references to this edition will appear in the text as *CP*.

45. Wallace Stevens, *The Palm at the End of the Mind: Selected Poems and a Play*, ed. Holly Stevens (New York: Vintage, 1972), 206. For a comparative discussion of Whitman and Stevens, see Diane Wood Middlebrook's *Walt Whitman and Wallace Stevens* (Ithaca: Cornell University Press, 1974). Middlebrook's argument is not concerned with an idea of influence but with "the relevance to Stevens of Whitman as an achieved myth-maker and as the American continuator of the Romantic tradition" (208). For evidence of Stevens's ambivalence toward Whitman, see *Letters of Wallace Stevens*, ed. Holly Stevens (New York: Alfred A. Knopf, 1966), 870–71, as quoted in Middlebrook, *Walt Whitman and Wallace Stevens*, 15.

46. James Perrin Warren, "The 'Real Grammar': Deverbal Style in 'Song of Myself,'" *American Literature* 56, no. 1 (Mar. 1984): 10, 11–12. See also Warren's study *Walt Whitman's Language Experiment* (University Park: Pennsylvania State University Press, 1990), as well as C. Carroll Hollis, *Language and Style in "Leaves of Grass"* (Baton Rouge: Louisiana State University Press, 1983), who discusses the syntax of Whitman's journalistic style (211–32). In this context, both Warren and Hollis acknowledge debts to Marie Borroff's important study *Language and the Poet: Verbal Artistry in Frost, Stevens, and Moore* (Chicago: University of Chicago Press, 1979).

47. Fussell, *Lucifer in Harness*, 24.

48. David Perkins, *A History of Modern Poetry: From the 1890s to the High Modernist Mode* (Cambridge, Mass.: Belknap Press, 1976) and *A History of Modern Poetry: Modernism and After* (Cambridge, Mass.: Belknap Press, 1987). Studies before Pearce's, such as Edmund Clarence Stedman's *Poets of America* (Boston: Houghton Mifflin, 1885) and Alfred Kreymborg's *Our Singing Strength: An Outline of American Poetry, 1620–1930* (New York: Coward-McCann, 1929) appeared too long ago to be of much use here. Two other surveys are Alan Shucard's *American Poetry: The Puritans through Walt Whitman* (Boston: Twayne, 1988) and its sequel, *Modern American Poetry, 1865–1950*, written by Shucard, Fred Moramarco, and William Sullivan (Boston: Twayne, 1989).

49. Mutlu Konuk Blasing, *American Poetry: The Rhetoric of Its Forms* (New Haven: Yale University Press, 1987), 2.

50. Peter Ackroyd, *T. S. Eliot: A Life* (New York: Simon and Schuster, 1984), 176–77.

CHAPTER TWO

1. For Whitman's accounts of his experiences at the theater and opera, see especially "Plays and Operas Too" in *Specimen Days* (1882; *PW* 1:19–21), "The Old Bowery" in *November Boughs* (1888; *PW* 2:591–97), and "Old Actors, Singers, Shows, &c., in New York" in *Good-Bye My Fancy* (1891; *PW* 2:693–99).

2. Horace Traubel, *With Walt Whitman in Camden* (Boston: Small, Maynard, 1906), 1:414. Although Whitman associates waves with nonmetricality here, elsewhere he invokes the sea iambically. Consider "Had I the Choice" ("Or breathe one breath of yours upon my verse, / And leave its odor there" [*CRE* 514]) and "With Husky-Haughty Lips, O Sea!" ("And rhythmic rasping of thy sands and waves" [*CRE* 518]).

3. Although it is hard to imagine Whitman not reading *Democracy in America*, Tocqueville's name does not appear in his *Prose Works*. In *The Foreground of "Leaves of Grass"* (Charlottesville: University Press of Virginia, 1974), 123–24, Floyd Stovall cites Bucke's list of Whitman's clippings, the sixth of which is a review of Tocqueville's *The Old Regime and the Revolution*, translated by John Bonner (1856).

4. Whitman quotes from "Hebrew Poetry" by Dr. Frederic de Sola Mendes, a rabbi in New York: "Dr. Mendes said 'that rhyming was not a characteristic of Hebrew poetry at all. Metre was not a necessary mark of poetry. Great poets discarded it; the early Jewish poets knew it not'" (*PW* 2:546). The source of Whitman's quotation has not been identified.

5. *Prose Writings of William Cullen Bryant*, ed. Parke Godwin (New York: D. Appleton, 1884), 1:34–35.

6. I prefer the term "triple-meter" to "anapestic" or "dactyllic" because, in poems without regular metrical norms, a given line, such as "The pavingman leans on his twohanded rammer" ("Song of Myself" [*CP* 40]"), can be construed as either anapestic (here acephalic with a feminine ending) or dactyllic (with anacrusis and catalexis). Pound's famous line from canto 81, "(To break the pentameter, that was the first heave)," employs the same triple-meter scheme as this line of Whitman's (x/xx/xx/xx/x). See discussion of Pound below.

7. See "Old Poets" in *Good-Bye My Fancy*: "Years ago I thought Emerson pre-eminent (and as to the last polish and intellectual cuteness may-be I think so still)—but, for reasons, I have been gradually tending to give the file-leading place for American native poesy to W. C. B." (*PW* 2:660).

8. *Interviews with William Carlos Williams: "Speaking Straight Ahead,"* ed. Linda Welshimer Wagner (New York: New Directions, 1976), 101–2.

9. For an extended examination of the ways in which Whitman's attitudes toward America led him to conceive of poems as "vehicles—or better yet, the occasion—for social cohesion" (xvi), see Kerry C. Larson, *Whitman's Drama of Consensus* (Chicago: University of Chicago Press, 1988). See also the social, political, and cultural studies of Whitman noted below.

10. For a brief discussion of Whitman's *Democratic Vistas* as a jeremiad, see Sacvan Bercovitch's *The American Jeremiad* (Madison: University of Wisconsin Press, 1987), 198–99. Bercovitch does not discuss "The Eighteenth Presidency!"

11. The literature on Whitman and the Civil War is vast. In addition to sections devoted to the war in studies noted elsewhere in this chapter, see Timothy Sweet, *Traces of War: Poetry, Photography, and the Crisis of the Union* (Baltimore: Johns Hopkins University Press, 1990), for a bibliography and the most recent contribution to this literature.

12. *Leaves of Grass: A Textual Variorum of the Printed Poems*, ed. Sculley

Bradley, Harold W. Blodgett, Arthur Golden, and William White (New York: New York University Press, 1980), 1:31.

13. According to Stovall, Whitman used an edition published in Philadelphia in 1854, undoubtedly a reprint of the original Edinburgh 1849 edition (*Foreground*, 195).

14. In a footnote to *Democratic Vistas*, Whitman acknowledges the side of himself that sympathizes, or has sympathized, with Carlyle: "I was at first roused to much anger and abuse by this essay ["Shooting Niagara"] from Mr. Carlyle, so insulting to the theory of America—but happening to think afterwards how I had more than once been in the like mood, during which his essay was evidently cast, and seen persons and things in the same light, (indeed some might say there are signs of the same feeling in these Vistas)—I have since read it again" (*PW* 2:375).

15. In "The Poetics of Union in Whitman and Lincoln: An Inquiry toward the Relationship of Art and Policy," Allen Grossman interprets the language and style of these two men. In my judgment, Grossman overestimates Whitman's "deletion of the metrical aspect of the line" and underestimates the "timeless *locus communis*" established by the biblical resonances of Whitman's style. See especially 188–89 in Grossman's essay, which appears in Walter Benn Michaels and Donald E. Pease, eds., *The American Renaissance Reconsidered: Selected Papers from the English Institute, 1982–83* (Baltimore: Johns Hopkins University Press, 1985).

16. Despite, or because of, his dismissal of them, Whitman's relationship to the English Romantics is complicated and has been most recently studied by Kenneth M. Price in *Whitman and Tradition: The Poet in His Century* (New Haven: Yale University Press, 1990). See especially Price's first chapter, " 'An American Bard at Last!'—Whitman's Persona and the English Heritage." See also Stuart Curran, *Poetic Form and British Romanticism* (New York: Oxford University Press, 1986), which demonstrates that form, though often dismissed by poets and critics alike, provides a significant key to understanding the Romantic period.

17. Two good examples, both important discussions, are M. Wynn Thomas's *The Lunar Light of Whitman's Poetry* (Cambridge, Mass.: Harvard University Press, 1987) and Betsy Erkkila's *Whitman the Political Poet* (New York: Oxford University Press, 1989). For illuminating chapters on Whitman within larger discussions, see Donald E. Pease's "Walt Whitman and the Vox Populi of the American Masses" in *Visionary Compacts: American Renaissance Writings in Cultural Context* (Madison: University of Wisconsin Press, 1987), as well as the sections devoted to Whitman by David S. Reynolds in *Beneath the American Renaissance: The Subversive Imagination in the Age of Emerson and Melville* (New York: Alfred A. Knopf, 1988). See also Philip Fisher, "Democratic Social Space: Whitman, Melville, and the Promise of American Transparency," *Representations* 24 (1988): 60–101.

18. Walt Whitman, *The Correspondence*, ed. Edwin Haviland Miller (New York: New York University Press, 1969), 5:73. See Justin Kaplan's *Walt Whitman: A Life* (New York: Simon and Schuster, 1980), 46–49, for commentary on the evidence of Whitman's paternity.

19. Of course, the converse of this last statement is also true. For an ex-

tended discussion of Whitman's sexual politics, see M. Jimmie Killingsworth, *Whitman's Poetry of the Body: Sexuality, Politics, and the Text* (Chapel Hill: University of North Carolina Press, 1989). For a discussion that connects the "politics of embodiment" with Whitman's lifelong commitment to revision, see Michael Moon, *Disseminating Whitman: Revision and Corporeality in "Leaves of Grass"* (Cambridge, Mass.: Harvard University Press, 1991).

20. *CRE* prints "And whether my friend"; *PW* prints "And whether my friends" (2:718).

21. The pairing of *president* and *prostitute* offers examples of what Kenneth Burke calls "colliteration" and "concealed alliteration by cognates." See his short but rich essay "On Musicality in Verse" in *The Philosophy of Literary Form: Studies in Symbolic Action*, 3d ed. (Berkeley: University of California Press, 1973), 369–78.

22. For example, Erkkila argues that this catalogue "undoes traditional hierarchies by presenting each person as part of a seemingly indiscriminate mass." *Whitman the Political Poet*, 88.

23. In her discussion of this poem, Erkkila assumes that the guidon flags are Union ones. Ibid., 215.

CHAPTER THREE

1. In the midst of remarks comparing Dickinson and Browning, Hollander comments: "In Dickinson's case, there is, of course, no meta-statement at all, save what can be extracted from the poems. We can find hundreds of metaphors for her choice of metrical mode, but no bald statement of it" (*Vision and Resonance*, 233).

2. See Cynthia Griffin Wolff, *Emily Dickinson* (New York: Knopf, 1986), 531, 209, 523, and Robert Sherwood, *Circumference and Circumstance: Stages in the Mind and Art of Emily Dickinson* (New York: Columbia University Press, 1968), 24.

3. *The Poems of Emily Dickinson*, ed. Thomas Johnson (Cambridge, Mass.: Belknap Press, 1955). Poems will be identified in the text by the number Johnson has given them. Other references to this edition will be identified as *P*. I find persuasive Wolff's suggestion that Johnson's dating of existing copies of Dickinson's poems by analyzing her handwriting may mean simply that the process of consolidating her poems, not necessarily of composing them, became most intense in 1862. See Wolff, *Emily Dickinson*, 576.

4. *The Letters of Emily Dickinson*, ed. Thomas Johnson and Theodora Ward (Cambridge, Mass.: Belknap Press, 1958), 2:408. Subsequent references to this edition will appear in the text as *L*.

5. Wolff, *Emily Dickinson*, 187.

6. See Hollander, *Vision and Resonance*, 227–31. This Emersonian fiction is part of the Romantic legacy inherited by Dickinson. For a full discussion of this legacy, see Joanne Feit Diehl, *Dickinson and the Romantic Imagination* (Princeton: Princeton University Press, 1981).

7. Traubel, *With Walt Whitman in Camden*, 1:414–15.

8. Which edition of Webster's did Dickinson use? For references to the lexi-

con, see Richard Sewall, *The Lyman Letters: New Light on Emily Dickinson and Her Family* (Amherst: University of Massachusetts Press, 1965), 12, 58. George Whicher argues that Dickinson used Webster's 1847 edition; *This Was a Poet* (New York: Charles Scribner's Sons, 1938), 232. Wolff argues for the 1828 (first) edition; *Emily Dickinson* 562. Willis J. Buckingham favors an 1844 edition published in Amherst by J. S. and C. Adams; "Emily Dickinson's Dictionary," *Harvard Library Bulletin* 25 (1977): 489–92. In "These Flames and Generosities of the Heart: Emily Dickinson and the Illogic of Sumptuary Values," Susan Howe claims that Dickinson owned an 1844 reprint of Webster's 1840 edition, while her family owned the 1828 edition; *Sulfur* 28 (Spring 1991): 140. In my judgment, an important consideration is not only which edition Dickinson owned but also which edition tells us the most about American English during the years she wrote. For this reason, I quote from the 1847 edition, revised and enlarged by Chauncey Goodrich four years after Webster's death in 1843.

9. For what Johnson calls "a semifinal draft" from which the two fair copies derive, see R. W. Franklin, ed., *The Manuscript Books of Emily Dickinson* (Cambridge, Mass.: Belknap Press, 1981), 1:253–55. Franklin disagrees with Johnson's dating, placing the part of fascicle 12 in which this poem appears in 1861 (1:226).

10. With respect to this poem, Shira Wolosky comments, "Time's arithmetic, an impressive figure for prosody, here entails the totality that governs linguistic and empirical pattern." *Emily Dickinson: A Voice of War* (New Haven: Yale University Press, 1984), 20.

11. See Wolff, *Emily Dickinson*, 564.

12. Edward Hitchcock, *The Highest Use of Learning: An Address Delivered at His Inauguration to the Presidency of Amherst College* (Amherst: J. S. and C. Adams, 1845), as quoted in Wolff, *Emily Dickinson*, 79.

13. Amy Lowell, *Poetry and Poets* (Boston: Houghton Mifflin, 1930), 88–89. See also David Porter, *Dickinson: The Modern Idiom* (Cambridge, Mass.: Harvard University Press, 1981), especially the final three chapters in which he considers Dickinson's "protomodernism."

14. Gay Wilson Allen, *American Prosody* (New York: American Book, 1935), 308, 310, 307; Robert Weisbuch, *Emily Dickinson's Poetry* (Chicago: University of Chicago Press, 1975), 73; Adrienne Rich, *Necessities of Life* (New York: Norton, 1966), 33.

15. For examples see David Porter, *The Art of Emily Dickinson's Early Poetry* (Cambridge, Mass.: Harvard University Press, 1966), 38–39; Sharon Cameron, *Lyric Time: Dickinson and the Limits of Genre* (Baltimore: Johns Hopkins University Press, 1979), 1; and Wolosky, *Voice of War*, xv.

16. Porter, *Art*, 8; Gelpi, *Tenth Muse*, 257. Discussions of Dickinson's metrics, as of her style in general, are indebted to Brita Lindberg-Seyersted, *The Voice of the Poet: Aspects of Style in the Poetry of Emily Dickinson* (Cambridge, Mass.: Harvard University Press, 1968). For an account of Dickinson's use of iambic pentameter, see A. R. C. Finch, "Dickinson and Patriarchal Meter: A Theory of Metrical Codes," *PMLA* 102 (Mar. 1987): 166–76.

17. Cristanne Miller also cites this letter for examples of meter. See *Emily*

Dickinson: A Poet's Grammar (Cambridge, Mass.: Harvard University Press, 1987), 11–12.

18. This poem also appears in a letter of February 1885 to Higginson (*L* 3:864), where it follows an often quoted sentence, "Biography first convinces us of the fleeing of the Biographied—." One could argue that the evolution toward verse continues, as the "you" addressed to Gilbert expands into a collective "you" addressed to all the subjects of biographies. Out of a personal letter had come a public elegy.

19. The publication of Judy Jo Small's thorough study *Positive as Sound: Emily Dickinson's Rhyme* (Athens: University of Georgia Press, 1990), which appeared after I had drafted my own remarks on rhyme, would make redundant an inventory of previous discussions. See Small's review of the critical literature from 1925 to 1988 in her introduction. In an attempt to prune back the tangle of terms commentators have used, I shall follow Small and distinguish between "full" and "partial" rhymes (see her table on 15). One type of rhyme Small does not include is what Mary Jo Salter calls "accordion rhyme" in "Puns and Accordions: Emily Dickinson and the Unsaid," *Yale Review* 79 (Winter 1990): 210–18.

20. Two important ones are Hollander's "Rhyme and the True Calling of Words" in *Vision and Resonance* and Donald Wesling's *The Chances of Rhyme: Device and Modernity* (Berkeley: University of California Press, 1980). Originally published in *Modern Language Quarterly* 5 (Sept. 1944), Wimsatt's essay has been reprinted in *The Verbal Icon: Studies in the Meaning of Poetry* (Lexington: University of Kentucky Press, 1954), 153–66.

21. Hollander, *Vision and Resonance*, 127.

22. Ibid., 118; Wesling, *Chances of Rhyme*, 120.

23. Porter claims that in the early poetry full rhyme, which he calls "exact," occurs with a frequency of one in two (*Art*, 194). Subsequently, Timothy Morris has determined that of the 4,840 rhymes in Dickinson's poems, 2,006 (41.4 percent) are full or exact; "The Development of Dickinson's Style," *American Literature* 60 (1988): 30.

24. For Small's reading of the phrase "Keyless Rhyme," see *Positive as Sound*, 65–66. For other comments on this poem, see 92–94.

25. Waggoner, *American Poets*, 214. For background on this discussion, as well as her own contributions to it, see Lindberg-Seyersted, *Voice of the Poet*, 184–96.

26. Isaac Watts, *The Psalms, Hymns, and Spiritual Songs, of the Rev. Isaac Watts, D.D. To Which Are Added, Select Hymns from Other Authors; and Directions for Musical Expression*, ed. Samuel Worcester (Boston: S. T. Armstrong 1827), vi–vii, as quoted in Porter, *Art*, 143.

27. Richard B. Sewall, *The Life of Emily Dickinson* (New York: Farrar, Straus, and Giroux, 1974), 349n.

28. Weisbuch, *Emily Dickinson's Poetry*, 73. Reynolds argues that the dash is a common stylistic feature of "the literature of misery" produced by American women in the 1850s (*Beneath the American Renaissance*, 415).

29. For example, see Pearce, *Continuity*, 180; Porter, *Art*, 144; Gelpi, *Tenth Muse*, 244, 246; Weisbuch, *Emily Dickinson's Poetry*, 73; Miller, *Poet's Gram-*

mar, 51–53; and Susan Howe, *My Emily Dickinson* (Berkeley: North Atlantic Books, 1985), 23.

30. In *L* Johnson gives the date of publication as February 17, 1866, but in *P* as February 14, 1866.

31. Allen, *American Prosody*, 310.

32. For chapters on enjambment see " 'Sense Variously Drawn Out': On English Enjambment" in Hollander's *Vision and Resonance*; "Commerce" in Justus Lawler's *Celestial Pantomime: Poetic Structures of Transcendence* (New Haven: Yale University Press, 1979); and "Why Have I Divided My Lines as I Have" in my own *William Carlos Williams and the Meanings of Measure*.

33. Sewall, *Lyman Letters*, 2, 63; Wolosky, *Voice of War*, 32, 34. In addition to studies cited elsewhere, see Barton Levi St. Armand, *Emily Dickinson and Her Culture: The Soul's Society* (Cambridge: Cambridge University Press, 1984), and Judith Farr, *The Passion of Emily Dickinson* (Cambridge, Mass.: Harvard University Press, 1992), for discussions that situate Dickinson in nineteenth-century American culture.

34. Wolff, *Emily Dickinson*, 123. Wolff's comments raise important issues beyond the scope of my discussion here. For a sample of the conversation among feminist critics of Dickinson, see Suzanne Juhasz, ed., *Feminist Critics Read Emily Dickinson* (Bloomington: Indiana University Press, 1983).

35. Sewall, *Lyman Letters*, 75.

36. Ibid., 71.

37. Karl Keller, in *The Only Kangaroo among the Beauty: Emily Dickinson and America* (Baltimore: Johns Hopkins University Press, 1979), is an exception. Although he does not discuss it in detail, he does quote the first stanza (101). See also his general remarks that introduce the chapter "Emily Dickinson and Harriet Beecher Stowe" (99–102).

CHAPTER FOUR

1. For quotation from this letter, as well as for other remarks about the "mutual distrust" of Pound and Stevens, see Perloff, *Dance of the Intellect*, 1. For the texts of Pound's radio broadcasts, see *"Ezra Pound Speaking": Radio Speeches of World War II*, ed. Leonard Doob (Westport, Conn.: Greenwood Press, 1978). Subsequent references to this edition will appear in the text as *EPS*.

2. Ezra Pound, *Selected Prose, 1909–1965*, ed. William Cookson (New York: New Directions, 1973), 145–46. All subsequent references to this edition will appear in the text as *SP*.

3. *Personae: The Collected Shorter Poems of Ezra Pound* (New York: New Directions, 1971), 89. Subsequent references to this edition will appear in the text as *P*.

4. See Bloom's introduction to *Ezra Pound* (New York: Chelsea House, 1987), 3 and passim.

5. A comparison with Williams is inevitable, for, like Pound, Williams both loved and hated Whitman, moving from an early infatuation with "Song of Myself" to a distant and grudging acknowledgment. Stephen Tapscott's *American Beauty: William Carlos Williams and the Modernist Whitman* (New York: Co-

lumbia University Press, 1984) examines the Whitman-Williams pairing in detail and includes occasional observations about the Whitman-Pound one.

6. Hugh Witemeyer, *The Poetry of Ezra Pound: Forms and Renewal, 1908–1920* (Berkeley: University of California Press, 1969), 135.

7. Pearce, *Continuity*, 90.

8. Blasing, *American Poetry*, 9.

9. Christine Brook-Rose, *A ZBC of Ezra Pound* (Berkeley: University of California Press, 1971), 66. Also see the rest of the chapter "I believe in technique as the test of a man's sincerity" (66–74).

10. Hugh Kenner, *The Pound Era* (Berkeley: University of California Press, 1971), 150.

11. *Literary Essays of Ezra Pound*, ed. T. S. Eliot (New York: New Directions, 1954), 32. Subsequent references to this edition appear in the text as *LE*.

12. James G. Frazer, *The Golden Bough: A Study in Magic and Religion*, abridged ed. (New York: Macmillan, 1922), 421, 426.

13. For another reference to this principle, see *Letters of Ezra Pound, 1907–1941*, ed. D. D. Paige (New York: Harcourt Brace, 1950), 216. Subsequent references to this edition appear in the text as *L*.

14. Samuel Taylor Coleridge, *Shakespearean Criticism*, ed. Thomas Middleton Raysor (New York: E. P. Dutton, 1960), 1:198.

15. *The Cantos of Ezra Pound* (New York: New Directions, 1972), 518. Subsequent references to this edition appear in the text as *C*. I recognize that some may argue for a scansion that stresses both "first" and "heave" or for one that stresses "heave" instead of "first." Both these readings need to be subjected to the test of relative stress. The sense of Pound's line is that the loosening, or breaking, of the pentameter is the *first* among many heaves, formal, political, economic, and social.

16. For a review of representative accounts of Pound's prosody, as well as for his own contribution to the conversation, see the chapter entitled "Prosody" in John Steven Childs, *Modernist Form: Pound's Style in the Early Cantos* (Selinsgrove, Pa.: Susquehanna University Press, 1986), 110–25. Not included by Childs is Antony Easthope's brief, and in my judgment unconvincing, discussion of "intonational metre" with respect to Pound in *Poetry as Discourse*, 153–59.

17. Kenner, *Pound Era*, 491.

18. As an example of the many statements in which Pound criticizes Milton, consider this comment to Laurence Binyon (May 4, 1938): "And I find your line with 'avaricious' *too* ti tum ti tum ti tum ti tum ti TUM. Might even be from that blighter Milton" (*L* 313).

19. Brook-Rose, *ZBC of Ezra Pound*, 43.

20. Blasing, *American Poetry*, 143, 231.

21. For Hollander's observation that Pound's "anti-Whitmanian move" is "to substitute the historical for the personal," see *Vision and Resonance*, 240–41. My argument so far should make it clear that I cannot wholly agree with the formulation that Pound's historical fiction stands at "the opposite pole" from organic fiction.

22. Herbert Schneidau attributes Pound's emphasis on function to his Puri-

tanism. See *Ezra Pound: The Image and the Real* (Baton Rouge: Louisiana State University Press, 1969), 178.

23. Ezra Pound, *ABC of Reading* (New York: New Directions, 1934), 27. All subsequent references to this edition will appear in the text as *ABCR*.

24. A sympathetic discussion of Pound's attempts to approximate classical meters by using their stress analogues is James A. Powell, "The Light of Vers Libre," *Paideuma* 8, no. 1 (Spring 1979): 3–34. Childs argues against Powell in ways that are both fair and persuasive (*Modernist Form*, 113–17).

25. *Selected Writings of Charles Olson*, ed. Robert Creeley (New York: New Directions, 1966), 22.

26. In the first number of *Poetry* (Oct. 1912), the epigraph from Whitman reads: "To have great poets there must be great audiences, too." This is the final sentence of "Ventures, on an Old Theme," published in *Specimen Days and Collect* (1882; *PW* 2:521). (Whitman's original sentence contains commas after "poets" and "audiences.") Whitman echoes this statement in "An Old Man's Rejoinder," published in *Good-Bye My Fancy* (1891): "Which perhaps leads to something: to have great heroic poetry we need great readers—a heroic appetite and audience" (*PW* 2:657).

27. Witemeyer, *Poetry of Ezra Pound*, 135.

28. Brook-Rose, *ZBC of Reading*, 67.

29. K. K. Ruthven, *A Guide to Ezra Pound's "Personae" (1926)* (Berkeley: University of California Press, 1969), 117.

30. For a discussion of Douglas's influence on Pound, see Ronald Bush, *The Genesis of Ezra Pound's "Cantos"* (Princeton: Princeton University Press, 1976), 277–90, and the chapter "The Emergence of the Economic Theme" in Peter Nicholls, *Ezra Pound: Politics, Economics, and Writing: A Study of "The Cantos"* (London: Macmillan, 1984), 20–46. For more theoretical treatment of Pound's economic theories, see Richard Sieburth, "In Pound We Trust: The Economy of Poetry/The Poetry of Economics," *Critical Inquiry* 14, no. 1 (Autumn 1987): 142–72.

31. Brita Lindberg-Seyersted, ed., *Pound/Ford: The Story of a Literary Friendship* (New York: New Directions, 1982), 44.

32. See *Paris Review* 28 (1962): 25. Commenting on the apparent change in his attitude, Pound points to the choruses in his translation of the *Trachiniae* (1956) as examples of his continued interest in form and the union "of the word and melody."

33. Nicholls discusses the later Pound's economic theories in his chapter "'The Toxicology of Money,'" in *Politics, Economics and Writing*, 138–60.

34. Doob quantifies the broadcasts as follows: "Of the 110 broadcasts, 77 were directed exclusively at American audiences, 29 at British audiences, and 4 at both" (*EPS* 418).

35. *Collected Early Poems of Ezra Pound*, ed. Michael King (New York: New Directions, 1976), 209. Subsequent references to this edition will appear in the text as *CEP*.

36. A good introduction to the problematic nature of Pound's Americanism is Benjamin T. Spencer's "Pound: The American Strain," *PMLA* 81, no. 7 (Dec.

1966): 457–66. See, too, Marion Montgomery's "Ezra Pound's Angry Love Affair with America," *Journal of Popular Culture*, 2, no. 3 (Winter 1968): 361–69. Also useful are occasional remarks in Daniel D. Pearlman's "Ezra Pound: America's Wandering Jew," originally published in *Paideuma* 9, no. 3 (Winter 1980) and reprinted in Bloom's *Ezra Pound*, 87–104. For biographical background, see J. J. Wilhelm, *The American Roots of Ezra Pound* (New York: Garland, 1985). Finally, Wendy Stallard Flory, in *The American Ezra Pound* (New Haven: Yale University Press, 1989), argues for the American character of Pound's aims and for the development of those aims out of the American jeremiac tradition. See especially her first chapter, "An American Childhood and the Ideal of Public Service" (13–41).

37. William Carlos Williams, *Imaginations*, ed. Webster Schott (New York: New Directions, 1970), 10.

38. For a different judgment, see Robert Casillo, *The Genealogy of Demons: Anti-Semitism, Fascism, and the Myths of Ezra Pound* (Evanston, Ill.: Northwestern University Press, 1988), 159: "For Pound America is basically feminine."

39. *Catullus, Tibullus, and Pervigilium Veneris*, ed. and trans. F. W. Cornish, J. P. Postgate, J. W. Mackail (Cambridge, Mass: Harvard University Press, 1962), 162. I have borrowed John Hollander's efficient translation (*Melodious Guile*, 43).

40. See "ambivalence" in *American Heritage Dictionary of the English Language*.

41. For a survey of these arguments, see Casillo, *Genealogy of Demons*, 8–15. Against many critics, Casillo maintains, quite persuasively, that Pound's anti-Semitism "cannot be understood in isolation from Pound's text." "Far more than any other of his themes, anti-Semitism exemplifies the inner contradictions of Pound's writing and discloses the incoherence of his psychology and values" (17, 22). For probing remarks about Pound's politics, especially his fascism, see Martin A. Kayman, *The Modernism of Ezra Pound: The Science of Poetry* (London: Macmillan, 1986), 18–32, 157–58. See also the chapters "Pound and Fascism" in Nicholls, *Politics, Economics and Writing*, 79–103, and "The *Cantos* of Ezra Pound, the Truth in Contradiction" in Jerome J. McGann, *Towards a Literature of Knowledge* (Chicago: University of Chicago Press, 1989), esp. 111–12.

CHAPTER FIVE

1. The most sustained treatment of the relationship between Bishop and Moore is David Kalstone's in *Becoming a Poet: Elizabeth Bishop with Marianne Moore and Robert Lowell* (New York: Farrar, Straus, and Giroux, 1989), 3–106. See also Jeredith Merrin, *An Enabling Humility: Marianne Moore, Elizabeth Bishop, and the Uses of Tradition* (New Brunswick, N.J.: Rutgers University Press, 1990), esp. 1–12, and the chapter "Miss Moore and Miss Bishop" in Lorrie Goldensohn, *Elizabeth Bishop: The Biography of a Poetry* (New York: Columbia University Press, 1992), 135–61.

2. Irvin Ehrenpreis, *Poetries of America: Essays on the Relation of Character to Style*, ed. Daniel Albright (Charlottesville: University Press of Virginia, 1989), 121.

3. Elizabeth Bishop, *The Collected Prose*, ed. Robert Giroux (New York: Farrar, Straus, and Giroux, 1984), 113. Subsequent references to this edition will appear in the text as *Prose*. All dates of composition are Giroux's.

4. Elizabeth Bishop, *Complete Poems, 1927–1979* (New York: Farrar, Straus, and Giroux, 1983), 133. Subsequent references to this edition will appear in the text as *Poems*. This poem has received little critical attention, although a welcome exception is Robert Dale Parker's discussion of it in *The Unbeliever: The Poetry of Elizabeth Bishop* (Urbana: University of Illinois Press, 1988), 114–19.

5. See Thomas Travisano, *Elizabeth Bishop: Her Artistic Development* (Charlottesville: University Press of Virginia, 1988), 173.

6. Henry David Thoreau, *Walden*, ed. J. Lyndon Shanley (Princeton: Princeton University Press, 1971), 153–54.

7. Longinus, *On the Sublime* 20.1–2, in *Classical Literary Criticism*, trans. T. S. Dorsch (Baltimore: Penguin, 1965), 130. *Princeton Encyclopedia of Poetry and Poetics*, 37. Longinus discusses anaphora but not epistrophe, commenting on the mimetic effect of a particular instance: "In this way the orator does just the same as the aggressor."

8. See Parker, *The Unbeliever*, 160n., for evidence that Bishop owned Iona and Peter Opie's edition of *The Oxford Dictionary of Nursery Rhymes* (1951; reprint, London: Oxford University Press, 1952). Subsequent references to this edition will appear in the text as "Opie." The long note following "This Is the House That Jack Built" in this edition comments that this rhyme "has probably been more parodied than any other nursery story" and cites W. Hone's *The Political House That Jack Built* (1819), illustrated by Cruikshank, as the earliest instance of political parody (231–32n.).

9. The letter is in the Houghton Library; quoted in Travisano, *Elizabeth Bishop*, 134.

10. For recent discussions of Bishop's life in Brazil, see Lloyd Schwartz, "Elizabeth Bishop and Brazil," *New Yorker*, Sept. 30, 1991, 85–97, and Goldensohn, *Biography of a Poetry*, 1–79.

11. Bruce Catton, *The American Heritage Picture History of the Civil War* (New York: American Heritage, 1960), 111.

12. For Trollope's narrative of his trip to America, see his *Autobiography* (New York: Harper and Brothers, 1883), 146–50.

13. Catton, *Civil War*, 250.

14. *The Letters of Anthony Trollope*, ed. Bradford Allen Booth (New York: Oxford University Press, 1951), 97. Whether or not Bishop knew this edition of Trollope's letters is unclear, but its appearance in 1951 coincides with the publication of "View of the Capitol" in July and her departure from the United States for Brazil in November.

15. Anthony Trollope, *North America*, ed. Donald Smalley and Bradford Allen Booth (New York: Knopf, 1951), 327.

16. See Parker, *The Unbeliever*, 117, for the comment that "these are visits

to herself or to some idealized (sainted) version of herself" and other remarks. See also Patricia Storace's review of Bishop's *Complete Poems, 1927–79* in *Parnassus* 12–13, nos. 2, 1 (Spring-Winter 1985): 163–78. Storace does not discuss the poem about Pound, but she calls the review "Visits to Saint Elizabeth's," suggesting the same self-referential possibilities of the title.

17. The letter is in the Washington University Libraries; quoted in Parker, *The Unbeliever*, 160.

18. As with the other poems I have been considering, this one has received little critical attention. Parker comments that Bishop, "almost as if dutifully, produced a poem called 'View of the Capitol from the Library of Congress'" (*The Unbeliever*, 70), and Travisano dismisses the poem as "comparatively slight" (*Elizabeth Bishop*, 98).

19. My understanding of this poem has benefited from the comments of several colleagues at the University of Virginia who listened carefully to some of these remarks and then pointed out that Bishop must also have in mind the "brasses," or military commanders, who want to enter the Korean War and go "*boom—boom.*"

20. For a representative instance, see Bishop's foreword to Candace MacMahon's *Elizabeth Bishop: A Bibliography, 1927–1979* (Charlottesville: University Press of Virginia, 1980), ix: "I am rather pleased to see I've written so much when I've always thought I'd written so little; on the other hand, I am rather appalled by how bad some of things I've written actually are."

21. In this context, Kalstone observes, "Brazil placed Bishop at an enabling distance from America" (*Becoming a Poet*, 152). From this enabling distance, Bishop can acknowledge her ties to America, as when she names a toucan, given to her as a gift, "Uncle Sam" (*Becoming a Poet*, 154).

22. Ashley Brown, "An Interview with Elizabeth Bishop" in *Elizabeth Bishop and Her Art*, ed. Lloyd Schwartz and Sybil P. Estess (Ann Arbor: University of Michigan Press, 1983), 292. Subsequent references to this edition will appear in the text as *Art*. This interview appeared originally in *Shenandoah* 17, no. 2 (Winter 1966): 3–19.

23. Bishop's statement here calls into question Helen Vendler's claim that she "resists the label 'American poet.'" *The Music of What Happens: Poems, Poets, Critics* (Cambridge, Mass.: Harvard University Press, 1988), 295.

24. See Parker, *The Unbeliever*, 133–44; Travisano, *Elizabeth Bishop*, 184–88; and essays by Kalstone, Vendler, Pinsky, Laurans, Costello, Schwartz, and Spiegelman in Schwartz and Estess, *Art*.

25. Nathan Scott, "Elizabeth Bishop: Poet without Myth," *Virginia Quarterly Review* 60, no. 2 (Spring 1984): 257.

26. Robert Alter, *The Art of Biblical Narrative* (New York: Basic Books, 1981), 26n. Both the *Oxford English Dictionary* and the *American Heritage Dictionary* define *parataxis* as the placing side by side of grammatical elements without any connecting words, not even *and*. Although I realize some may insist on this narrower definition, I also want to include Alter's broader one because of its specific relevance to the syntax of biblical narrative. For other treatments of parataxis, see Richard Bridgman's *The Colloquial Style in America* (New York: Oxford University Press, 1966) and Tony Tanner's *The Reign of Wonder:*

Naivety and Reality in American Literature (Cambridge: Cambridge University Press, 1965).

27. Alter, *Biblical Narrative*, 27. In making these formulations, Alter acknowledges his debt to Herbert Schneidau's *Sacred Discontent* (Baton Rouge: Lousiana State University Press, 1977).

28. Travisano remarks that Bishop "composed poems out of a succession of linked images, usually without supplying explicit connectives" (*Elizabeth Bishop*, 56).

29. Robert Lowell, *History* (New York: Farrar, Straus, and Giroux, 1973), 198.

30. Alter, *Biblical Narrative*, 21. In these remarks, Alter follows Tzvetan Todorov in *The Poetics of Prose*, trans. Richard Howard (Ithaca: Cornell University Press, 1977), 53–65.

31. As Penelope Laurans has shown in " 'Old Correspondences': Prosodic Transformations in Elizabeth Bishop," included in *Art*, "Bishop likes as much fluctuation and variation in her poems as possible" (94n3). Compare Laurans's accurate observation with Bishop's typically self-effacing description of her formal practices: "Sometimes I'm amazed at people's comparing me to you when all I'm doing is some kind of blank verse—can't they *see* how different it is?" This statement comes in a letter to Marianne Moore, dated October 24, 1954 (the letter is in the Rosenbach Museum; as quoted in Kalstone, *Becoming a Poet*, 4). Of course, Bishop's verse differs formally from Moore's syllabics; yet "some kind of blank verse" is hardly "all" she does.

32. In addition to Scott's remarks in "Elizabeth Bishop: Poet Without Myth," see, for example, Anne Stevenson, *Elizabeth Bishop* (New York: Twayne, 1966), 31.

33. Easthope, *Poetry as Discourse*, 134.

34. In his afterword to *Becoming a Poet*, James Merrill suggests that Kalstone would have discussed this poem if he had lived to finish his book. It is regretable that such a discussion is missing from Kalstone's superb treatment of Bishop's relationship to Lowell (109–250). For another discussion of this relationship, see Goldensohn, *Biography of a Poetry*, 162–91. Goldensohn considers this poem (274–77), as does Bonnie Costello, *Elizabeth Bishop: Questions of Mastery* (Cambridge, Mass.: Harvard University Press, 1991), 209–13. Both provide useful background, quoting letters and journals, but neither associates the opening italicized stanza with a voice other than Bishop's.

35. Susan Schweik discusses "Roosters" as a war poem in *A Gulf So Deeply Cut: American Women Poets and the Second World War* (Madison: University of Wisconsin Press, 1991), 214–34.

36. See "Love from Emily," *New Republic*, Aug. 27, 1951, 20–21, Bishop's review of *Emily Dickinson's Letters to Dr. and Mrs. Josiah Gilbert Holland*, ed. Theodora Van Wagenen Ward (Cambridge, Mass.: Harvard University Press, 1951). In her essay "Bishop's Sexual Poetics," Joanne Feit Diehl remarks on Bishop's affinities with Dickinson. See *Women Poets and the American Sublime* (Bloomington: Indiana University Press, 1990), 92–93.

37. "Elizabeth Bishop: Influences," *American Poetry Review* (Jan.-Feb. 1985): 13.

38. The question "Which is which?" provides an excellent example of Hollander's assertion that "the kind of poem which might be called *ekphrastic*, which addresses a particular visual image in order to give a reading of it, has frequent recourse to the interrogative mode." See *Melodious Guile*, 34–36. See also Costello's chapter "Art as Commemoration," in *Questions of Mastery*, 214–33, for a thorough discussion of Bishop's ekphrastic poems.

39. Robert Lowell, *Day by Day* (New York: Farrar, Straus, and Giroux, 1977), 127.

40. In his reading of "Anaphora," which he also considers an *ars poetica*, Kalstone makes a similar connection between Bishop's poem and Stevens's "Notes" (*Becoming a Poet*, 96).

41. See Stevenson, *Elizabeth Bishop*, 35.

42. For an excellent discussion of refrain, see Hollander's chapter "Breaking into Song: Some Notes on Refrain" in *Melodious Guile*, 130–47.

43. Hollander's chapter "Garlands of Her Own: Bondage, Work, and Freedom" in *Melodious Guile*, 85–110, contains illuminating discussions of these and other sonnets about the sonnet. "Sonnet" has been discussed by many critics recently, especially though not exclusively in the context of Bishop's sexuality. In addition to remarks by Parker, Diehl, Costello, and Goldensohn, see Adrienne Rich, "The Eye of the Outsider: The Poetry of Elizabeth Bishop," *Boston Review* (Apr. 1983): 15–17.

44. Compare Bishop's comment on Moore with Hollander's insight that "in art, freedom paradoxically manifests itself in the imagination's unbridled propensity to design new bridles for itself" (*Melodious Guile* 90). For commentary on "In Prison," see David Lehman, " 'In Prison': A Paradox Regained" (*Art* 61–74).

45. See Blasing, *American Poetry*, 111, for a reading of this reversal in a different context.

46. *Princeton Encyclopedia of Poetry and Poetics*, 764–65.

47. MacMahon, *Bibliography*, 143.

48. Ibid., 144.

49. In "Domestication, Domesticity, and the Otherworldly," first printed in *World Literature Today* 1 (Winter 1977) and reprinted in *Part of Nature, Part of Us* (Cambridge, Mass.: Harvard University Press, 1980), 97–110, Helen Vendler identifies the tears as the "strange component, which finally renders the whole house unnatural" (*Art* 32).

CHAPTER SIX

1. A. R. Ammons, *Sumerian Vistas* (New York: Norton, 1987), 28. All subsequent references to this edition will appear in the text as *SV*. This poem appeared originally in *Hudson Review* 36, no. 1 (Spring 1983): 75–110.

2. A. R. Ammons, foreword to *Ommateum* (Philadelphia: Dorrance, 1955).

3. A. R. Ammons, *Collected Poems, 1951–1971* (New York: Norton, 1972), 260. Subsequent references to this edition will appear in the text as *CP*. In *CP* Ammons shortens the title of this poem to "Summer Session."

4. See definitions in both the *Oxford English Dictionary* and *Princeton En-*

cyclopedia of Poetry and Poetics. In naming this device *epanalepsis*, I am aware that I am modifying these definitions somewhat.

5. A. R. Ammons, *Lake Effect Country* (New York: Norton, 1983), 8. The didactic tone of the passage from "The Ridge Farm" is characteristic of much of Ammons's poetry. See Willard Spiegelman's clarifying chapter "Myths of Concretion, Myths of Abstraction: The Case of A. R. Ammons" in *The Didactic Muse: Scenes of Instruction in Contemporary American Poetry* (Princeton: Princeton University Press, 1989), 110–46.

6. A. R. Ammons, *The Snow Poems* (New York: Norton, 1977), 203. Subsequent references to this edition will appear in the text as *SP*.

7. See Justus Lawler, *Celestial Pantomime: Poetic Structures of Transcendence* (New Haven: Yale University Press, 1979), 53, 59.

8. Hollander, *Vision and Resonance*, 230–31. Although phonemically linked by Ammons, the words *rigid* and *ridge*, like *error* and *eros*, are etymologically unrelated.

9. Harold Bloom, "A. R. Ammons: 'When You Consider the Radiance,'" *The Ringers in the Tower* (Chicago: University of Chicago Press, 1971), 257.

10. In *Corsons Inlet* and *Selected Poems, 1951–1977*, these last three lines read "so that I make / no form of / formlessness." The absence of "of" in *Collected Poems* is a printer's error.

11. Bloom, *Ringers*, 275. William Carlos Williams, *Selected Essays* (New York: New Directions, 1954), 286. Subsequent references to this edition will appear in the text as *SE*.

12. As in the nod to Williams in "Essay on Poetics," discussed below, Ammons's direct engagement with Williams is indisputable. He plays on the image of a poem as a "machine made of words," a phrase from Williams's "Author's Preface" to *The Wedge* (1944), revising it in *SP* to "a poem is a machine made out of worlds" (43). Also in *SP*, he closes the poem about his fiftieth birthday (February 18, 1976) with this echo: "A half-century inscribed / birthday cake, promises / of presents, a wheelbarrow / (red, rained on) and stereo!" (157).

13. Although he does not treat these particular lines this way, Alan Holder would argue, if I read him correctly, for this paraphrase; *A. R. Ammons* (Boston: Twayne, 1978). Setting up two groups, or clusters, that "constitute the poles between which Ammons's sensibility oscillates," he associates formlessness with the One (Unity) and form with the Many (Multiplicity). See 68. For a discussion of "Corsons Inlet" as an example of the "walk poem," see Roger Gilbert, *Walks in the World: Representation and Experience in Modern American Poetry* (Princeton: Princeton University Press, 1991), 212–24.

14. A. R. Ammons, *Sphere: The Form of a Motion* (New York: Norton, 1974), 16. Subsequent references to this edition will appear in the text as *S*.

15. Pagination differs in various printings of *Paterson* (New York: New Directions, 1963). In the fourth, for example, this passage appears on 65, in the twelfth, on 50.

16. *The Collected Poems of William Carlos Williams, Volume I: 1909–1939*, ed. A. Walton Litz and Christopher MacGowan (New York: New Directions, 1986), 339.

17. Hoffman, *Harvard Guide*, 576.

18. These pieces appeared respectively in *Poetry* 102 (June 1963): 202–3; and in *Epoch* 33, no. 1 (Fall-Winter 1983): 38–39. The second has been reprinted in David Lehman, ed., *Ecstatic Occasions, Expedient Forms* (New York: Macmillan, 1987), 1–2. See Holder's bibliography (*A. R. Ammons*, 171) for citations of other prose before 1978.

19. "'A Place You Can Live': An Interview with A. R. Ammons," *Manhattan Review* 1, no. 2 (Fall 1980): 11.

20. Williams makes this statement in "The Tortuous Straightness of Chas. Henri Ford," first published in 1939; yet the year before, in a letter of January 23, 1938, Williams writes James Laughlin that the sonnets of Merrill Moore have "given me the lie." See Hugh Witemeyer, ed., *William Carlos Williams and James Laughlin: Selected Letters* (New York: Norton, 1989), 25–26.

21. *Tape for the Turn of the Year* (New York: Norton, 1972), 32. Subsequent references to this edition will appear in the text as *T*.

22. The figurative meanings Ammons sees in the typography of his poems receive their clearest statement in "The Limit," grouped in the 1966–71 section of *CP* (266–67) and included in *Briefings*.

23. Hollander, *Vision and Resonance*, 229; Wesling, *Chances of Rhyme*, 1–2. For a lucid account of previous discussions of organicism, as well as for Wesling's own original contribution to them, see 12–18.

24. Hyatt Waggoner, "On A. R. Ammons," in *Contemporary Poetry in America: Essays and Interviews*, ed. Robert Boyers (New York: Schocken Books, 1974), 334.

25. Holder, *A. R. Ammons*, 122.

26. Henry Sayre, *The Visual Text of William Carlos Williams* (Urbana: University of Illinois Press, 1983), 53.

27. See Paul Fussell, *Poetic Meter and Poetic Form*, rev. ed. (New York: Random House, 1979), 155.

28. This, at least, is Pound's formulation in his "Treatise on Metre," *ABC of Reading*, 199–200.

29. Bloom, *Ringers*, 283.

30. Waggoner, *American Poets*, 622–23.

31. Waggoner applauds *Tape for the Turn of the Year*, calling it "good Emerson," but doesn't "much like" "Summer Session." Holder ranks "Summer Session" "among Ammons' most interesting poems," while in *Tape* he finds "egregious examples of the imitative fallacy," "verbal doodling," and tastelessness. Waggoner, "On A. R. Ammons," 334, 338; Holder, *A. R. Ammons*, 118–20, 123.

32. Hayden Carruth, "Reader Participation Invited," *The New York Times Book Review*, Sept. 25, 1977, 30.

33. Vendler, *Part of Nature*, 370.

34. Michael McFee, "A. R. Ammons and *The Snow Poems* Reconsidered," *Chicago Review* 33, no. 1 (Summer 1981): 32, 35.

35. Ibid., 36.

36. A. R. Ammons, *Selected Poems* (Ithaca, N.Y.: Cornell University Press, 1968); *The Selected Poems, 1951–1977* (New York: Norton, 1977); *The Selected Poems: Expanded Edition* (New York: Norton, 1986). In *Selected Poems*,

1951–1977, for example, Ammons includes two poems that appear consecutively in his *Collected Poems*, "Mountain Talk" and "Loss." However, in *Collected Poems* these two poems follow "Belief," which bears the dedication "for JFK" and focuses its meditation on Kennedy's funeral in November 1963. Of course, Ammons is entitled to select any poems he chooses, but the relative placement of these three poems demonstrates that his two sides coexist at a given moment in his career; it also suggests that the widely anthologized "Loss" may benefit from reading in a larger context.

37. "Summer Place," *Hudson Review* 30, no. 2 (Summer 1977): 173. Subsequent references to this printing will appear in the text as *SPl*.

38. See acknowledgments in *Selected Longer Poems* (New York: Norton, 1980).

39. Although not as explicit a meditation on America as the passages from *Sphere* and "Summer Place," Ammons's long poem "Garbage," written in 1989, signals his return to the long poem, a return made more dramatic by the appearance of *The Really Short Poems of A. R. Ammons* (New York: Norton, 1990). As the title "Garbage" suggests, the meditation on trash, which opens in section 129 of *Sphere* and continues through "Summer Place," extends Ammons's attention to the present realities of actual America. "Garbage" appeared in *American Poetry Review*, 21, no. 2 (Mar.-Apr. 1992): 36–41.

40. See Holder, *A. R. Ammons*, 22, for a brief discussion of what he calls Ammons's "Mesopotamian posture."

ENVOI

1. Henry James, "Mr. Walt Whitman," *The Nation*, Nov. 16, 1865, 625–26.

2. Timothy Steele, *Missing Measures: Modern Poetry and the Revolt Against Meter* (Fayetteville: University of Arkansas Press), 1990; Joseph M. Conte, *Unending Design: The Forms of Postmodern Poetry* (Ithaca: Cornell University Press, 1991). See especially the conclusions to these books.

3. Gwendolyn Brooks, "Poets Who Are Negroes," *Phylon* 11, no. 4 (Dec. 1950): 312. I am grateful to Kimberly Benston for pointing me toward this piece.

4. Rae Dalven, trans., *The Complete Poems of Cavafy* (New York: Harcourt Brace Jovanovich, 1976), 290.

INDEX

Ackroyd, Peter, 22
Adams, John, 100, 108
Aeolian harp, 171
Allen, Gay Wilson, on Dickinson's formal techniques, 50, 63
Alter, Robert, on parataxis, 127, 132
American literature, Tocqueville on, 3
"Americanness" of American poetry, 8, 9, 10; literary critics on, 9–10, 192n17; search for, 10, 15, 18
American poetry: critical assessments of, 7–8; form and technique in, 187, 188; localism and regionalism of, 72. *See also* "Americanness" of American poetry
American poets: characteristics of, 7–8, 9; and American attitudes toward, 189–90
American poets, and form: and self-evaluation, 22–23; valuation of, 4, 6, 7, 14
American poets, and style: characteristics of, 3–4; and idea of America, 5, 18, 19, 20–21. *See also* names of individual poets
Ammons, A. R.: on America, 175, 181, 182–83; and Americanness of, 24, 175–76, 182; on artifice and artificiality in poetry, 167, 168, 169, 170; and ars poetica, poetry as, 149, 150, 156, 158, 161, 162, 163; and chiasmus, use of, 152, 159; and colon (punctuation mark), 186; and duality of, 175, 176, 210n36; and Emerson, 156, 177; and enjambment, use of, 159–60, 170; and epanalepsis, use of, 150, 154, 207–8n4; and fiction of form, 24, 178; and form, 150–54, 156, 159, 168–69, 172, 173; on form, 149–51, 157, 162, 163–65, 169; formalism of, 23–24; and formlessness, 152, 156, 159; and free verse, 151–52; and natural form, 153–54, 161, 163, 166; and natural imagery in, 163, 164–65; and organicism, 166–67, 168, 169, 170, 172; and parallelism, use of, 152, 159; and poems, length of, 179, 183, 210n39; as poet, 179, 180–81; and regular stanza, use of, 159–60, 167; and role as poet, 171–72; on

stanza, 170–72, 173, 175; and Stevens, 179, 180; and structure, 162–63, 168–69; visual patterns in, 151, 155, 209n22; water imagery in, 167–68, 170, 171; and Whitman, 160, 161, 163, 177–78; and Williams, 154–55, 156–58, 162, 163, 167, 168, 169, 208n12. Works: *Collected Poems*, arrangement of, 210n36; "Corsons Inlet": on form, 155–56, 161; on formlessness, 156; forms of motion in, 158; and Williams, 155; "Essay on Poetics": on form, 169; and organicism, 167–68, 169; and regular stanzas in, 167; and Williams, response to in, 167–68, 169; "Extremes and Moderations": Aeolian harp, imagery in, 171–72; and role as poet, 172; on stanza, 170–71; and water imagery in, 170, 171; "Four Motions for the Pea Vines": as ars poetica, 165, 166; rhythm in, 165, 166; and typography in, 166; "Garbage": on America, 210n39; "Hibernaculum": and artificiality, 169, 170; on form, 169–70; "A Note on Prosody": on structure, 162–63; *Ommateum*: and form, 149, 150; visual patterns in, 155; and voice in, 154–55; "The Ridge Farm": and chiasmus in, 152; and form, 149, 150, 151–54, 156; and formlessness, 156; and parallelism in, 152; and "ridge line" boundaries, 153, 154; and tone in, 208n5; *The Snow Poems*: and antiformalism, 172; as ars poetica, 174–75; critical assessment of, 172; and form, 172, 173–74, 175; on readership, 176–77; *Sphere: The Form of a Motion*: chiasmus in, 159; and enjambment, use of, 159–60; and form, 157, 158, 161; and measure, 160, 161; parallelism in, 159; on political parties, 177; and regular stanza, use of, 159–60, 167; repetition in, 158–59; and Whitman, "Song of Myself," 160, 161; *Sumerian Vistas*: on America, 183, 184–85; dates in titles, 184, 185; natural imagery in, 184–86; "Summer Place": on America, 181,